THE LAST GREAT TOUR?

TRAVELLING WITH THE 2005 LIONS

Paul Daly, a law graduate of University
College Cork has been short-listed for the
ESB National Media Award in the Regional
Sports Journalist of the Year category.
His first book, *Reflections of Cork,*
was published in 2004.

This is, if we're being honest about it,
the last great Lions' tour.
Sir Clive Woodward, Auckland, 1 June 2005

Guide me, O Thou great Redeemer
Pilgrim through this barren land
I am weak but Thou art mighty
Hold me with Thy powerful hand.
Bread of Heaven

THE LAST GREAT TOUR?

TRAVELLING WITH THE 2005 LIONS

PAUL DALY

The Collins Press

Published in 2005 by
The Collins Press
West Link Park
Doughcloyne
Wilton
Cork

British Library Cataloguing in Publication Data

Daly, Paul
        Travelling with Lions
        1. Lions (Rugby team) 2. Rugby Union
        football - Ireland
        3. Rugby Union football - New Zealand
        I. Title
        796.3'3364'0993

ISBN: 1903464935

Typesetting: The Collins Press

Font: Helvetica, 10 point

Printed in Ireland by Colour Books

Cover images: Rugby ball and All Blacks, courtesy of Getty Images

Table of Contents

Acknowledgements

First of all, some apologies. Given the timeframe in which I have had to put this book together, it is not perfect (hopefully, by the time you're reading this, you've already paid). Any errors are the author's.

There are so many people to thank that it's hard to know where to begin. Two of my teachers have had a profound influence on my life: Mr Damien Keane, now the principal at St Joseph's National School on the Mardyke in Cork; and, especially, Mr Seamus Bruton, who taught me English in Christian Brothers College, Cork. Only a pity that, instead of repaying him with an A1 in Leaving Cert English – don't ask – I've had to get published. Both of them were foolish enough to encourage me in my endeavours.

Dr Michael O'Sullivan's decision to prescribe contact lenses allowed a youngster to – pardon me – see the light as far as rugby was concerned. Mr Eddie Lyons, as he keeps reminding me, gave me my break. Mr Ken O'Connor inadvertently rescued me, something for which I'm sure everyone reading this is grateful, and I much enjoyed my spell with the Evening Echo. It being my first time on a tour in any capacity, the friendliness of many members of the press corps was very much appreciated. Thanks to Dave Ferguson, Dave Kelly, Ciaran Cronin, David Barnes, Simon Lewis, Andrew Innes, Paul Morgan, Andy Howell, Mark Scott, Will Downey, Alison Donnelly, Alasdair Reid, Liam Heagney, Derek Foley, David Long, Matt Johnson, David Hands, Rob Kitson, Akfi Ladal, Brendan Fanning, Brendan Moran, Ron Roby, Peter Jackson, Barry Gold, Eddie Butler and Jim Kayes for taking the time to say hello and, in some cases, a little more than that. Huw Richards deserves a sentence of thanks all on its own; as does Oisín Langan for putting up with me for nearly three weeks – a record, I think. Mention must be made too of the NZRU's excellent communications team: Joe Locke, Meredith Keys, Brian Finn and Josyln 'Where's your badge' Titus.

Thanks as well to the O'Connor brothers, Dave and Bryan of Diesel, North Main Street, for keeping me in clobber. It only remains to thank my family and friends. You know who you are!

PAUL DALY
October 2005

The Lions' Squad

Neil Back, flanker, Leicester, England, 66 *caps*, 83 *points*
Iain Balshaw*, full-back/wing, Bath, England, 24, 60
Gordon Bulloch, hooker, Glasgow, Scotland, 75, 20
Shane Byrne, hooker, Leinster, Ireland, 38, 15
Gareth Cooper, scrum-half, Newport-Gwent Dragons, Wales, 26, 30
Martin Corry, back-row/second-row, Leicester, England, 37, 15
Chris Cusiter, scrum-half, The Borders, Scotland, 16, 5
Gordon D'Arcy, centre/wing/full-back, Leinster, Ireland, 12, 10
Lawrence Dallaglio **b**, flanker/number eight, London Wasps, England, 73, 75
Matt Dawson, scrum-half, London Wasps, England, 70, 96
Will Greenwood, centre, NEC Harlequins, England, 55, 155
Danny Grewcock **g**, second-row, Bath, England, 57, 10
John Hayes, prop, Munster, Ireland, 54, 10
Gavin Henson, centre/fly-half/full-back, Neath-Swansea Ospreys, Wales, 16, 124
Denis Hickie, wing, Leinster, Ireland, 51, 125
Richard Hill **f**, flanker, Saracens, England, 71, 60
Charlie Hodgson, fly-half, Sale, England, 19, 154

The Last Great Tour?

Shane Horgan, centre/wing, Leinster, Ireland, 37, 60
Gethin Jenkins, prop, Cardiff Blues, Wales, 31, 15
Stephen Jones, fly-half, Clermont-Auvergne, Wales, 48, 441
Ben Kay, second-row, Leicester, England, 40, 10
Josh Lewsey, full-back/wing, London Wasps, England, 34, 105
Lewis Moody, flanker, Leicester, England, 31, 40
Geordan Murphy, full-back/wing, Leicester, Ireland, 31, 80
Donncha O'Callaghan, second-row, Munster, Ireland, 16, 0
Paul O'Connell, second-row, Munster, Ireland, 29, 20
Brian O'Driscolle, centre, Leinster, Ireland, 59, 147 (captain)
Ronan O'Gara, fly-half, Munster, Ireland, 52, 525
Malcolm O'Kelly **a**, second-row, Leinster, Ireland, 73, 35
Michael Owen, number eight/flanker, Newport-Gwent Dragons, Wales, 24, 5
Dwayne Peel, scrum-half, Llanelli Scarlets, Wales, 41, 20
Jason Robinson, wing/full-back/centre, Sale, England, 39, 110
Graham Rowntree, prop, Leicester, England, 52, 0
Tom Shanklin **h**, centre/wing, Cardiff Blues, Wales, 33, 75
Andy Sheridan, prop, Sale, England, 1, 0
Ollie Smith, centre, Leicester, England, 5, 0
Matt Stevens, prop, Bath, England, 5, 0
Simon Taylord, number eight/flanker, Edinburgh, Scotland, 38, 25
Gareth Thomas, wing/full-back/centre, Toulouse, Wales, 83, 170
Steve Thompson, hooker, Northampton, England, 39, 15
Andy Titterrell, hooker, Sale, England, 4, 0
Julian White, prop, Leicester, England, 28, 0
Jonny Wilkinson **y**, fly-half/centre, Newcastle, England, 52, 817

The Lions' Squad

* injured and replaced, pre-tour, by Mark Cueto, Sale, England, 3, 20

b injured and replaced, June 5, by Simon Easterby, flanker, Llanelli Scarlets, Ireland, 42, 20

g suspended and replaced, June 27, by Brent Cockbain, second-row, Neath-Swansea Ospreys, Wales, 20, 5

f injured and replaced, June 27, by Jason White, Sale, Scotland, 46, 20

e injured, June 26, not replaced

a injured and replaced, June 2, by Simon Shaw, second-row, London Wasps, England, 28, 10

h injured, June 26, not replaced

d injured and replaced, June 10, by Ryan Jones, number eight/flanker, Neath-Swansea Ospreys, Wales, 8, 5

y added to initial selection of forty-four players in May

Tour Itinerary

Monday 23 May, Millennium Stadium, Cardiff, V Argentina, drew 23-23

Saturday 4 June, Rotorua International Stadium, Rotorua, V Bay of Plenty, won 34-20

Wednesday 8 June, Yarrow Stadium, New Plymouth, V Taranaki, won 36-14

Saturday 11 June, Waikato Stadium, Hamilton, V New Zealand Maori, lost 13-19

Wednesday 15 June, Westpac Stadium, Wellington, V Wellington, won 23-6

Saturday 18 June, Carisbrook, Dunedin, V Otago, won 30-19

Tuesday 21 June, Rugby Park Stadium, Invercargill, V Southland, won 26-16

Saturday 25 June, Jade Stadium, Christchurch, V New Zealand, lost 3-21

Tuesday 28 June, FMG Stadium, Palmerston North, V Manawatu, won 109-6

Saturday 2 July, Westpac Stadium, Wellington, V New Zealand, lost 18-48

Tuesday 5 July, Eden Park, Auckland, V Auckland, won 17-13

Saturday 9 July, Eden Park, Auckland, V New Zealand, lost 19-38

Preface

IT FELT LIKE SOMETHING SPECIAL WAS GOING TO HAPPEN

Saturday 2 July 2005, Wellington, 4.53pm
Intercontinental Hotel

Outside the Intercontinental Hotel in central Wellington, hundreds of people, bedecked in red and the colours of the individual home nations, gathered to sing and cheer. The Saint George's Cross, the Red Dragon, the Tricolour, Saint Andrew's Saltire and the Union Jack were fluttered and draped and found themselves flapped and hoisted and waved. A piece of A4 paper taped to a pillar announced that the team would be leaving, 'any time after 5.15pm'. Barriers held the masses back as they craned their necks and raised their noses, hoping to glimpse a familiar face through the plate glass, the security and the lucky ones milling expectantly in the lobby.

And then, they burst into song. 'Lions! Lions! Lions!' they bellowed, people from high and low in four nations, from the tops of tower blocks to villas by the sea, from skyscraper offices to coal pits in the valleys, all singing in the same, curious accent, hailing maybe from the West Country of England.

'The Fields of Athenry' was belted out, 'Flower of Scotland' too, 'Ireland's Call', 'Bread of Heaven'. Even, 'Show me the way to Amarillo'. 'Who egg'd our van?' asked a sign held aloft by two fair-haired Englishmen. 'When are they coming out, Dad?' wondered a fair-haired boy in an Ireland jersey, cheeks declaring, 'Lions'.

'Alfie do the 'tolah, Alfie do the 'tolah', a group began to chant, in honour of the Lions' new captain, Gareth 'Alfie' Thomas and the celebration he embarks on whenever he scores: 'Dancing the Ayatollah', first performed on the terraces of Cardiff City Football Club.

'Lions! Lions! Lions!' they continued on, hundreds in deafening unison. A crisp winter's day was being stolen away by twilight, and darkness was beginning to fall.

Westpac Stadium, 7.17pm

Alfie's doing the 'Tolah! Just over 100 seconds have gone and Gareth Thomas has scored underneath the posts. With a simple conversion to come, Jonny Wilkinson will add two points and the Lions will lead by seven.

'Lions! Lions! Lions!' It seemed as if the stadium itself was bellowing, a song rising from the depths of a sea of red. The fans were swaying this way and that; the ground seemed to be shifting as well and when a beleaguered New Zealand team gathered underneath the posts, their captain, Tana Umaga, had to bellow to make himself heard. Even before the first whistle, the Westpac was a bubbling cauldron; the Haka had been drowned out by Lions' fans roaring themselves hoarse; even earlier, when Umaga's name had been read out, the cheers of the home crowd competed valiantly but failed to subdue the raucous boos of the travelling support. Umaga had a hand in the incident that led to the Lions' original captain, Brian O'Driscoll, leaving the field on a medical cart in the First Test and the Lions' fans weren't too happy about that: all week, they've been sporting T-shirts bearing Umaga's face and the slogan, 'Wanted for the assassination of Brian O'Driscoll'. The All Blacks weren't too happy either: all week, Umaga was the centre of unwanted attention. 'There wouldn't be enough space on the [dressing room] wall for all that crap,' his coach, Graham Henry, had growled, when asked if it would be a motivating factor. By which he meant to say, too bloody right it would be a motivating factor.

Under the posts, Umaga must not have bellowed loud enough: from the restart after Thomas' try, the Lions' scrum-half, Dwayne Peel, ran 60 yards and won a penalty. Even though Wilkinson's effort came back off the post, Jason Robinson, the smallest of them all, rose above three men to claim. Another penalty was about to be awarded, five metres out. Three more easy points. Something special was happening.

Then second-row forward Paul O'Connell dived shoulder-first into the ruck. Penalty reversed. It was never the same after that.

Intercontinental Hotel, 5.17pm

The crowd a little quieter now, the anticipation, though feverish, channelled into nervous fidgeting and laughter. This is it boys. Lose tonight and it's time to pack the bags. There are two games in Auckland next week but if the Lions don't win this one, they will count for next to nothing. Only pride would be at stake; for a team here to win, playing for mere pride would represent an almighty fall. They were, their coach said, 'the best-prepared'

The Last Great Tour?

Lions' team ever, embarking on maybe, 'the last great Lions' tour.' Tonight, it will be triumph or disaster; one will lead to rejoicing, the other to despair and a long, lonely week in Auckland.

'Here they come!' exclaimed a voice. And Thomas strode out to lead his men onto the coach, marching purposefully forward through a chorus of adulation. His eyes, rigid, fixed dead ahead, didn't stray from the doors of the bus but full-back, Englishman Josh Lewsey's head was jolted back by the deafening blast. He swivelled his neck, looked around and drank it in. Stephen Jones, the Welsh fly-half, was almost embarrassed to look, out of the corner of his eye; so too his compatriot and namesake, number eight, Ryan Jones. The rest kept their heads bowed and pretended not to notice but even with their game faces on, flickers of surprise showed here and there: there was a twitch in the face of one, Simon Easterby, captain of Llanelli and Ireland's blindside flanker.

The players safely boarded, their management team followed. Sir Clive Woodward, the head coach, was the man who had made all these great proclamations on their behalf, the one who had built the squad up as the one that would win, for only the second time in the Lions' proud history, a Test series against the mighty All Blacks of New Zealand. He said, two weeks ago, that he had a 'warm feeling'; he urged anyone who was listening to jump on a plane and travel the 12,000 miles to the land of the Long White Cloud because 'something special' was about to happen. And, standing amidst the colour, the flags and banners, with emotion pouring forth, it was a fight to keep one's feet. Yes, 'something special' was about to happen.

Here's the story of how it all went wrong.

Part 1

Getting There

JUST WHO IS THIS GUY?

Sunday 29 May 2005, Schipol Airport, Amsterdam
I hated rugby once, you know. In first year at secondary school, we hauled our bags up to the top of St Patrick's Hill every Monday afternoon, to run around in the freezing muck. Christian Brothers' College, Cork, is a rugby-playing school with a proud history on the playing fields of Munster, but, to be honest, at the age of thirteen, I could hardly have cared less.

It didn't help that I was no great physical specimen. From my mother's side of the family, I had inherited a pair of legs best described as 'spindles', while the paternal genes had lumbered me with defective eyesight that remains to this day; like most people, I can't see past my own nose, but it's purely for ophthalmic reasons.

In those days, I treated the rugby ball like a hand grenade: it wasn't that there was any risk of the ball itself exploding in my hands, but once that oval shape approached, it seemed to attract guided missiles twice my weight from all around. 'Run, run, run,' the voices in my head screamed. 'Not towards him! Towards the touchline!'

Back then, there seemed little chance I'd ever take up rugby seriously, that it would remain forever a mystery, 'a game played by gentlemen with odd-shaped balls', good only for the occasional half-day from school when there was a big cup game to go to. The glasses, of course, were the main problem.

But to borrow from a former British Prime Minister, there's no legislating for 'events, dear boy, events'. By the time my fourteenth birthday came around, Dr Michael O'Sullivan had scribbled out a prescription for a pair of contact lenses. Irregular enough for a boy my age but hell, I didn't care much about potential long-term consequences: the shanks of metal that had been attached to my face ever since I had failed to see a classroom blackboard at the age of seven were gone. I could ride a bike with the wind tracing the contours of my face; I didn't have to spend my spare time with a screwdriver and sellotape, piecing my glasses back together; and, I could drop my body into a crouch, brace myself for impact, allow a fourteen-stone prop forward to crunch into my shoulder, and not worry in the slightest about a pair of cheap spectacles working their way free, to be swallowed by mud or trampled underfoot.

Better yet, I enjoyed somewhat of a rise. By the following year, I had graduated to a regular position on the 'B' team, making one try-scoring appearance for the Firsts, on a curious weekend which featured a combination of other wingers succumbing to illness, injury and family bereavement, but I missed out on the panel for the Junior Cup.

Academic life – to which, most of my coaches will agree, I was, and am, more suited – began to take over and so, my hikes to Lansdowne grew fewer in number, until, after a bad run of form in my last year, my boots graced the turf for the final time. Exams meant less time for training, so it was off to the far more laissez-faire attitudes of the Old Christians club, from where I had once travelled the few miles down to Mayfield in my Uncle Barry's car with seven team-mates crammed inside and my head sticking out the sunroof.

A year later came my greatest sporting triumph. An Under-18 Old Christians team packed with stars – and vice-captained by me – rampaged to the final of, wait for it, the South Munster Under-18 'B' Cup. It was my first – and probably last – competitive game in Musgrave Park, Cork's premier rugby ground, and also my first taste of one of those barely tangible things that make professional sportsmen tick.

We were leading – and dominating – Bandon, who had given us a pasting earlier in the season, by 12-0. There were about ten minutes to go when a lovely shimmy allowed their fly-half to skip through our midfield. His inside centre came up in support and it looked like curtains. As full-back, I was the last line of defence. It might have been 30 metres from our posts, but it was as close to an open goal as the game of rugby knows. Simple pass: a tap-in. Under the posts, 12-7, and a nervy, nervy end to the game.

Although I once suffered the indignity of skewing a ball over the bar for Wilton United Under-14s from about half a yard in front of the goal line, and I knew how thin the line between success and failure can be, I wasn't about to stick that night's booze money on me being in a position to ensure that Bandon stayed stuck on nil.

But the fly-half didn't draw me wide enough: I never committed myself to the tackle; and I drifted off and hauled down the centre. As I got to my feet, that barely tangible other became a very real thing: the hum of the crowd's appreciation in my ears, the claps, the shouts, the roars, the congratulations. 'Dowtcha, kid.' Sure, there were only about 100 people there, but the feelings something like that stirs in you are the same in front of 30,000 or 40,000. It might be louder if you're Brian O'Driscoll or Paul O'Connell, but the feeling of pride swelling in the gut is the same.

That's it for rugby high points, though. College came soon after, with its attendant distractions – as one of my former classmates, the journalist, T.P. O'Mahony, once acknowledged, 'many of them in mini-skirts' – and the oval ball began to flit out of my life. The drudgery of training was replaced by the delirium induced by a six-pack of Dutch Gold. Muck, wind and rain are nothing compared to a raucous, carefree students' night out. Apart from the odd appearance for the Old Christians' seconds, at a basement level where the only performance-enhancing drugs are nicotine and Panadol, that was that.

Until writing came along, in the form of an old classmate. Ken O'Connor was covering schoolboy soccer for the *Evening Echo*, the biggest-selling local evening newspaper in the country, and he needed a hand trudging the highways and byways of the city to watch little boys running around in shorts. It was time for another event. I'd done a bit of writing while in secondary school, for *Inside Cork*, another of the locals. Name in paper equals reputation.

So Ken, in need of help, decided to give me a call and one day, outside the library came the typical Cork job offer: 'Can ya gimme a hand?' Schoolboy soccer turned into schoolboy GAA turned into local GAA turned into national GAA turned into local rugby turned into national rugby.

My law degree continued apace and my writing continued to diversify. Then, during my second year exams, I got a phone call from the *Echo*'s Chief Executive. Would I come in and have a chat? They had something in mind for me during the summer.

'How would you feel about writing a book?'

I picked my jaw up from the floor, mumbled, 'I'll think about it', then said, 'Yes, of course' a few days later. I signed off on *Reflections of Cork* after an odyssey around Cork in the summer of 2004, arranging, conducting and editing 100 interviews with people from around the city and county.

Which, minus the swearwords, brings me to where I am now. From an Under-13 FAI Cup game between Everton and Tallow in Everton Park in February 2003 to an airport lounge in Schipol in May 2005 tapping away on a rickety old laptop, wondering why the hell I've persuaded someone that a 22 year-old student could travel halfway around the world and write a book about it. It's going to be a long six weeks.

*M*onday 30 May 2005, Changi Airport, Singapore
I think it's Monday, but I'm not sure. I am, however, convinced it's not Sunday. It's been Sunday for the last two days at least, so surely, it can't be three-in-a-row.

But most importantly, a week after finishing my exams, my mind is free again to wander to the great issues of the day, to ponder the future of the world. Or, I could just think about the Lions. They certainly enjoyed a more comfortable trip from Europe: two chartered jumbo jets flew them from Heathrow to New Zealand and boy, did they need two chartered jumbo jets.

To start with, there's the playing squad of 45, bigger than any Lions' panel put together in the past. Three of them weren't on the initial flight: Jason Robinson remains at home with his pregnant wife, while Gareth Thomas and Stephen Jones have club commitments in France. But even with that trio in Europe, the 42 who caught the flight make a healthy number. Then there are the two separate coaching teams. Sir Clive Woodward, Eddie O'Sullivan, the Irish international coach, Andy Robinson, the English international coach and Phil Larder, the legendary defence coach, will prepare the selected teams for the Saturday games and Test matches. Another legend, Ian McGeechan, heads the brains' trust that will oversee the midweek sides; he is joined by Llanelli's Gareth Jenkins and defence coach, Mike Ford. It is the first time in history that two squads within a squad will operate under the Lions' banner.

Kicking coach Dave Alred, and fitness coaches Dave Reddin and Craig White, are in the touring party too, as is former international referee, Irishman, Dave McHugh. Two video analysts, Tony Biscombe and Gavin Scott, will be combing through the tapes, while a medical team led by Dr James Robson, featuring doctor, Gary O'Driscoll, physiotherapist Phil Pask, physio/masseurs, Stuart Barton and Bob Stewart and masseur Richard Wegrzyk, will keep the squad as close to fit as is possible, full fitness being rarer than uncooked fillet steak in the attritional world of professional rugby.

The most high-profile member of the off-field section of the touring party is probably spin-doctor Alastair Campbell, a former advisor to British Prime Minister, Tony Blair. Campbell is joined by a media manager, Louisa Cheetham, and two assistants, Ben Wilson and Marcus Jansa. That Campbell is the most high-profile is no slight on the Tour Manager, Bill Beaumont, who himself toured with the Lions before going on to be a well-respected rugby administrator and successful businessman. He's the Tour Manager, but there's also a Team Manager, Louise Ramsay. The Lions' Chief Executive John Feehan, obviously has to travel while Woodward has brought along barrister Richard Smith, QC, an expert on sports law, to take care of any legal issues that may arise, a chef, Dave Campbell, whose role is pretty self-explanatory, and two kit technicians, Dave Tennison and David Pearson – again, figuring out what their roles encompass doesn't require much imagination.

Phew! It's easy to see why cynics might see this as overkill, a classic case of too many chiefs, where the hell are the bloody Indians? But, Woodward could counter, borrowing from Corkman Roy Keane: 'Fail to prepare, prepare to fail.' The head coach has attempted to cover almost every possible angle: the Lions even commissioned a special song, 'The Power of Four', to be performed before the New Zealand national anthem at all the matchday venues. According to Woodward, who consulted former Lions on the matter, having no anthem of your own gives the opposition a psychological advantage.

'I make no apology for saying this is the best-prepared Lions' tour in history and this squad have the making of a great Lions' Test side,' Woodward said on their arrival in New Zealand. 'But nobody is underestimating the scale of the challenge ahead.

The Last Great Tour?

'So why have I put so much emphasis on the preparation? I look clearly at the history of the Lions and we have been to New Zealand ten times and lost nine, not a great record. That's why I put these plans in place. I would like to reverse that tide of history, but to do that we have to be at our very best ... In my view if the British and Irish Lions were successful in New Zealand, that would surpass anything any of us have achieved in the past.'

Then there's the playing party, the cream of the British and Irish crop, led by Brian O'Driscoll, the brilliant Irish centre. The squad is dominated by the Englishmen who won the World Cup under Woodward two years ago: Lawrence Dallaglio, one of that side's key figures, is, though his international days are now behind him, included after a stellar club season. Of the team that lined out in the final against Australia, only the retired Martin Johnson – who, it is rumoured, Woodward attempted to persuade to travel – the out-of-form Ben Cohen and the injured trio of Phil Vickery, Trevor Woodman and Mike Tindall aren't in the Lions' panel. While Cohen was left out, there are a few Englishmen in the squad who haven't been hitting the high notes of late. Jonny Wilkinson, whose late drop goal sealed that World Cup win, was only parachuted in as forty-fifth man after proving his fitness in a club game; Richard Hill too has had injury problems; Ben Kay, Danny Grewcock and Will Greenwood haven't fired on all cylinders for a while; Robinson hasn't scored a try in months; and flanker, Neil Back is 36 and retired from international rugby. Most of the remaining Englishmen played in an international side that finished fourth in the Six Nations this year and a few more, Matt Stevens, Ollie Smith, Andy Titterrell, Andy Sheridan and Mark Cueto, are novices at the highest level. Of the 21 players England provide to the squad only Dallaglio, the athletic full-back, Josh Lewsey, Martin Corry – the teak-tough Leicester number eight, powerful hooker, Steve Thompson, and Julian White – Vickery's successor at tighthead prop – are genuine front-runners for places in the Test team. Matt Dawson and Graham Rowntree bring experience to the touring party, Charlie Hodgson a dash of panache and Sheridan, Lewis Moody and Smith a strong whiff of untapped potential.

The Welsh, of course, won the championship and yet, at ten, boast less of a representation than either Ireland or England. Kevin Morgan, Rhys Williams, Brent Cockbain and Adam Jones of the Grand Slam-winning team can all count themselves unlucky not to be included. Jones, Gavin Henson, whose dyed hair and colourful boots make him instantly recognisable – and whose winning penalty against England made him an instant Welsh hero – Shane Williams, Tom Shanklin, Martyn Williams, Dwayne Peel, Thomas, Gethin Jenkins and Michael Owen all shone this season and will hope to do so again in New Zealand.

While Ireland won the Triple Crown last year, finished third this season and beat the Tri Nations champions, South Africa, last autumn, at least one of their eleven also owes his place to past deeds: centre Gordon D'Arcy, the player of the 2004 Six Nations, has struggled with injury all year and has played only a handful of games. But, apart from him, the Irish contingent is promising: Donncha O'Callaghan has lots of potential, while the two second-rows ahead of him in the international pecking order, Malcolm O'Kelly and Paul O'Connell, are highly regarded – indeed, O'Connell was spoken about as a potential Lions' captain – hooker, Shane Byrne, is the best lineout thrower in the squad and full-back, Geordan Murphy, was once described by former England and Lions number eight, Dean Richards, as the 'George Best of rugby'. Ronan O'Gara and Shane Horgan could be dark horses for a Test cap, but only friends and family would consider Denis Hickie and John Hayes serious contenders.

Three Scots, the skilful but injury-prone back-row Simon Taylor – another who, if the medical exams were a little more stringent, would be rising at dawn to watch the Lions' tour – sniping scrum-half, Chris Cusiter, and their hooker and captain, Gordon Bulloch, complete the touring party. It's Scotland's poorest-ever representation in a Lions' squad but these days, they find themselves perpetually competing against Italy for the Six Nations' wooden spoon; only Chris Paterson, Jason White and, maybe, Seán Lamont will have been surprised not to be included.

While the scale of the task facing Woodward's men cannot be overstated, the coach was defiant: 'We have world-class players, the challenge for us in the coming weeks before the tests is for the coaches and myself to blend them into a world class side'.

It is certainly an almighty task. One can quibble over the exact number of times a British and Irish selection has toured the Land of the Long White Cloud: arguably, if the 1888 vintage is taken into consideration, this is the twelfth tour, although the 1904 team was the first to play a Test against the natives. But one cannot quibble over how difficult those tours have proved: the only Lions' squad to emerge victorious from New Zealand was that which travelled the country in 1971. Coached by the legendary Carwyn James, that was a remarkable team, with the great Willie John McBride as its forward totem and, in the backs, a who's who of rugby greats: Gareth Edwards, Barry John, Mike Gibson, Gerald Davies and J.P.R. Williams. But even then, facing a crop of non-vintage All Blacks led by an ageing Colin Meads, the Lions needed a late Williams' drop-goal in the Fourth Test to secure victory. As McBride commented in a documentary prior to this tour: 'J.P.R. Williams hasn't kicked a drop-goal before or since!'

'When we take the field,' captain Brian O'Driscoll commented, 'everyone understands the passion of New Zealand rugby. We will respect all our opponents, but we will not fear them. We realise if we train well, prepare well and play well, we can win. That's the challenge at hand and I know I speak for the whole squad when I say it's a challenge we are looking forward to. The last month has been a long wait and it's great it's finally arrived.'

Exactly a week ago, they were in Cardiff, facing a depleted Argentinean side in a warm-up game. Their display there would hardly have sent a shiver down the spine of the watching All Blacks' management team: only a late Jonny Wilkinson penalty salvaged a 25-25 draw for a stuttering Lions' selection.

Such are the difficulties in the modern era: getting the right blend together before 25 June, when they face the All Blacks for the first time, is a momentous task. It was beyond the Lions four years ago in Australia when, after winning the First Test, they lost the next two, finding themselves in severe injury trouble in the final week: some estimates put the figure at only eight fit players, while things got so bad that Scottish scrum-half, Andy Nicol, down under on holiday, was called into the squad as emergency cover. The Lions did win their Test series against South Africa in 1997, two years after the dawn of the professional era, but, even then, they were helped enormously by the wayward place-kicking of their opponents.

While Woodward, O'Driscoll and the battalion of assistants have to get their ship ready to sail into battle, they must also plan for what the All Blacks will throw at them in the Test series. While New Zealand fell at the penultimate hurdle in the 2003 World Cup, beaten in the semi-final by Australia, the crop of exceptionally talented young players that featured in that tournament has continued to flourish: Richie McCaw, the openside flanker, Chris Jack, the second-row, Dan Carter, the fly-half, and centre, Aaron Mauger, all have the look of All-Black greats. Already sitting in the pantheon is their veteran captain, Tana Umaga, and plenty of other members of the current squad will fancy their chances of winning a place there in the not-so-distant future.

In Paris last autumn, they demolished France, destroying them up front and running them ragged out wide for a 45-6 victory. It was a performance of brutish intensity, combined with raw aggression and wonderful skill. Even though the All Blacks struggled in last season's Tri Nations, they showed great form in Paris and elsewhere on their autumn tour, which suggests that the management team of head coach Graham Henry and his assistants, Steve Hansen and Wayne Smith, are capable of converting talent into results. More importantly, they appear to have married the forward intensity of the northern hemisphere game with the backline skills favoured by the Super 12 competition in which teams from New Zealand, South Africa and Australia compete. It's questionable how many of the players could truly be described as 'world-class: O'Driscoll, obviously, is a household name, as is Dallaglio. Apart from that pair, however, and the Englishmen who won the World Cup, there are very few of international renown. It's easy to imagine a New Zealand rugby fan leafing through the Lions' squad list: 'Never heard of him, never heard of him, O'Driscoll – he's not bad – never heard of him, never heard of him, never heard of him, Dallaglio – he's a bit old, isn't he? – never heard of him, Henson – that the lad with the fake tan, going out with Charlotte Church? – never heard of him …'

It doesn't help the Lions' cause that Henry's two assistants have experience of European rugby: Hansen was his right-hand man in Wales and took over when Henry left in 2002, while Smith, himself a former All Black coach, coached the English club side, Northampton, for a spell. Still, the Lions, with a well-drilled set-piece and a battle-hardened pack of forwards, will expect to have an advantage up front, allowing them to play a kicking game to suffocate the All Blacks. We shall see.

The fact that Henry, then in charge of the Welsh national team, coached the Lions in defeat in Australia four years ago adds an extra spice to this Tour. Although the late 1990s turn-around in Welsh fortunes that Henry mastermined saw him hailed in the valleys as the 'Great Redeemer', at the time, Woodward felt that he, not Henry, ought to be the man at the helm; his displeasure at the selection and of the New Zealanders' management of that trip has only ever been thinly veiled. For either man, victory will be sweet.

But the most important thing about this Lions' tour is that it is actually a proper tour. Not since South Africa embarked on a fourteen-game trek in 1994 has an international side travelled to New Zealand to play a Test series of three matches after a succession of midweek games against provincial sides. The physical rigours of modern rugby, and, in many cases, the bank balances of the club sides to whom some players are contracted, make such long jaunts prohibitively difficult to organise. This is a real tour; not only do the six games prior to the First Test give the players a chance to stake their claims to starting positions, but they will bring the game to the furthest-flung corners of New Zealand, from Auckland at the top of the North Island, to Invercargill, at the very bottom of the South Island. For now though, the focus is on the opening game against the Bay of Plenty, for which the team was selected yesterday morning.

'It will be a tremendous honour for me to have the opportunity to pull on a Lions' jersey for the first time,' said Paul O'Connell. 'Looking at the team sheet, it is really exciting to play alongside players of such quality, names like Lawrence Dallaglio and Martyn Williams, who I have admired for such a long time. It will be a great experience and an important test for both me and for the team.'

'Every game is a big game on this tour and we want to put in a good performance against the Bay of Plenty,' added Gordon Bulloch. 'It was great to train in New Zealand for the first time today and the players are very excited about our first match. We are still working on gelling as a team but things are coming together and with a lot of talent on the field for Saturday's game, we are hopeful we can get the tour off to a good start.'

Rugby Mad New Zealand

Tuesday 31 May, Manukau

Everywhere you go in New Zealand there's an opinion hanging in the air, waiting to be imparted. On the question of the Lions, no one is silent; they all have something to say. On the plane from Singapore, I had the pleasure of stretching out alongside a heavy-set farmer from the northern tip of the North Island.

'Oh, you're Irish, are you?'

I asked him about the Lions: 'Is there much of a buzz around the place?'

'Well, you know when you go through immigration? Well, this time, there's a line just for people following the Lions. Strip search. Rubber glove job. But yeah, the Lions are something special. Australia, South Africa? Play them every year. Beat 'em too. Lions are different. Once every twelve years. Mind you, they haven't a chance of winning'.

I should have known. Kiwi knows best. Once Singapore Airlines flight SQ328 levelled off, I was fiddling with my TV screen and seat adjuster. The mere fiddling irritated the Kiwi, because Kiwi knows best. Without warning, he reached across me with a beefy arm, probed beneath my seat and wrenched the TV skyward.

'There you go, mate.'

Now, just to turn on some music and get some shut-eye.

'Let me show you how the machine works.'

It would have been rude to protest that really, I just wanted to sleep, and, in any case, I had figured out how to use the contraption on the last flight.

'Ya see? Ya see?'

He was brash, overbearing and confident about his place

in the world; maybe not the character traits you'd throw into a lonely hearts ad, but it was offset by his friendliness. As long as I didn't diss the rugby team.

In Auckland airport, they pour you free tea and coffee while you wait at the baggage carousel.

'It's the only airport in the world that offers it,' boasted a lady named Dorothy, blue eyes flashing, 'Hello' from a wizened face. 'There's 140 of us. We do four hours each a week.'

There was a tag with her name on it that read, 'Volunteer'.

'And it's all voluntary?'

'Oh yes.' And it was as if her chest puffed right out.

It transpired that she was from Scotland originally, but her adopted home had seeped into her bones.

'Do you follow the rugby?'

The irony is that traditionally, New Zealand were famed for their forward power; while they have relied mainly on the spectacular skills of their backs to win games over the past decade or so, for many years, they pioneered the 'ten-man', territorial game built on dominating the opposition up front.

'Of course I do.'

'So, have the Lions got a chance?'

'Well, a lot depends on the First Test. If that goes well, anything can happen.'

'Business or pleasure?' the lady asked at immigration control.

'I'm here for the pleasure of watching the Lions beat the All Blacks.'

'Yeah, right. Enjoy your stay.' Sarcasm dripped from every word.

At a security point though, I encountered New Zealand

humility for the first time.

'Oh, I think you have a real chance, mate. I don't think you can read too much into the Argentina game and I worry about the All Blacks. I wonder is the belief there. Oh yeah, you guys have a real chance,' said the imposing security guard, only too happy to have a quick word. It was, after all, rugby related. When it comes to such matters, the safety of the nation, presumably, can wait until after the final whistle.

And then, I'm in. Welcome to Auckland. One epic voyage has ended and another one is about to begin. It's going to be rugby, rugby, rugby, writ large and everywhere for the next six weeks. Everyone will have an opinion. No one will be shy of sharing.

A Thousand Welcomes
Wednesday 1 June 2005, Auckland

The 1905 New Zealand side that toured the British Isles was the first to be called the 'All Blacks'. They went on to sweep all before them, but, on departure, they were already legends in their own land. In *Stand Up and Fight: When Munster Beat the All Blacks*, Alan English writes that they were hailed as heroes wherever they went. In the less upmarket parts of town, ladies raised their skirts whenever an All Black approached. From the Auckland farmer to the Scottish airport volunteer, they're rather fond of their rugby in New Zealand and, even though the sight of a Lions' tracksuit – in any part of town – is unlikely to warrant the sort of greeting that could result in legal action, on their first appearance on these shores since 1993 the Lions expect to be hot property.

The Last Great Tour?

In Rotorua, hundreds received them at the airport; a traditional Maori welcome later on was 'quite staggering', according to Sir Clive Woodward; and when they held a public training session in the North Harbour Stadium near Auckland, the *New Zealand Herald* counted the attendance at approximately 5,000. 'Fresh' from the airplane, I arrived at the ground yesterday, five hours after the Lions did their thing: they came, they trained, they signed autographs. Later amidst the quiet, a groundsman sat atop his lawnmower, the crowds long since dispersed, his beloved turf scarcely disturbed by a workout which barely deserved the term.

Throughout Auckland, flags flap on thousands of lampposts. On one side they proclaim, 'Welcome to Auckland', on the other, 'Lions Supporters: Make Yourself 100% at Home'. In each of the match venues, special facilities will be laid on for the expected influx of 20,000 fans, what the media here have taken to calling, the 'Barmy Army'. Everywhere, the New Zealanders are genial. 'Here for the Lions, are you?' asked the man in the electrical shop from which I bought an adaptor for my laptop. Even though, after mild interrogation, it turned out he knew absolutely nothing about rugby, save that it involved an oval ball and lots of guys with mud on their shirts, he still knew that the Lions were in town and was able to match my accent. This was in Manukau, a city suburb of Auckland, where rugby league vies with union for the hearts and minds of the natives; it's also a place the Lions will visit only for a brief session of autograph signing and yet, he still knew enough to make small talk.

Gordon D'Arcy described his early experiences thus: 'It's great; everyone's been really accepting and warm to us, but that's what the New Zealand people are like: they're really friendly, really welcoming. They'll give you a shout from the other side of the street, which is amazing. It's great to be here, been really enjoyable, but it will be interesting to see what it's like come Test week!'

The Lions have been roaming free amongst the natives. Sometimes, they don't even travel in convoy. Early this afternoon, Irish hooker Shane Byrne, decked out in his Lions tracksuit, was marching purposefully back towards the Hilton Hotel before training. Nobody raised their skirt, or if they had, Byrne wasn't telling.

But the welcome hasn't been universal. The front page of yesterday's edition of the weekly *North Shore Times* is dominated by the powerful image of a locked gate, a set of rugby goalposts fuzzy and out of focus in the distance. The picture is that of the Onewa Domain, which will be the Lions' training base while they're in Auckland, re-developed at the expense of the local ratepayers. Landscape gardeners were called in, creating rockeries and planting trees, while painters spruced up the clubhouses. A new fence was erected around the perimeter, two metres high, with a metal sheet painted red to proclaim that the Lions are in town, but *in camera*. To make doubly sure that no one catches an illicit glimpse of the Lions training, police are on duty.

Indeed, inside the paper, an angry letter thunders forth: 'Who is paying for it all? Presumably the ratepayers of the North Shore. Who can tell, because the fancy facelift seems to have proceeded unannounced and unpublicised.'

Vern Cotter, the coach of the Lions' first opponents, the Bay of Plenty, added: 'You think back to past tours and the way

Lions players got out into the community, built some bridges and fostered rugby. It's disappointing from a community point of view, no doubt about that.'

The point is well put by both. The Lions have come to the other side of the world and sure, the aim of the tour is to bring a series victory back home with them, but where's their sense of fun? They are only allowing the public to view two training sessions, one in Auckland, the other in Christchurch; everywhere else, the long arm of the law will be stretched around their training facilities.

Clive Woodward responded: 'The training base that we're using has been developed at a large cost to the local authority. We're conscious of that and we want to give something back in return. So, we're doing a lot of coaching sessions with the local kids and we've had one proper public session.' Back in your box, Mr Ratepayer!

'It was good fun,' said D'Arcy of the open training session. 'One of the things about this tour is that we're not going to be stuck in the hotel, we're going to go out and actually try to be as accessible as possible, and yesterday was a great chance for the kids to come along and get a few autographs and a couple of them were lucky enough to join in the training session with us. You can't really put a price on what that means to kids.'

That, really, is that. And can the head coach be blamed for paranoia? On the last tour, the Lions were convinced that the hosts secretly watched them train, bolstered in that belief by the way the Australians managed to crack their line-out code in the final, critical test. Who can forget the way Justin Harrison soared high to pluck that late line-out, rising high and in front of Martin Johnson to secure a series victory for the Wallabies?

Getting There

There can be no repeat. So, there are only two open training sessions and if you're determined to catch a glimpse of the Lions' secret plotting, you'll just have to check the yellow pages under 'Blimp Hire'.

His detractors have always complained that Woodward sees himself as somewhat messianic: as the old joke goes, 'What's the difference between God and Sir Clive Woodward? God doesn't think he's Sir Clive Woodward.' And, early in the tour, there's a touch of the evangelical about him, a little bit of the preacher, speaking of giving something back, but also of how the tour – which he described a few days ago as 'the last of the great tours' – will benefit the players. Responding for the umpteenth time to questioners who wonder if his selection of a record 45 players would bring the old cliché about too many cooks spoiling the broth into play, he said: 'People complain about the number of players we have, but I wish we had 60 or 70. All of the players out here will learn a lot from New Zealand and it's a pity that more can't have the same opportunity. This is, if we're being honest about it, the last great Lions' tour and I want to maximise the benefits to all four countries. The players can learn from the other players, as well as the different coaches, and they can learn from New Zealand as well, particularly the intensity about rugby here, which is far more than back home. The numbers have, in my view, been really over-hyped'.

Far from shivering in an underground bunker in the Hilton, as Cotter suggests, getting out into the community and trying to make this tour unique is very much a part of the head coach's philosophy: 'The number one goal out here is to win the Tests, but there's a bigger picture too. I'd like everyone to learn something from the tour; I'd like to think everyone will go home having learned something new, even the medical guys.'

But let's not get carried away. The Lions are down under to win. If they can do some good deeds on the way, great; if not, well, they aren't going to be too concerned. And, if good deeds morph into distractions, that's no good. History remembers the odd Florence Nightingale, but it prefers victorious warriors.

A more hard-nosed view came from England's Martin Corry. 'Honestly,' he replied when I asked why, if the public sessions were so enjoyable for the players, there weren't more of them, 'we understand that there's a media element and there's a public relations element to it all but when you're playing and you've a game to focus on at the weekend, then you just want to get down and focus on that. Yes, it's lovely to have all the support and all the interest, but let's face facts, we're rugby players and we want to be focusing on what happens at the weekend. Having said that, it was a great experience and it's nice to see that kind of support for us.' Even Cotter acknowledged, 'Let's face it, it's very much a corporate-professional approach to the game. They're here for 80 minutes of rugby and that's basically it.'

Important and all as getting out and meeting people will be on this tour, it's a case of striking a balance between not getting distracted by the attention on the one hand, and feeding off the hype and the chance to escape the confines of the hotel on the other. D'Arcy was happy to acknowledge the point: 'With the management team we have here, between Alastair [Campbell] and Clive, they'll strike a perfect balance. They're both at the top of what they do. They'll get the balance right and we trust them to do that.'

On the whole, a friendly country has extended a warm

welcome: Lions and followers alike can expect a happy few weeks. For their part, D'Arcy and Corry sounded genuinely enthusiastic about the prospect of coaching with the local kids.

On the tour itinerary, there are five hours of local activity before every game; however, all that local activity will be performed by players who aren't in the squad for the following day. It's about striking a balance: the Lions could play at being ambassadors 24 hours a day and this might cause the locals to hitch up their skirts whenever the familiar crest comes into view, but they're here for the serious business of winning rugby matches. So, if you wouldn't mind standing back from the fence, please, sir. Certainly, officer.

Meet the Press
June 1 2005, Auckland

Any idiot could get in here, I was thinking to myself as a ginger-haired man passed by, giving me a strange smile on the way. I thought nothing of it; just another hanger-on in a Lions' tracksuit. Could be any one of the dozens of backup staff that Woodward has brought down under with him.

Then it dawned on me. Oh Jesus, I've just snubbed Alastair Campbell, the Lions' Media Consultant; the former overlord of 10 Downing Street! And I walked right by him! Here's a man who has helped to elect three governments, who has been the closest confidant of one of Britain's most successful post-War Prime Ministers, who controlled the Westminster Press Corps with an iron fist for most of the last decade. He even smiled: a whole lifetime can pass without getting the chance to introduce yourself to the most powerful people in society; well, I've had my chance. Downhill from here.

Oh well. As I had been thinking, any schmuck could get in. The Hilton Hotel, situated on Prince's Wharf on the waterfront, is the Lions' base during their time in Auckland. It is slightly hidden away, but requires no more than a five-minute stroll off the street.

And yet, security is a touch lax. It's easy to find the exact location of the press conference. All you have to do is look out for a group of badly-shaven, scruffy men with laptop cases. *Voilà*: meet the rugby writers of the world, almost exclusively male.

Silhouetted behind tinted sliding doors, such a gathering was visible: here was the Hilton's exhibition space, the location of the Lions' Auckland media activity. There was one security man on duty. Had I turned lengthways, I would just about have stretched from one of his arms to the other. But he didn't even ask me who I was. I just clutched my briefcase, put on the air of someone who had a God-given entitlement to be there and marched right through. I poured myself a cup of coffee – I was disappointed to see that there were no sandwiches – and waited for the festivities to begin. Then, I dissed Alastair Campbell.

Even if there were no sandwiches, I had high hopes for this operation. As I suspected, it proved to be extraordinarily well-managed. Woodward assumed his position at the top table first, read a statement and took questions. When Lawrence Dallaglio and Brian O'Driscoll joined later on they fielded questions as well. But the best part was yet to come, with players milling around at ease, happy to talk to all and sundry. Malcolm O'Kelly, Gordon D'Arcy, Martin Corry, Gavin Henson, Steve Thomson, Matt Dawson, Matt Stevens, Gethin Jenkins,

Getting There

Dwayne Peel, Tom Shanklin, Ben Kay, Andrew Sheridan, Charlie Hodgson and Josh Lewsey had all made an appearance within an hour of the head coach standing down.

The whole afternoon was run with military precision. Campbell's assistants scurried around with clipboards in hand.

'Mr O'Kelly, you have a five-minute radio slot now.'

'Can I have just a moment with him, please?'

'Well ... go on then, but quickly.'

Here, no one seems to know how to say, 'No'. Sure, scrums formed around particular players, but it was all very organised and mannerly; the players went there of their own volition too, it appeared: as they flitted in and out, materialising as if by magic from the white walls of the Hilton, nobody was particularly guarded or defensive.

But then, why would they be? These are the British and Irish Lions, the elite of the elite. All of them are stars for club and country. They've had to deal with the media at all levels, print, radio and television, for years now. And they are the elite: self-doubt was not in evidence amongst this gathering as they swaggered from interview to interview. Kay sat in a chair, threw his arms back and stretched; when one of the older members of the press corps came over to have a word, Kay reached out a mammoth paw and grabbed a chair for him. Henson's hair was red today, but his face a sea of calm and tranquillity as he relaxed before a phalanx of microphones. Nobody on edge, everybody courteous and polite.

All the time, though, Campbell lurked. He has three assistants working for him and they are very much working for him. At one stage, Dallaglio, O'Driscoll and Woodward were posing for photographs outside, looking out onto Auckland Harbour. An assistant looked at Campbell. Nothing. He waited a moment and turned back to look at his boss again. Once more, no response. A few moments more, and the assistant glanced back. Campbell, barely perceptively, flicked his head to the side, in the manner of a particularly idiosyncratic bidder raising his offer at an auction.

'OK, that's enough, folks, that's enough,' barked the assistant instantly. And Campbell drifted away, melting back into the hotel. Later on, he hovered everywhere. Even where he isn't, his presence is. It's like being in a room with the Mona Lisa: no matter where you are, those eyes seem to be piercing into your back. Surely, the players sense that too; it's hard to see there being any repeat of the last tour, where any unrest was communicated to the media, sometimes in player diaries. This time, any diaries will travel via Campbell and his three assistants, and one fears for the player, who, having uttered something indiscreet to the media, has to face the Lions' Media Consultant's legendary wrath.

Only the security could be faulted, but even that gives the lie to any suggestion that the Lions are hunkered down and hiding out. It all seems very laid-back and relaxed. Even Campbell, though his eyes swept the room like a satellite, didn't look in the least bit drawn or stressed. Everything is under control.

The Craic Shack
Wednesday 1 June 2005, Northcote, Auckland
Across the road from the Onewa Domain are two big Guinness signs, attached to a wall. The pub – well, it's hardly anything else – is painted a welcoming shade of green. It's within walking distance of the campsite which now contains

my campervan and so, from the moment it caught my eye, a visit was inevitable.

'Alright mate?' An enthusiastic welcome. The music a little loud, the place was virtually empty: an old guy sat at one side of the counter, sipping a half pint of lager; in an alcove, a couple were gazing into one another's eyes; outside, a group ate at a table. Still, I thought, it can't hurt to stay a while.

'The Guinness sign and the green were like a beacon to the thirsty traveller,' I announced.

'OK. Do you want some of this?' He pointed to a tap labelled, 'Shite Lager'. Hmmm.

'Is it any good?'

'Nah, it's shite.'

'Well, I'll have to have some then.'

As it turned out, the barman-cum-comedian's name was Simon and the old guy was Stan. The latter's touch of deafness, lack of hearing aid, and the decibel-level Nirvana were churning out of the speakers made it hard to explain why the British and Irish Lions are the British and Irish Lions, not just the British Lions.

'But it's all the one country, isn't it?' The prospect of explaining the intricacies of the Irish political situation to a deaf man in a loud bar is never a particularly palatable one.

'Yes, it's a funny one, Stan.' He seemed happy enough with that explanation.

By then, two more patrons had joined us at the counter, a pair of Welsh ex-pats, Mike and 'Tucker'. Mike hadn't seen Wales play in about fifteen years, but Tucker, well, Tucker is the sort of guy I'm looking out for.

'Ay, I'm picking up my campervan tomorrow and we're 'ittin'

the road then. Down to Taupo, then to Napier for the All Blacks'
trial and up to Rotorua.'

'How many?'

'Four altogether.'

Tucker, it turns out, is from a place called Brynaman, near
Swansea in Wales, the home town of the diminutive, but daz-
zlingly skilful Lions winger, Shane Williams.

'I used to drink with 'is dad back home, y'know? Y'wouldn't
think it, but 'is dad is about six foot four and twenty stone. 'e
was a truck driver.'

'So, he couldn't sidestep quite like Shane then?' Chuckles
all round.

'Nah. 'e's not fat, Shane's dad though, just big. Anyway, no
one in Wales is fat: we all just 'ave collapsed chests.'

Tucker and I swapped numbers and made a solemn oath and
vow to meet in Napier on Friday night after the All Blacks' trial.

I was not quite finished with the Craic Shack though. Just
then, two teenagers walked in. Nothing unusual about that. But
they were male and were wearing skirts. Simon runs a special
Wednesday night promotion: wear a skirt and get a jug of 'Shite'
for five dollars. New Zealanders definitely have a sense of
humour in there somewhere.

'What time are you open 'til, Simon?' I wondered.

'Ah, until whenever I decide to bugger off.'

'Ah yeah, but what time do you absolutely have to close,
according to the law?'

Simon paused, for once unable to give a smart answer.

'You know, no one's ever asked me that before.' They
might have a sense of humour, but they don't drink like we do
back home.

Who are you then?

Thursday 2 June 2005, Northcote, Auckland

What would happen, my irate letter-writing friend had wondered in his letter to the *North Shore Times*, if someone turned up in the vicinity of the Onewa Domain while the Lions were training? He speculated that, with so many baton-wielding policemen around, it wouldn't be particularly pleasant. Only one way to find out.

At ten in the morning at Takapuna's club grounds, the dull thwack of boot on ball carried over the red sheeting. People passed by, non-plussed. The clubhouse itself was deserted, with only a few empty cars for company. There were no police on duty either, nor was there any security to be seen. The gates remained impressively padlocked, but as they crashed back and forth in the wind anyone could walk up and peer through one of the many gaps.

Three Lions were practicing their kicking: Ronan O'Gara, who starts at fly-half on Saturday, Charlie Hodgson, who's on the bench, and the red-haired, red-booted Gavin Henson, who has been given the number twelve shirt for the opener against the Bay of Plenty. Each player had someone with them to retrieve balls and whisper encouragement. While I was peeping through the fence, Dave Alred, the Lions' kicking coach, was advising Henson. His sage words weren't audible above the howling wind, but after one punt, he happily exclaimed, 'Now you've got it!'

Down in one corner, arms folded, Sir Clive stood impassively. So much for the great lockout. Then again, any Kiwi spy is unlikely to learn much from watching kicking practice: 'O'Gara kicks right footed, does he? Thank you, Mr Bond, but that's hardly MI6 material.'

The Last Great Tour?

It turned out that there was no press conference today. Apparently yesterday's was 'the big one'. There was a medical update in the morning but those of us marooned far from the Hilton, without ready access to email, just have to shrug our shoulders and get on with it. Perhaps the glorious relaxation and unfettered access of yesterday may not be the norm after all.

There's nothing uptight about the Hilton's general security arrangements. Outside the main door of the hotel when I got there, a lady was resting against a pillar, a Lions' ball and jersey clutched in her hands. She had a marker too and, judging by the black scrawls, she'd been fairly successful at grabbing players for autographs.

'I have all of them now, except for Brian O'Driscoll,' she announced, proudly. Apparently, the Lions are all very accommodating and the security men are happy to stand back. But, standing in the shade in Auckland in July, even though it's a mild winter by northern European standards, can get a bit chilly.

'Oh, I'm freezing. I've been here since nine o'clock this morning [by then, it was lunchtime]. I've been living here for a few years and I've got used to the warm weather. I think I'll call it a day now.' And the little English ex-pat tottered off into the heart of Auckland, still clutching her memorabilia and black marker.

Even though Gordon D'Arcy said yesterday that the locals had been known to shout out from across the street whenever they saw the Lions, I'm not convinced. Apart from the English World Cup winners, the readily-identifiable Henson and O'Driscoll, logic suggests that few of the squad are recognisable to the vast majority of New Zealanders. D'Arcy has never even played against the All Blacks: why would they recognise him? They might know him by deed after his exploits during Ireland's win in Twickenham in 2004, but recognise his face? Probably not.

My suspicions were confirmed later in the afternoon. With no press conference to attend, I was free to walk around the centre of Auckland. Wandering out of one shop, something caught my eye: a group of four men walking, slower than normal. Their gait and dress seemed a little unusual. Then, the faces registered: Stephen Jones, Dwayne Peel, Tom Shanklin and Martyn Williams, four Welsh Lions. All were dressed in civilian gear; indeed, Shanklin was wearing a pair of long, baggy shorts to which the word unflattering can't quite do justice. Neither the shorts nor the players drew any glances. I followed them about 400 metres up the street, at a safe distance, watching closely for the slightest sign of interest. No heads turned, no faces creased into smiles, no strides were checked. Nobody asked for an autograph.

Nobody knows who they are.

All four had helped Wales to the Grand Slam a few months previously. Jones, Williams and Shanklin were all inspirational throughout the season, Williams as the roving openside flanker, lubricating Wales' fluid running game, Jones a steady hand on the tiller at number ten and Shanklin the hard-running centre in midfield. And Peel? Well, Wales might have had fifteen stars in every game, but none shone brighter than the lively Llanelli scrum-half. He was a key man for his country in their spring triumph, so good during that campaign that he seems a shoo-in for a Lions Test jersey; at the very least, he's the front-runner in a four-man race for the number nine shirt. With his spiky hair and slight frame, he ought to be recognisable too.

And yet, nobody knows who he is. It's possible that they do know, but are just keeping schtum, leaving the Lions to browse the streets of Auckland, burning energy wondering why no one's paying any attention. But if we are to believe D'Arcy, the locals don't feel in the least bit inhibited about bellowing a greeting from across the street. So, it seems that nobody knows who they are.

Even in a thriving, busy city like Auckland, which, with its noise, smells and dozens of ethnic groups, brings New York to mind, this is unusual. Maybe that particular 400 metres was a barren stretch for rugby fans. Maybe the sports shop along the tour Lions' route was full of soccer-mad New Zealanders just then. Or maybe the answer is the simplest one: nobody knows who they are in their civvies, they are just another group of tourists.

There is a new test for the Lions then: to be recognised. When they return to Auckland in July after their trek around the provinces of New Zealand, will they be able to walk the streets unknown? Whether they are or not will, of itself, tell much of the story of the tour.

Look at that
Friday 3 June 2005, Napier

The road from Taupo to Napier winds through the mountains like a rolled-out ball of wool that someone tied down so they could find their way home. Right and left, mountains rise up to the skies and water crashes into the valleys below. There are interlocking spurs, doldrums, things you think you'd only ever see in geography books, and forests of conifers teetering on mountainsides, as the road swoops down among the rockfalls and waterfalls and swings back up towards the sky, where the clouds are puffs of white before a backdrop of blue.

Then, as if someone had turned on a tap, the skies began to open. Rain lashed the windscreen; on cue, the scenery became less scenic too: just bursts of gorse now, clinging to rocky outcrops. Cold, crisp and glorious, to wet, windy and miserable. It's easy to see now why, at the moment, the bush-fire danger on the roadside signs is placed as low as it can ever go. New Zealand is a thing of beauty but a thing too of unrelenting savagery. As a mist fell into the valleys, cloaking the dozens of contours of the dozens of hills, the territory began to look forbidding, a friend of no invader, but a world of refuge for the brave and valiant native.

But the sun came out again, peeping over snow-topped hills. Well it might have: Mother Nature has shown what she can do. The curtain was pulled back again; everything returns to normal. But there can be no doubt that this land of friend-ly people, spectacular scenery and happy views is not a land only of welcomes.

***

Driving out of Auckland at half-seven that morning, the defi-ciencies in my approach to the business of covering the tour became painfully apparent. Not only had I missed the press briefing there was yesterday, I had also missed out on a mas-sive news item.

'Ireland lock Malcolm O'Kelly is on his way home from New

Zealand this morning,' the newscaster intoned. England's Simon Shaw had already been summoned as a replacement. O'Kelly had towered over me on Wednesday and seemed in good shape. Later that day though he was withdrawn from the bench for the Bay of Plenty game and, yesterday night, he was ruled out of the rest of the tour.

'I am obviously very disappointed that for me the tour is over,' he said. 'I have had this problem for a while but had managed to keep it at bay. I have to be philosophical and accept the judgement of the doctors. It is as well just to accept it and go home, and let the coaches and players get on with the job of trying to win the series against New Zealand. They are a great bunch and though I am sorry I will no longer be part of it, I wish them all the best.'

Clive Woodward said: 'Mal is a terrific player and it is always very sad when a top-class player loses out to injury like this. We spoke after he saw the specialist today and agreed there was no chance of him being fit enough to play and it was better for the tour if a replacement was called out. It is very sad for Mal but his attitude has been first-class. Even now, he has put the broader interests of the Lions first.'

'All of us, but perhaps most of all Mal's Irish team mates, are obviously saddened at the news,' said his Leinster and Ireland colleague, Brian O'Driscoll. 'We've known about his injury but like him hoped it would not flare up like this. It is typical of Mal that he has taken it in the spirit he has.'

STAKING A CLAIM
All Blacks' Final Trial
New Zealand Probables V Possibles
*F*riday 3 June 2005, MacLean Park, Napier

Probables 32
Tries: S. Sivivatu (2), D. Howlett, R. So'oialo
Convs: N. Evans (3)
Pens: N. Evans (2)

Possibles 37
Tries: M. Nonu (2), B. Atiga, S. Hamilton, B. Ward
Convs: S. Donald (3)
Pens: S. Donald (2)

A few weeks ago, the Irish rugby team had something like this final trial before picking the squad to travel to play two Tests against Japan. It had to be abandoned well before the end, for fear that the stretcher-bearers would collapse, such was the rate of attrition. In bygone days, the final trials were a big thing, allowing youngsters to emerge from nowhere and elderly international staples to fall by the wayside. In New Zealand, the final trial remains a major event. Tonight's attendance at MacLean Park was 20,000; the official capacity is 16,000, which makes the figure somewhat more impressive. That isn't even the whole story: the Canterbury Crusaders' front-line players were allowed time off after their defeat of the New South Wales Waratahs in the Super 12 final while several more Test contenders were playing for the New Zealand Maori against Fiji. It got worse: Mils Muliaina, Keven Mealamu, Rodney So'oialo and Jerry Collins, all front-runners for Test berths against the Lions, were only on the bench and, to cap it all, injury had ruled out hooker Anton Oliver, vying with Mealamu for a start against the Lions, as well as captain, Tana Umaga.

Then, there was the weather. In Fiji earlier today, they complained about the heat. The New Zealand Maori carved out a two-point victory, but had melted into the dressing room at half-time; as an aside, there was little there that the Lions could take, with their game against the Maori taking place on 11 June. Back in Napier, it was bitterly cold, 'bloody freezing, mate', according to the locals. While for the handful of supporters and journalists from the home nations interested enough to take in the game it was bracing, for the native masses used to rather more sultry conditions it was yet another reason to sit in front of the fire, in the company of a cup of cocoa and the remote control rather than several thousand other shivering fans. So, 20,000 was a remarkable figure.

Of course, even in the cold, there was plenty at stake. The All Blacks will warm up for the Test series with a game against Fiji on 10 June and the squad for that game will be named tomorrow morning. And, despite the absentees, there was plenty of talent on display. Doug Howlett, Byron Kelleher, Ali Williams and Tony Woodcock, for the Probables, and Conrad Smith and Ma'a Nonu, for the Possibles, will all expect to hear Graham Henry call out their names for the Fiji squad. In addition, Sosene Anesi and Sitiveni Sivivatu of the Waikato Chiefs enjoyed tremendous Super 12 campaigns and are considered, in New Zealand language, 'bolters' for the Fiji and Lions' squads; as it turned out, seeing those two in action was worth the admission price alone.

That said, the atmosphere was surreal. The stadium announcer did his best to gee up the supporters, but the teams were greeted with only mild applause. The odd piece of individual brilliance inspired the odd lukewarm cheer, but the crowd seemed happy to sit back and let the rugby wash over them. There was a bit of mischief in the air too. Towards the end, Collins remained on the bench; indeed, of the Probables, only he and Mealamu, the other top international in their reserves, remained fully tracksuited. 'Jerry! Jerry! Jerry!' the crowd chanted, anxious that the muscular back-row forward see some action – and, maybe, crack some skulls. On cue, 'Jerry' turned around and raised a finger to his lips. 'Sssshhh.'

On the pitch though the honours were hotly-contested in a fine match. It took only eleven minutes for the game to spring into life. Sivivatu picked up the ball in his own half, on the left touchline and weaved his way upfield over for the game's opening score, at one stage gripping the ball in one hand, teasing and taunting the defence, and swatting away would-be tacklers with the other. Ten minutes later, the Fijian-born winger drew another cheer from the crowd. This time, Anesi made the incision, allowing his team-mate to slip over with ease. By then, the Probables led by 17-0 and the crowd had fallen virtually silent, a soft requiem for the Possibles playing over in their heads.

Just before half-time though they struck back. Nonu, who, up until then, had looked dynamic and dangerous without ever threatening the Probables' dominance, made another half-break in midfield. Again, his offload out of the tackle was perfect and, this time, it found full-back Ben Atiga in support. Try for the Possibles and the interval deficit was reduced to a manageable twelve points.

The Last Great Tour?

The 20,000 who had paid in were certainly getting their money's worth: the pace of the game was remarkably high and the skill levels supreme. Sivivatu and Anesi were graceful in open play, as was their fly-half, Nick Evans, while Sione Lauaki, the flanker, was rampaging around the field with ball in hand. For the Possibles, Nonu was the stand-out performer although, given that he had played on the wing during the Super 12, his centre partner, Conrad Smith and openside Josh Blackie found themselves doing plenty of covering work in defence.

Four minutes after the restart though Nonu showed that his repertoire of offensive skills more than make up for any defensive shortcomings, again making a half-break and offload that this time led to a try for Scott Hamilton. But the Probables stretched their lead again. Once more, Sivivatu was the key man, breaking clear down the left and kicking ahead. It looked like he was going to complete a spectacular hat-trick, but, unsportingly, Howlett beat him to the touchdown. Soon after, the two-try winger was substituted to loud applause. That score came fourteen minutes into the second half and the Probables, though it appeared as if they were set to canter away to victory, weren't to cross the line again until the very end. The reason was Nonu. Presumably tired of making space for others, first he powered over from close range after Smith had made the initial break and then he ran through midfield to notch a second try. So, Nonu too got a well-deserved cheer when he departed with fifteen minutes left on the clock.

With replacements entering the fray from all corners of MacLean Park, the game became a little fractured, but a try from Brent Ward gave the Possibles a ten-point lead and, when So'oialo came off the bench to stroll over late on, the result was already beyond doubt.

One of those who emerged from the reserves was the great Andrew Mehrtens. Sadly, there was nothing great about the 25 minutes the fly-half was on the pitch: simple passes went awry; kicks were aimless, from hand and tee; tackles were missed and balls were dropped. He looked like a man who knew that time had, long ago, been called on his All-Black career. Still, he may yet feature against the Lions: New Zealand aren't possessed of much depth in the fly-half position. Aaron Mauger, usually the inside centre, can play there, but, on the evidence of their displays tonight, the other pretenders, Evans and Steve Donald, don't have the ability to kick the ball well enough to survive in a Test series. So, by a strange process of elimination, the bell need not be tolling for Mehrtens just yet.

Tonight's style of play was the most impressive aspect though: the game was full of fast, open rugby. 'You've got to look at what our natural skills are in this country,' the All Blacks' assistant coach, Steve Hansen, said afterwards. 'We've a lot of natural, running backs. They've just come out of a [training] programme that's encouraged that and they've got the skill to do it, so, why not? Perhaps, because we haven't been together for too long, defensive systems weren't as good as they could have been, which allowed free, running rugby, but that's just the way it is'. And there was a conviction about Hansen as he said it that suggested the All Blacks are gearing up for just that sort of approach to the Test series: how will the Lions respond tomorrow?

Probables: S. Anesi; D. Howlett, C. Laulala, S. Mapusua, S. Sivivatu; N. Evans, B. Kelleher; S. Bates (c), C. Newby, S. Lauaki; A. Williams, J. Ryan; C. Johnstone, D. Witcombe, T. Woodcock.
Subs: J. Cowan for Kelleher 44, A. Mehrtens for Sivivatu 57, B. Mika for Ryan 70, R. So'oialo for Lauaki 74.

Possibles: B. Atiga; S. Hamilton, C. Smith, M. Nonu, B. Ward; S. Donald, S. Devine; N. Williams, J. Blackie, C. Masoe; K. O'Neill, T. Donnelly; J. Afoa, A. Hore (c), S. Taumoepeau.
Subs: T. Kopelani for Hore 72, J. Gopperth for Donald 72, C. Hoeft for Taumoepeau 73, J. Nutbrown for Devine 73.

Referee: L. Bray (Wellington).

I met Tucker afterwards, as arranged. He had picked up his mate Justin and two fine-looking blondes, Helen and Vicky. Vicky, being sensible, is making a break for it after the Bay of Plenty game, but Helen, bless her, is interrupting her year of backpacking to travel on the rest of the tour with Justin, Tucker and another friend of theirs.

"is name's Dai,' she moaned, 'and I'm told that he sweats profusely. And I'm sharing a bed with 'im!'

Both girls complained about the sub-zero temperatures they had to endure in the van the night before: 'It were freezing. And Justin was too pissed to turn on the gas.'

I was forced to admit that my sympathies lay with the ladies. 'Hey, lads,' I bellowed, 'now that's not on, letting the girls freeze like that.'

The Rugby Begins

'Yeah, well,' said Justin, a glint in his eye, 'why don't you ask them what they were doing when the lady at the campervan place was showing us how to use the gas, waste disposal and all that?'

A silence fell, so Justin continued. 'Inside, looking at the bloody mirror, that's what: "Ooh, I look so thin".' Which rather put a different complexion on things.

While my heart went out to Helen and her predicament, at least she has a bed to share. A group of New Zealand rugby fans were wandering around Napier wearing the sort of T-shirts normally associated with a stag night. 'Balmy Army', read the back, with nine names listed. On the other half of the back of the shirts were inscribed the words 'Paddy', 'Taffy', 'Jock' and 'Pommy'.

'You're Irish, are you? Well, that's you there, look.' And the charming gentleman turned, twisted his arm and pointed to one of the names. 'Paddy, see, eh?' The man's name was Brody and, like the other eight, he was a Wellingtonian.

'That's the best city in New Zealand.'

'What about Auckland?'

'Nah. Shower of wankers.'

After a few beers, it seemed only fair to wind Brody up about the relationship between the two cities.

'Brody here's a very proud Auckland man.'

'I bloody am not!' Brody nearly exploded, eyes nearly popping right out of his head. 'Get this straight: I'm not from bloody Auckland'.

Brody is the driver of a four-berth campervan that will follow the Lions' Tour. The four-berth van will have nine inhabitants for the duration of the trip, which means that at least one would be happy to swap places with Helen.

'You going tomorrow?' he asked me.

'Of course I am. Up the road to Rotorua.'

'Rotten-rua, you mean'.

'Sorry?'

'Rottenrua, they call it, because of the smell. It's the sulphur, from all the volcanic activity. It's bloody awful.'

Later in the evening, some of the All Blacks rolled in for a few beers. Remarkably, the only people who went anywhere near them were – perhaps predictably – the Welsh. Tucker and Justin badgered them for autographs and gossip, while the girls, well, the girls thought about what girls think about when there are professional sportsmen in the room.

'Ooooh, I'd like to grab myself an All Black'.

'What about 'im, there?'

'Ooooh, yes, I think so.' But no one else approached the players.

'Ah, they probably get that all the time. Why bother them?' said two of the locals when asked why they weren't even making eye contact with the trialists, never mind pestering them for autographs. In Ireland, players go nightclubbing in specially sealed-off areas on the premises for fear they might get mobbed by beer-swilling revellers; here, the players' space is respected: not only are they not encircled, it's as if a five-foot force-field extends around them.

Part Two

The Rugby Begins

THE MYTHICAL TAXIS OF ROTTENRUA

Saturday 4 June 2005, Rotorua

The streets of Rotorua were alive and colourful at four in the afternoon, red jerseys everywhere, almost tumbling backwards under the weight of dozens of crates of beer bottles.

'Starting early, lads?'

'Naw, mate.' They seemed slightly affronted. 'It's four o'clock.'

By six night had replaced twilight and the vibrant sunshine of late afternoon was a distant memory. With half of the city's 52,000 population heading to Rotorua International Stadium for the Lions' opening game, even the lightest footfalls echoed in the empty streets.

Very kindly, the local information bureau took it upon itself to offer free buses from town to the stadium. With the handful of taxis that Rotorua boasts booked out, however, the buses were a tad over-subscribed: a queue stretched half the length of the village green, and it seemed like every machine on four wheels that could rattle its way the couple of miles to the venue had been enlisted. A rickety minibus – smaller than my campervan – pulled up and the crowd swarmed forward. The natives were a touch docile, though. Shifty-eyed Irishmen, fresh from arriving on the scene, sized up the line and decided there was nothing to be lost by trying to slip in at the front; at worst, they might have been ordered to the back. So, in slid a slightly-built Irishman, clutching his briefcase. There wasn't a murmur from those around. Back home, there would have been kicking, screaming and a decent risk of being hung, drawn and quartered.

Around Auckland, there were signs advertising the All Blacks' Test against Fiji on 10 June. 'Event starts 6.30pm,' they read. Event? As the free bus wound its way to the ground, fireworks burst into the skies around us. Fireworks? Nice, but not quite an event in itself. As it turned out though, even the word 'event' didn't quite capture the occasion: this was a show. Welcome to New Zealand, boys and girls.

The Rotorua International Stadium seems to be cut into the earth: huge grassy banks drop down towards the pitch in a manner that would cause a fire safety officer to break out in a cold sweat; the playing surface is at the bottom of a bowl, or, perhaps, a cauldron, with walls of supporters and a stand rising up from it; at the very top, houses are dotted round the perimeter; people finish their dinner, crack open a bottle of wine and watch the show from the comfort of their dining room. If it's warm enough, they sit on the wall, beer bottle swinging lightly in hand.

The show that Rotorua put on for the 33,000 fans was entrancing. Dozens – maybe hundreds – of scantily clad girls pranced about – music blaring from perfectly-maintained and - balanced speakers – amidst flames shooting upwards around them. It was like Riverdance with fire and even less clothing. Riverdance, Kiwi-style, was followed by a Maori war dance of such ferocity that, in the press box, pens froze over paper and jaws began to sag.

'Event.' No wonder the streets were deserted.

Every possible method of prodding the crowd into violent support of the home team was employed. DHL, the sponsors of the whole series of Lions' games, have a 'ball delivery' competition for each match: one lucky winner gets to run out onto the pitch and place the ball on the centre spot, where it will rest in the tumult, quietly awaiting the kick-off. The 33,000 had been whipped into a frenzy by the fire and the war dance by the time 'little Matthew Jones!' ran out, ball tucked under his arm, greeted by a tumultuous roar. Was little Matthew fazed in the slightest? Not at all. Without breaking stride, he planted the ball one-handed – technique perfect – and waved triumphantly to the audience. Oh, how they loved that.

'Nearly time for kick-off!' howled the public address system. Another roar. And then, Vivaldi's 'Four Seasons' to welcome the Lions. A modest show of support from their fans: the odd tricolour, Union Jack and St George's Cross fluttering rather than being waved frantically. Predictably, the tempo lifted for the arrival of the Bay of Plenty, with some strange, loud dance-rock hybrid churning out of the speakers. The blast of noise that welcomed them onto the pitch sounded like what little Matthew got, multiplied by fifteen.

The New Zealand national anthem was sung with gusto. The 'Lions' Song' got as much of a rendition from the fans as it did from the players, which is to say, none. Paul Honiss, the referee, was introduced to the crowd. Cue round booing for Mr Honiss and finally, air thick with anticipation, we were ready to go.

Throughout the game, the man on the public address left nothing to chance. Every time there was a break in play, the music began to thump again. Just when the crowd had nothing to cheer, nothing to clap along to, just when they were settling back in their seats, boom, boom, went the speakers. From the first minute to the last, the 33,000 were whirled along a roller-coaster of noise and emotion.

'Beats Croke Park on a wet Sunday in September, doesn't it?' I asked a fellow Irish traveller on the bus back to town.

'Aah, knocks the bollix out of it,' he replied, his agreement joined by an easy laugh that suggested he'd never seen anything like it before. Event? No, definitely more of a show; perhaps even a performance.

Afterwards, in the pub designated as the 'Barmy Army Headquarters', Hennessy's Irish Bar, things were surprisingly subdued. Well, maybe not so surprisingly: the drink had been flowing since the afternoon and, in New Zealand, there's no difficulty in buying alcohol in the stadium, bringing it back to your seat, consuming it and then charging back for more. So the patrons were glassy-eyed, even by half-ten in the evening. Mindful of the fact that I was lodged far, far away from town, having trawled the streets for a familiar 'Taxi' sign, I finally found one and muscled into a cab. The driver confided in me that there are just 34 taxis in the whole of Rotorua.

'We're going to be busy tonight. Normally, we have to look for work. Not tonight!'

He seemed remarkably relaxed, even though there was little chance that he or his colleagues would see the inside of their beds before dawn. Back home, there would be complaints, complaints, complaints. This guy didn't even moan about the sulphuric stench.

'How do you get used to the smell?'

Brody was right. Rotorua stinks the way a four-berth campervan with nine inhabitants would the morning after a night on the Guinness. It's the tourist capital of New Zealand, but the geothermal activity that makes it a place of beauty and wonder also brings a foul odour.

'Ah, you just get used to it, I suppose.' All very laid-back, the Rotoruans. But they can whip themselves into a frenzy if they want.

Game 1: British & Irish Lions V Bay of Plenty
Saturday 4 June 2005, Rotorua International Stadium, Rotorua

Bay of Plenty 20
Tries: C. Bourke, M. Williams
Convs: M. Williams (2)
Pens: M. Williams (2)

British & Irish Lions 34
Tries: J. Lewsey (2), M. Cueto, T. Shanklin, D. Peel, G. D'Arcy
Convs: R. O'Gara (2)

The man in the luminous jacket on duty outside the VIP

entrance flashed me a toothy smile.

'If they don't win tonight, they might as well pack up and go home.'

He was speaking of the Lions, of course: the Bay of Plenty finished third in last season's National Provincial Championship (NPC) and held the Ranfurly Shield at one stage as well; however, the teams in the NPC perform at a far lower level than those in the Super 12 and tonight, a smattering of Super 12 stars were joined by honest part-timers getting their one shot at the big time.

They were joined too by 33,000 supporters in a ground that was swelled to more than capacity. How often does Rotorua International Stadium see a crowd of this size?

'Haha! Never!' the toothy one cackled.

Never might have been a bit off the mark: when the Lions played here in 1983, 35,000 paid in to watch. Nonetheless, this was a special occasion. Up and down the Tudor streets of Rotorua, blue and yellow bunting hung from lampposts, rear-view mirrors and shopfronts and, inside the ground, the pre-match entertainment had whipped the crowd into a violent frenzy.

The Bay have a good record against the Lions as well; while they've never been successful against a touring party from Britain and Ireland, they've always performed admirably. Now, the farmers and bank clerks lining out with Super 12 team-mates would get the chance to show that the Bay spirit survives in the modern age, the era of cut-throat professional rugby. Could romance survive?

After fifteen minutes, it looked like romance, along with the famous Bay spirit, was going to get an almighty mauling. A bar in Rotorua was advertising $1 pints of beer from kick-off until the first try. It turned out that the barman wouldn't have been particularly over-worked: Josh Lewsey opened the Lions' 2005 account after just two and a half minutes.

In their first attack, the Lions swept this way and that, before working enough space to send the full-back over in the corner. 'We hit the ground running, hit the ground really well,' said assistant coach, Eddie O'Sullivan, afterwards. 'Perhaps too well. It was like bringing stuff straight off the training paddock and onto the field.'

Ronan O'Gara was at ease, running onto zippy passes from Dwayne Peel. The Lions had set plays, with O'Gara and centre, Gavin Henson, alternating depending on which side they wished to attack. Then, all at once, Henson would swing from one side to the other and launch out a long, looping pass, catching the opposition unawares.

For fifteen minutes, the Lions kept ploughing forward into Bay territory. Lewsey scored again and Mark Cueto collected an O'Gara cross-kick to flop over for a third try. It was 17-0 and the Lions were coasting. As O'Sullivan suggested, perhaps they had started too well. In any case, the famous Bay spirit was about to take a bow. After their first sustained attack, they were celebrating a try. Given the chance to redeem themselves, they moved the ball with real pace, carried it with purpose and hit rucks with savage intensity. The Lions' defence certainly didn't look as handsome as their attack: flanker Nili Latu brushed off the tackle of O'Gara and popped a pass to his back-row colleague, Colin Bourke, who scored in the corner.

Then, disaster really struck for the Lions. Before the 20-minute mark, the Bay continued to attack and press. Centre Grant McQuoid was wrapped up by Brian O'Driscoll and

The Last Great Tour?

Lawrence Dallaglio came charging across to assist his captain, but as he went to join the tackle, his right ankle went from under him. As play went on, he writhed in agony on the ground, before the Lions' doctor, James Robson, raced out and called for a medical cart to remove Dallaglio from the fray. His tour was over, less than half an hour after it had begun, his ankle fractured and dislocated.

While nothing could match the personal anguish that the injury caused to Dallaglio, it was a crushing blow to the Lions as well. Dallaglio has won every honour in the game, has captained his country and, in the days before the first game, had looked in menacing physical condition. He is unquestionably, as Lewsey, his club team-mate at London Wasps later put it, 'one of the greatest leaders the game of rugby has ever seen'.

Still, the head coach, though the camera trained on his face captured his own despair as the news of the severity of the injury was relayed to him, was already thinking ahead. 'Obviously we're disappointed but you're going to pick up injuries along the way,' Woodward said. 'There's been a lot said about the number of players we're bringing with us but to me it's quite obvious that when you're coming to New Zealand for games of this intensity, you've got to come with a large squad. He's a world-class player. I'm gutted for him but it's over, so you just have to move on very, very quickly. You can't dwell on it. The preparations for the Taranaki game are now underway.'

The loss of Dallaglio might have affected the Lions on the pitch as well. The Bay continued to pound away, led by the powerful Latu and hooker Aleki Lutui up front, the sniping Kevin Senio at scrum-half, and the skilful midfield partnership of McQuoid and Alan Bunting, all expertly orchestrated by debutant fly-half Murray Williams.

Things began to go wrong for the Lions: for about ten minutes they suffered an almost complete systems' breakdown: passes went astray or forward; balls were knocked on; kicks were skewed into touch; and, worryingly, the penalty count, the best measure of a team's composure and discipline, began to rise. Perhaps most worryingly though, the Lions' midfield defence looked alarmingly porous.

'I think when we got our match together, our plays and got good forward momentum, there was a lot of space out wide at times,' said the Bay's one-time All Black full-back, Adrian Cashmore. 'We don't have the quickest wingers in the Bay, but we created some opportunities.'

O'Gara will doubtless ship most of the post-match media and supporter criticism, but Henson, openside flanker Martyn Williams, who should be his fly-half's wing-man, and even the great O'Driscoll found themselves struggling too. 'Phil [Larder, the defence coach] had a word with Henson at half-time, and O'Gara too,' said Woodward of the midfield defence's difficulties.

Murray Williams knocked over a penalty and it was no surprise when he sidestepped over for his side's second try and slotted the conversion to leave the sides level at the break, 17-17. It was no surprise either that the Bay were roared to the dressing room.

'We got sloppy,' O'Sullivan admitted afterwards. 'We lost a bit of composure in the set-piece and turned over some ball, gave away some silly penalties and gave the Bay something to play with. And they're a good side. The key was, it was a good baptism of fire and showed what happens in New Zealand if you don't control the football when you have it. Not that we didn't know, but we know we've got to work harder.'

That was the polite way to put it. I am writing this on Sunday afternoon and, this morning when I was sitting down, having a coffee and reading the uncomplimentary verdict of the New Zealand press, a Maori lady came over to check the Lotto numbers. Inevitably, we started talking about rugby. 'Boy, can they swear,' she said of the Lions, explaining that a microphone in the dressing room captured the half-time team talk.

Whatever was said, it resulted in a much better performance after the interval; in fact, it resulted in an entire change of game plan. The words of Steve Hansen after the All Blacks' trial the previous night now seem uncanny: 'They'll probably play running rugby [against the provincial sides] and the question is whether the provinces are going to be strong enough to really challenge them. Hopefully they are, but there is a question mark about that. When Test time comes around, they'll play a kicking game, I'm sure. As Graham [Henry] has alluded to on previous occasions, they'll try to strangle us up front.'

Here, with the game on the line, the Lions ditched the running game of the early stages and reached for the garrotte: O'Gara began to kick everything, pinning the Bay down in their own half. O'Sullivan described it as 'a masterclass in tactical kicking' and the head coach was impressed as well. 'Second half, I thought O'Gara was the outstanding player. He tightened up, he controlled the game and got us field position and territory. He allowed us to get a lot of composure back and I thought he kept his head very well, so I think he had a great game.'

O'Gara's opposite number, Williams, turned in a plucky performance, but on the several occasions he missed touch in the second half, the Lions' back-three, led by the outstanding

Lewsey, ran the ball right back at their hosts. The pressure kept mounting.

Early on, Tom Shanklin couldn't hold a scoring pass, but, on 52 minutes, he made amends, finishing off a move started when Murray Williams failed to find the relief of the sideline. O'Gara missed the conversion though, and the Bay, still roared on by a passionate crowd, remained in the contest; they maintained a stubborn aggression in defence and prevented the Lions from developing any real fluidity in attack. Another Williams penalty closed the gap to two points but that merely served to mark one of the rare occasions that the Bay entered Lions' territory in the second half. Even when Williams did manage to find touch, Lewsey took a quick throw-in and ran the ball back once more.

Amateurs against professionals could not deal with such levels of intensity. Sure enough, on 70 minutes, the Lions notched a fifth try. By now, Andrew Sheridan and Steve Thompson, the English front-row forwards, had joined the fray and made an immediate impression. 'If he scrums every time he gets to the scrum like he did today, he'll have a huge impact, won't he?' said forwards' coach, Andy Robinson, of Sheridan the international novice widely tipped for Test selection. They shunted the Bay back three times in the scrum and, on the final occasion, with the home side's fatigue beginning to show, Peel slipped in for the try. O'Gara missed the conversion, leaving only seven points – one score – between the sides, but it never looked like the Bay could rescue the contest. Two critical errors, the concession of a penalty and a line kick that went beyond the end line, were the sign of a tired team and simply allowed the Lions to ratchet up the pressure still further.

With four minutes to go, Lewsey burst through a gap in midfield and, though he might have completed his hat-trick, passed to substitute Gordon D'Arcy to touch down. O'Gara knocked over the extras for a fourteen-point win that, in reality, didn't flatter the victors.

'We had one poor twenty minutes and three good twenty minutes,' was how Woodward put it. 'We just wanted to win and move on. We've moved on from the Argentina game and to see the guys who are playing on Wednesday in the dressing room, they're really buzzing now, so we've got some momentum. Clearly, the pluses far outweigh the minuses.'

The Lions players – in contrast to the rough 'n ready Bay of Plenty stars – were scrubbed up and besuited by the time they faced the media and echoed the head coach's view. 'I think you have to take the positives out of every game,' said his captain. 'The way we started was exactly how we wanted to. There are aspects of our game that need a lot of fine-tuning, but I'm not one to dwell on negativity: we've got to move on, understand where we need to improve but realise where we've done well and make sure we continue in that vein.'

Lewsey, the game's outstanding player, struck a similar note: 'For this squad, it's about developing week-in, week-out. Today was a bit uncohesive at certain times if we're absolutely honest, but we'll focus on the positives and realise that when we played some rugby, went through the phases, we looked dangerous and scored some good tries.'

It is fitting to end with a tribute to Lewsey's performance. Shortly after the full-time whistle, the group of *Sunday Times* rugby writers detailed to give their analysis of the game, Stephen Jones, Stuart Barnes and David Walsh, gathered to discuss what they would do.

'So, that's settled then,' Jones announced. 'You'll do Lewsey, I'll do Lewsey and Barnsey'll do Lewsey.' In everything he did, the full-back was magnificent. The knowledge of the game he exhibited at the press conference was remarkable too but showed a man who thinks deeply about his own game. Many have thought Lewsey to be simply an outstanding athlete who had become a rugby player; his performance on and off the pitch disproved that theory: clearly, this was a man who analyses his and his team's faults to a degree that would see most sane people break out in a cold sweat.

He conducted himself like a gentleman too, admitting that being handed his jersey by coach, Gareth Jenkins, was a 'choky-throat moment'. With his head raised high above the Dictaphones before him, he dealt with questions patiently, politely and courteously. Alastair Campbell hovered alongside. Three times he signalled that Lewsey had said enough; on each occasion, the player disagreed, quietly accepting more questions: 'There's a lot been said about what it means to be a Lion and I wanted to make sure that it wasn't just lip service'.

Bay of Plenty: A. Cashmore; F. Bolavucu, A. Bunting, G. McQuoid, A. Tahana; M. Williams, K. Senio; C. Bourke, N. Latu, W. Ormond (c); B. Upton, M. Sorensen; B. Castle, A. Lutui, S. Davison.
Subs: W. Smith for Bourke 48, A. Stewart for Bolavucu 53, T. Filise for Davison 62, P. Tupai for Sorensen 62.

Lions: J. Lewsey; M. Cueto, B. O'Driscoll (c), G. Henson, T. Shanklin; R. O'Gara, D. Peel; L. Dallaglio, M. Williams, R. Hill;

The Last Great Tour?

P. O'Connell, B. Kay; M. Stevens, G. Bulloch, G. Jenkins.
Subs: M. Curry for Dallaghlio 16; S. Thompson for Bulloch 65, A. Sheridan for Stevens 65, G. D'Arcy for Henson 68, M. Dawson for Shanklin 76.

Referee: P. Honiss (New Zealand)

What's that Smell?
Sunday 5 June 2005, Rotorua

First things first. It looks like I was right about the Lions' security not being of presidential motorcade proportions: some time during the week, an intrepid reporter managed to gain access to one of the touring party's private rooms, stocked with laptop computers and freshly laundered gear. A nice story for the *Herald on Sunday*.

I spent the morning wandering around Waimangu Volcanic Valley, formed by the Tarawera volcano which has erupted five times in the last 18,000 years: that's pretty good going for a volcano. Rotorua is a hotbed – pun intended – of geothermal activity: clouds of sulphur spurt up from the ground all over the town, masking road signs pointing the way to hidden valleys and naturally-heated spas. Waimangu renders the word, 'spectacular' utterly redundant. Craters formed by eruptions past are filled with water that ranges from azure to green; boiling hot water trickles over marble ledges which the hands of time have streaked with red and black; and tropical plants, tinged every colour of the rainbow, cling to the sides of the valley. Quite a place for a three-hour stroll.

Doing no such strolling was Lawrence Dallaglio, confined

to a hospital bed in Auckland. The comments that came through the Lions' media team were emailed in the form of big chunks of text and are worth parroting almost in full:

I knew my leg had been caught in the ground and it wasn't facing in the right direction after the incident. I had fractured and dislocated it. I was in a lot of pain and James [Robson] was able to put it back in on the pitch. He had never had to do that before and once the ankle was back in, the pain subsided.

I was lying there thinking, 'I have never been taken off on a stretcher before in my career!' There is a first time for everything and even when I did my knee in 2001, I still played on. I knew straight away that my tour was over – there was no messing around because I realised the severity of the problem. My three children thought it was very funny that Daddy had to be taken off on a golf cart.

I knew that if it was an injury that I couldn't get up from then it was pretty serious. My natural defence mechanism told me the tour was over. It is just an unfortunate coincidence that I have been injured on successive Lions' tours and had to go home early ... [Dallaglio was flown out of Australia in 2001 as well, having started in all three Tests in South Africa in 1997]

We can win the Test series against the All Blacks and this tour isn't about any one player. The guys have the firepower to achieve a series win, even though everyone in this country is saying otherwise because the locals are very good at sticking up for themselves.

No one is guaranteed anything on a tour like this and I know that better than most. There are a number of players who will now have to step up in terms of leadership but we do have that kind of quality in the squad and there is a great strength in depth. Players will rise to the challenge and that's the beauty of this kind of tour: players relish the chance to put themselves forward. Players will come to the fore in, at times, the most peculiar of situations.

England won here after 30 years of trying in 2003 and that proved it is possible and there aren't many bigger things in rugby than to be remembered as having been part of a Lions' tour that won a series in New Zealand …

In terms of the squad, this injury is the kind of thing that can happen on tour and if anything justifies what Clive has been saying all along about the number of players needed out here, then this is it. People continually seem to be criticising this aspect of the tour, but we have now lost players in the first week of the trip and that just highlights the need for the current structure …

Yes, the team did go off the boil against Bay of Plenty after the injury and that's natural. I still think it was a great start to the tour and one the best wins ever in an opening game by the Lions. There were real signs of the potential in this squad and each game is building towards the Test series.

The Rugby Begins

We will have a clear idea after Saturday's game with the New Zealand Maori which direction this tour is going in. I believe we showed enough in the first game to suggest we are going to have an exciting tour. We have so many match-winners across the team – with two or three still to arrive [two, in fact: Stephen Jones has landed, while Gareth Thomas and Jason Robinson remain in Europe] – and that's why it is so frustrating because I realise we have a chance of being very successful and I wanted to be part of that.

Fighting words. The loss of Dallaglio's physical presence, ability and leadership is huge, however. There are very few names in the Lions' touring party that will strike fear into the hearts of the New Zealand public; in fact, not even fear: the natives are unlikely to be struck down with the merest tinge of anxiety. Few of them will have heard of Simon Easterby either, the man snatched almost from the runway at Shannon Airport – he was due to travel to Japan with the Irish squad – to replace Dallaglio.

Yesterday's announcement of the New Zealand squad to face Fiji wasn't quite a show of strength; rather, a show of strength in depth. There was no room for Andrew Mehrtens, but, of the other trialists, Ma'a Nonu, Conrad Smith, Sitiveni Sivivatu and Sosene Anesi, the latter pair for the first time, all made it. Sione Lauaki, while not among the 23 named by Henry, will train with the squad in the lead-up to the Fiji game. Prop Campbell Johnstone and hooker Derren Witcombe were also named in an international squad for the first time; Friday night was not one on which front-row forwards would ever stand out, but seasoned observers of the murky world that such players inhabit reckoned they had been impressive. The fifth player to receive his first call-up was second-row, James Ryan. Plenty of fresh blood, plenty of hunger and out wide, plenty of gas. Woodward protested that he hadn't been paying attention, but it's hard to believe that the dynamic trio of Nonu, Anesi and Sivivatu didn't catch his eye. The quintet of new faces joined a host of seasoned internationals in Henry's selection: it's a formidable panel.

All Black Squad V Fiji: Sosene Anesi, Dan Carter, Jerry Collins, Doug Howlett, Chris Jack, Byron Kelleher, Richie McCaw, Justin Marshall, Aaron Mauger, Keven Mealamu, Mils Muliaina, Ma'a Nonu, James Ryan, Sitiveni Sivivatu, Conrad Smith, Greg Somerville, Rodney So'oialo, Campbell Johnstone, Mose Tuiali'i, Tana Umaga (Captain), Ali Williams, Tony Woodcock, Derren Witcombe.

The Calm After the Storm
Monday 6 June 2005, Waitomo

On Saturday night, Hennessy's Irish Bar was packed to the attic insulation with glassy-eyed, wobbly revellers. By Monday afternoon – the annual Queen's Birthday public holiday on the now-deserted streets of Rotorua – only about twenty Lions' fans remained, most of them over the age of 45.

'Oh, it was crazy,' the barmaid said, gesturing at the empty fridges. Well, they weren't quite empty, but the only beer that was fully stocked was Corona Extra. The bar went through 250 kegs during the weekend and had to make inroads into its emergency supplies. The threat of the 'Barmy Army' leadership to pick a three-pub town – they won't say which, but will show up without warning – on the South Island and literally drink it dry *en route* to a game now looks far from idle.

The Rugby Channel – and, in this country, of course they have a channel entirely dedicated to rugby – was showing, for the umpteenth time, the New Zealand Maori V Fiji game. Near me, a Welshman got up from his table, a stack of plates in his hand and headed towards the bar to return them.

"Ere,' piped up an English accent from the table across, 'take these as well, will you?' Back in the Home Nations, such a suggestion would have got, at best, a scowl and, depending on the location, might ultimately have required a hospital visit for one or both parties. An Englishman lording it over a Welshman? Even jokingly? Here, the Welshman gave a hearty chuckle. 'Alright, mate.'

What is it about the concept of the Lions that allows men of different cultures and different countries, who will call each other bad things when their homelands collide in the Six Nations Championship, to come together like this? The history of the Lions is one element, of course: British and Irish selections have been testing themselves against the best the southern hemisphere has to offer for well over 100 years; given that rugby's inaugural World Cup was held only in 1987, in the period before that, Welsh, Scottish, English and Irish stars could only be recognised as true greats if they performed in the Lions' jersey and, arguably, the best of the All Blacks, Springboks and Wallabies only acceded to greatness and international renown if they starred against the Lions. The memories of those who went before remain and the thought that emulating those feats will hear a player spoken of in the same breath as legends of the game is, surely, ever present.

There's always something of the underdog about the Lions as well: knitting the four countries together is a delicate task, undertaken in the hostile, partisan territory south of the equator, where New Zealand and South Africa – and latterly Australia – view themselves as the powerhouses of world rugby. There's something special about socking it to the SAN-ZAR nations on their own turf, against all the odds. To be a part of a grand project like that is a temptation for any player; it's a temptation for any man at all: to feel that one belongs to something is a primeval human urge and to feel that one is amongst friends fighting an improbably strong foe stirs feelings of kinship and togetherness.

And then there's the equally primeval human urge for fun: when the bread is made, it's time for the circus. This has an effect on the concept of the Lions as well. A clue came from the composition of the remainder of the patrons in Hennessy's. There were three women in the bar, quite easily outnumbered by the contingent of smiling, laughing, middle-aged men. Remember the fridge as well: only Corona, a fancy beer consumed by young fancy dans – they serve it with a slice of lemon or lime, for God's sake – remained in any great number. On today's evidence, a Lions' tour is an excuse for a married, settled man to kiss goodbye to responsibility for six weeks and go on the piss. The resulting atmosphere was carefree and it felt like, at any moment, in that bar, on a public holiday in the New Zealand winter, that carefree would turn to euphoric and, freed of all worldly constraints, one of the drinkers would dance to the middle of the floor and turn a perfect cartwheel for sheer joy.

At the information centre too, everything was returning to

normal. 'Everywhere was booked out,' the girl told me, but it wasn't like Rotorua isn't used to such crowds. 'It gets packed like this during the summer as well'. Perhaps not with the same ferocity though: it's hard to imagine the holidaying Aucklanders threatening Mr Hennessy's emergency supplies to quite the same extent.

Forgotten About
Tuesday 7 June 2005, Stratford

The 'Forgotten World' Highway runs between the towns of Taumarunui and Stratford on the North Island. And it's certainly forgotten about. For four, maybe five hours – and you wouldn't be too bothered about counting either – what can be loosely described as a road snakes up the sides of mountains and curves down into deep valleys, rushing upwards as gullies fall away right and left, and tumbles into narrow gorges and eerie one-way tunnels. It contains views that defy the thesaurus and numb the mind; there should be road signs: do not drink in the scenery and drive.

About twenty kilometres of the track are just that: track. Here and there, gravel is strewn on upmarket muck. Nearing the end, you may see an oxymoron: a road maintenance crew: surely, there has to be a road to maintain in the first place ...

The scenery continues to slacken the jaw and then, a road sign catches the eye. 'Whangamonoma', it says. Nothing unusual about that. Except, it's printed on cardboard material and, scrawled to one side, slightly above the name, is, 'Pop. 40'. And then, the next sign: 'Republic of Whangamonoma'.

At the Whangamonoma Hotel, the man behind the bar said

the population is currently closer to 34, but it swells to several hundred when the weekend rolls around and the city dwellers come, from north and south, seeking refuge amidst the mountains. A collage of clippings on one of the walls tells the story of the Republic of Whangamonoma: already almost abandoned by the rest of the world – the last passenger train stopped there in 1983 – in 1989, it was removed from the map of Taranaki and moved to neighbouring Manawatu, which caused outcry in the town. They promptly declared independence, going so far as to elect a president. It became more surreal when the Manawatu Council appointed that president as an official ambassador to Manawatu. And more surreal still when the first holder of the office stood down and a goat was elected in his place, until his (Billy the Goat's) untimely death in 2001.

Every year, thousands flock to Whangamonoma for Independence Day, when the town's handful of streets become a blaze of colour and life. This afternoon, it was deathly quiet.

'And do you field a rugby team?' I asked. The eyes behind the bar blazed with indignation. A quivering finger sh ' out.

'Of course we do. Look at the wall behind you, he barked. Sure enough, dozens of sepia photographs of Whangamonoma teams from down the ages lined the wall.

'See that photograph? The Deans Cup? That's the oldest rugby trophy in New Zealand. Played for by three clubs out here,' he said, proudly.

'How do you manage to field a team with only 34 people?'

'Ah, with the hinterland, it's about a hundred more.' Just like home, where every weekend, groups of grown men line out to defend the honour of tiny, far-flung hamlets.

'And where's the cup now?'

'Down the road.' He seemed a touch downbeat that I'd had to bring that up; maybe there was bad blood.

'With the mortal enemy?'

'Nah, I wouldn't say enemy: we're all New Zealanders at the end of the day. And we're all rugby players.' Just like home again. Your lads might spend three-quarters of the year flaking lumps out of the lads from the next parish, but once they pull on the county jersey, you'll cheer all of them on.

Friendship is only race-deep
Tuesday, June 7 2005, New Plymouth

For some reason, a 'Barmy Army Harmonies' booklet has turned up in my briefcase. Where it came from, I do not know; where it will go, I am sure: the bin. The original songs in there are almost universally appalling; a particularly egregious example is one ditty which attempts to rhyme 'eyeliner' – a dig at the often make-upped Ma'a Nonu – and 'hairdryer' – a none-too-funny joke at another All Black winger, the hirsute Doug Howlett.

But amongst these back-of-a-beer mat compositions are the national anthems of the Home Nations. Well, 'Ireland's Call' replaces 'Amhrán na bhFiann', but that's another debate entirely. In any event, it was heartening to see, in Peggy Gordon's pub next door to the marquee and Portaloos masquerading as the 'Barmy Army HQ', Scots, English, Irish and Welsh joining together in belting out 'Ireland's Call', 'Flower of Scotland', 'Land of My Fathers' and 'God Save the Queen'.

The songs were dispatched with passion and verve,

almost drowning out the blues band making an almost equally valiant effort to thump out the Beatles' 'Eight Days a Week'. Without the slightest hint of a shadow of a doubt the anthems are altogether more likely to stiffen the sinew and summon up the blood than the pitiful 'Lions' Song', which is to be performed before each game. While Woodward's rationale for commissioning the song was the demoralising effect of having to listen to the opposition belt out their own anthem, having listened to the 'Lions' Song' live in Rotorua, it's not at all clear that inflicting it on the players will be any less demoralising.

I was having this discussion with Rick, a self-employed carpenter from Epsom who is travelling the world before getting saddled with a wife, kids, mortgage, several hire purchase items and some household pets.

'It'd be nice if they could have an Irish anthem for the Lions Rick, but most of our songs are about killing you guys. I like "Flower of Scotland", though.' I'd temporarily forgotten the context of the Scottish national anthem, and Rick was quick to correct me.

'Yeah, but 'Flower of Scotland' is about killing Englishmen as well'.

So, 'Flower of Scotland' wouldn't do as a Lions' anthem. I held my hands up apologetically.

'Of course. Sorry, Rick'.

'Ah, all that's in the past now anyway, innit?'

Later on though, with a few more pints of the local brew settling in his stomach, Rick passed a comment which suggested that, whatever the marketeers might say, undercurrents of enmity run deep beneath still waters.

'Look at 'im,' Rick said, pointing out a Welshman. 'I can't

stand that.' The Welshman's crime was to wear a Welsh jersey, rather than a Lions' replica shirt. 'That's just tight, that is. He's only wearing that because it's red. He should go out and buy a proper shirt.' In fairness to Rick, he noticed the incongruity of his own words when set beside what he had said earlier. 'I'm just saying, that's all'. He may well have been mindful too of the lack of red displayed on my body; I felt that, as a – ahem – chronicler of the tour, it would be wrong to wear a red jersey. Also I was, well, too tight to fork out the $140 most stores were charging. Instead, I was wearing the DHL Lions' Series polo shirt that the New Zealand Rugby Union had given out in their media bags. I puffed my chest out so the badge was clearly visible.

'Yeah, you're wearing something. That's alright, mate,' was Rick's imprimatur.

Like me, Rick was travelling alone, in a campervan. Another of his mates was another Englishman, Jim.

'He's travelling with his girlfriend, right, but she's not well at the moment,' Rick explained before we were introduced. Sure enough, Jim seemed a touch distant.

'What's wrong with his girlfriend?' I asked, while Jim was getting his round in.

'Well, it's not so much his girlfriend,' Rick answered, dropping his voice. 'Her Dad's going into hospital for a triple bypass. She's wondering whether she should go back.'

Ah.

'Jim's said it's a decision only she can make'. Very commendable. 'But, like, it's a triple bypass and that's hardly groundbreaking these days, is it? And Jim reckons ...' and here, his voice dropped to lower than a whisper '... that if they go back, they won't come back out again.' Not so commendable. And yet, perfectly understandable: a Lions' tour of New Zealand comes around every twelve years at best; in twelve years' time, there may not even be another tour; certainly, Jim will be twelve years older and, either it's twelve years of success with family planning, or Jim will be weighed down by a few smaller versions of himself, though, hopefully, with more hair. His desire to stay is perfectly natural. And leaving it up to her is certainly the gentlemanly thing to do.

A lad from Drogheda I met on the way back from the game in Rotorua was travelling the world too. 'Quit the job, sold the car, kissed the girlfriend goodbye. Good luck!' The two stories suggest there's something special about a Lions' tour. Would Jim even be giving a second thought to flying back from, say, Marbella for such an operation? I doubt it.

There were New Zealanders there too, one of whom was decked out in a black and yellow rugby jersey which brought a certain Limerick rugby club to mind.

'What's that jersey? Young Munster is it?'

'Naw, mate,' he replied pleasantly, after fixing me with a quizzical look and asking me to repeat myself. 'You have to wear your colours when you're drinking with Poms'. So, the Taranaki jersey just happens to resemble the kit of one of Limerick's most famous clubs.

'How come you all hate Auckland so much?' Out in the provinces, it seemed like a good idea to explore further the tension between the capital and the rest of the country.

'Too many corral-hoppers, mate. Too many Islanders,' came the reply, a reference to the amount of Fijians, Tongans and Samoans – Pacific Islanders – who ply their trade in the Auckland jersey. Before I even got the chance to note that this is a bit rich coming from a man who's going to cheer on an All Blacks' team full of 'corral-hoppers', the statement was qualified.

'A few is OK. Everyone needs a few. But they're overrun.'

It might seem racist – in the less malignant sense – but in reality, nestled away on the coast, it's a small town with a chip on its shoulder. Later on, another local pointed out a bespectacled man in the crowd. Apparently he had either coached Auckland at one time, or had been on the shortlist to do so. Either way, my informant said, 'he was shafted'. Apparently, 'we do things differently down here, and they don't like it that much'.

Of course, come 25 June in Christchurch, the Taranaki hordes will be bellowing their support for Aucklanders Tony Woodcock, Keven Mealamu, Mils Muliaina and, if they make the squad, Doug Howlett and Joe Rokocoko, as well as several more with Pacific Islands' heritage: Rodney So'oialo, Jerry Collins, Sitiveni Sivivatu, Ma'a Nonu and, of course, the captain, Tana Umaga. Oh, they'll be bellowed on, no doubt. A small town with a chip on its shoulder is still a small town in the same country as the big town. The inverse is true of Rick's little lapse: a big town with an occasional disdain for the smaller towns around it is still part of the same country.

The most visible attempt to knit all the relationships that form over the course of a Lions' Tour into something cohesive is being made by the 'Barmy Army'. There was no reference that I can recall in the Irish press about such a grouping before the tour commenced; the first time I heard the phrase mentioned was on an Auckland radio station. While it may not have surfaced back home, in New Zealand it has been ubiquitous, because of the enormous capacity its organisers have for gaining publicity, and also because it gives the New Zealand media a convenient label to slap on the thousands of visitors who are expected to follow the Lions.

Basically, the 'Barmy Army' evolved from English cricket supporters who, to hide from individual despair, banded together on a 1990s' tour to Australia during which their boys were being roundly thumped by the home team. The name took hold and followed the cricket supporters around. It might well have petered out – reports reach me that the English cricket team is even winning the occasional game now – but for the contribution of an English entrepreneur, Freddie Parker. The Lions' 'Barmy Army' was born. Parker, a policeman on a career break, and his team arranged to have headquarters set up in each city on the Lions' itinerary, with a marquee, live music and lots of drink; not to mention the official 'Barmy Army' merchandise truck parked alongside it. It's hard to know whether or not Freddie's heart is in the right place, or his right pocket, nestling close to his wallet.

It's not clear how successful the 'Barmy Army' concept will be. It's hard to imagine it going down well with Irish fans, for a start, and the Welsh and Scottish probably won't have much time for it either, but we will have to wait and see. If nothing else, the HQs in each of the towns will feature a guaranteed party and a good chance to get well sozzled. But it's not like the Lions' fans are here to get sozzled all the time. Sure, there will be murderous amounts of drink consumed, but New Zealand is a country of such immense beauty that it would be criminal to spend six weeks in the pub.

And even when it's time to drink, the travelling contingent is still prepared to seek out any place with a quirk. A few doors up from Peggy Gordon's is a place called the White Hart Hotel. Rick met a few middle-aged Leicester supporters in one of the motor camps he stayed in: they told me that this is their third Lions' tour, and, to a man, they had a glint in their eye. .

'I met this guy last night. He said that he'd have a band and topless barmaids.'

'Topless barmaids?' Rick and I wondered in unison.

'Oh yeah.'

Sure enough, there were topless barmaids. That description, however, doesn't quite capture the White Hart Hotel experience. For some reason, in all probability a legal loophole, the premises avoided the nationwide ban on smoking in public places that was enacted in December 2004. Just as well too, otherwise, the smell could have been overwhelming: bearded, middle-aged bikers in leather jackets, with dirt in every crevice of their creased faces, bopped along to the beat, every now and then prising some grime out from beneath their fingernails in time to the music. A few women – rougher than sandpaper – danced among them. It was not the sort of place in which you would go out of your way to make eye contact; I got the distinct impression that an incident that might start with me spilling someone's drink could very easily end with yours truly on the end of a rope tied to the back end of a Harley Davidson being driven at speed down the main street.

And there were only two topless barmaids, one of whom was quite pretty and the other, well, not quite so easy on the eye. In fact, she was so large that her frame didn't quite fit when I looked at her with one eye. And even the attractive topless barmaid was a little strange: one breast was slightly different from the other – not that we were looking or anything.

As all this suggests, the Lions' supporters have proved to be no slouches when it comes to alcohol consumption: come nightfall, the wine, whiskey and beer have been flowing. Good news for Freddie: those of us previously too tight to buy any pricey merchandise might, some drunken night, come over all maudlin, and, ridden with a combination of guilt and pride, reach for our own wallet, exchanging hard-earned cash for Freddie's fine produce. Then, Rick would have nothing to worry about.

Shakespeare Country
Wednesday 8 June 2005, Stratford
'It's a load of bollocks, innit?'

I was having a chat about the 'Barmy Army' with two of the travelling supporters, a pair from Essex in England. Not only were they Essex boys, but they had Essex teeth as well.

'Naw. We found a lovely pub. Nearest pub to the ground actually. It's only, what, $3 for a pitcher of beer? Don't know about this "Barmy Army" business: none of the proper supporters have any time for it.' Emphasis on 'proper'.

Both of these self-styled proper supporters from Canvey Island RFC were in their mid-twenties. 'Travelling in a van?'

'Naw. Car and a tent.' One of them was even intent on staying out.

'I'm not going to go back at all. It's so laid-back here, so easy going. Some places don't open 'til ten in the morning. Naw, I'm gonna stay out here a while. Work a bit, save a bit of money. Easy does it.'

It's places like Stratford, a sleepy town which seems to drift down from the slopes of Mount Taranaki, half an hour north of New Plymouth, that can cause a visitor to fall in love with New

Zealand's peace, serenity and pace of life, what the French call, *le rythme de vie*.

Many of the town's streets are named after characters from Shakespeare; beautiful alleyways paved with red slink off the main street; and a Glockenspiel tower rises highest on the sky-line. There's an air of sluggishness about the place, as if noth-ing ever happens and, if on the off chance something does, it will happen slowly. For someone seeking the quiet life, Stratford is as good a place as any.

Today something was happening, although nobody seemed to know about it. The Lions were visiting a training session conducted by the Taranaki development officer with players drawn from four different high schools in the area. But nobody seemed to know about it.

'We might have got a crowd, if it was advertised,' said one of the headmasters. As it was, by the time the Lions were due to arrive in Victoria Park – a monument to those who fell under the Anzac flag in the Great War – the crowd had swollen to several dozen, its peak. Many of them were, like the Essex boys, Lions' supporters hunting for autographs.

Still, several dozen can be quite intimidating for the self-conscious teenager. They swaggered up to tackle bags and into passing drills, trying to conduct themselves with the effortless cool a self-conscious teenager imagines that the Lions train with. They ran from here to there with a disaffected insouciance, never pushing themselves harder than a trot. Too cool, man.

When Brian O'Driscoll, Simon Shaw, Shane Williams, Mark Cueto, Matt Dawson, Stephen Jones and four backroom staff turned up, the pace dropped even further and the swag-gers became even more pronounced. Getting things wrong in front of a crowd is one thing, but getting something wrong in the presence of professional rugby players, internationals, icons, idols? Not for me, man. So, they tossed their curls and shook their hips through a half hour of skill work, nobody wanting to be known forever as the guy who couldn't. A handful suffered the mortification of being singled out; it could have been worse though: for all their swagger and style, their rucking technique was appallingly bad, so bad that it brought to mind a story of my father's from his spell as a selector with the Munster Junior Rugby side. One evening, driven to distraction by the failure of his forwards to get sufficiently low as they hit the ruck, the by now deranged coach fetched a corner flag and held it above the ball, an improbably low distance from the ground. If a player was unable – quite often, as it turned out – to get his head under the stick, he was rewarded with a clatter; offenders to whom the coach took a particular dislike got a stroke across the backside as a bonus.

But even he might have been understanding in Stratford. Quite apart from the soothing effect of the town's poetic rhythm – hardly conducive to good, old-fashioned rucking – being in the glare of the limelight like that is extraordinarily difficult for a teenager: there were journalists there, but even a man with a notebook isn't so bad, unless he's accompanied by a camera. A camera! And there were plenty of cameras there, going snap, snap, snap. Better toss those curls, baby! And whatever you do, don't screw up! So the players went through what they thought were the motions, waiting for the session to end so they could get some autographs, and the Lions milled about, chatting and joking to one another, giving only a vague, detached attention to the drills being carried out before them, but never once turning their backs on either the play or the cameras. It was no wonder the mind drifted. Stratford, like many of the rural towns that dot New Zealand, reminds one of the sleepy approach to life in Irish villages ten years ago – an approach that remains in places, but has been steadily eroded over the past decade – and its drowsiness carried into Victoria Park this afternoon.

There are two standard journalistic approaches to such events. One is to collar a local and get them to say something like: 'Oh, it's a wonderful occasion. Everyone in the town has really been looking forward to it. I'm sure the children will cherish it for years to come.' (Getting people to say something is an old journalistic trick, which generally involves the journalist making a statement, the interviewee nodding, and the journalist then attributing the statement to the person.

'Isn't it a wonderful occasion?'

'Oh, yeah.'

'I bet everyone in the town has really been looking forward to it.'

'Sure!'

'And the children will cherish it for years to come.'

'Definitely.' And, there's a workable quote. A famous example is that of the legendary Shamrock Rovers' midfield hardman, Gino Lawless, being quoted as saying that a tackle was 'injudicious, but scarcely malicious.'

The second is to take a cynical approach: 'Oh, look at the Lions playing up to the media, look at these poor kids, like peasants being granted a token audience with royalty. It's all very pathetic really, isn't it? Sir Clive attempts to appease the locals, worm his way into their affections.' Coming towards the end of the training session, I remained in the second camp. It looked like a PR exercise: the Lions didn't look particularly bothered, giving off the disaffected air of young relatives sitting through a christening ceremony. They hadn't offered any advice, except on one occasion when Matt Dawson clapped his hands and shouted something which sounded slightly sarcastic. Half an hour's training while the Lions watch? Hardly the sort of stuff that makes this a 'great Lions' tour' contender.

But then, it all ended: the session finished and my cynicism was washed away. The crowd of several dozen was to line up beneath a rusty old stand and file dutifully past a line of rickety chairs that the Lions would sit on. Autograph? Sure, no problem. But before any signing happened, the Lions mingled with the players. At last, the youngsters, free from the watching eyes of the media and their friends and family, were at ease. For ten magical minutes they talked and joked with professional rugby players. Even the jet-lagged Shaw, just off the plane, took part in the banter. The teenagers' eyes twinkled and danced as they presented shirts, shorts, scraps of paper, anything, to be signed. And as they chatted away, a sense of something different, something almost – yes, let's get swallowed whole by cliché – magical, fell over a damp little corner of rural New Zealand. It is, genuinely, something the two-dozen lucky ones will talk about, not only in the schoolyard tomorrow, but for the rest of their lives. The day the Lions came to town.

And it wasn't just a PR exercise. There was only one British or Irish journalist present: me. A few local reporters ran here and there, but no great effort was made to harvest great forests of newspaper coverage. Perhaps this was the most uplifting thing of all: the players were happy and at ease doing good deeds even when the glare of the cameras weren't upon them. Each of them looked, as Malcolm O'Kelly said before he had to leave for home, like 'an ambassador for rugby'. No cynicism here today. Better instead to be cynical about genuine PR stunts.

Game 2: British & Irish Lions V Taranaki
Wednesday 8 June, Yarrow Stadium

Taranaki 14
Tries: C. Masoe, B. Watt
Convs: B. Watt (2)

British & Irish Lions 36
Tries: G. Murphy (2), M. Corry, S. Horgan
Convs: C. Hodgson (2)
Pens: C. Hodgson (4)

'We scored the first try and the last try. So we won.' So spoke a jocular Taranaki fan, a happy streak of yellow and black shouting across to an Irish friend as the crowd filed out after the final whistle. Of course, Taranaki didn't win, but, at half-time, it looked as if they almost might. Once again, the Lions were struggling against the sheer passion and commitment of a team of part-timers. 'Our guys are pipe-fitters and plumbers,' one of the locals put it the previous evening, but pipe-fitters and plumbers, when they get their one shot at glory, tend to be pretty feisty.

Ian McGeechan, the coach of the Wednesday teams, alluded to this after the game: 'This is the game of their lives for our opponents. It's something we have to get used to.' By the time the interval whistle turned Yarrow Stadium into a tumult of yellow and black, it looked like the visitors had little conception of what exactly they found themselves up against. In the weeks leading up to the tour, former All Blacks' coach, Laurie Mains, described this Lions' squad as the worst in living memory. Those words sprung all around New Plymouth during the interval.

However, Mains' assessment is a little on the harsh side. While they might not have had a true conception of what they were up against, the Lions did know what they were trying to do. The ferocity of the Taranaki approach though forced them into handling mistakes and rattled them into unforced errors. They knew their game plan and tried to implement it, but, with the hosts swarming all over them, like a hive of bees pestering an intruder, it proved impossible. In addition, there were continuing problems at the breakdown.

'Well, it happens eighteen inches lower for a start,' sighed McGeechan, when asked about the differences between the tackle area in the northern and southern hemispheres. The breakdown, for the uninitiated, is what happens when a player with the ball gets tackled. When he falls to the ground and other players compete for the ball, that's the breakdown. Unless he passes the ball away, or pops it upwards – something the New Zealanders are very good at – then a ruck will form once other players arrive on the scene; which is where it gets complicated. The rules governing when players are allowed to put their hands on the ball and try and claim it in a breakdown situation aren't rules as you would normally know them: it all depends on the interpretation of the individual referee. One of the challenges for the Lions is to adapt to the refereeing of the breakdown. The other challenge is to adapt to the New Zealand approach to the breakdown: in Europe, the key man in most teams wears number ten; down here, the poster-boys are openside flankers, and, the more aggressive they are at the breakdown, the more posters they adorn. Referees and number sevens – generally, the first forward to arrive at the ruck and a specialist in trying to turn over posses-sion – are combining to give the Lions a desperately hard time.

The Lions are on a very steep learning curve as it is, strug-gling to adapt to these differences, but when crazy farmers like the rugged Gordon Slater, who also propped against the Lions in 1993, his front-row counterpart, All Black, Andrew Hore, and the animalistic second-row forward, Paul Tito, are thundering into the ruck, the curve stretches upwards dizzyingly, almost to vertical. Getting them to the ground so that a ruck could actual-ly be formed in the first place was a momentous task as the pumped up Taranaki XV thundered and thumped their way for-ward. Pumped-up they very much were. Both Hore and Tito played games last weekend, Tito for the New Zealand Maori in the punishing heat of Suva against Fiji, and Hore for the Possibles in the All Blacks' final trial; there was never any doubt though that they would even have considered not lining out for the 'Naki as well: gladly, they would have died for the priviledge of wearing the yellow and black.

So it again became a case of, pin 'em down and grind them into submission. Towards the end of the first half, it became clear that the Lions had realised this, centre Will Greenwood electing to grubber-kick the ball twenty metres rather than keep it in the hand. In fact, that had been the fashion from early in the game. The all-Irish back three of Geordan Murphy, Denis Hickie and Shane Horgan, showed a lack of willingness to run the ball back at Taranaki, even after receiving loose kicks, despite the fact that this tactic had worked so well against the Bay of Plenty. One was tempted to conclude that they simply didn't have the dynamism of the trio that lined out against the Bay, but, as McGeechan explained, 'The guys are smart. They know when to attack. They know when it's on and when it's not'. In the opening period, with Taranaki in killer bee mode, it was rarely on. And, by the time the second period began, the Lions were trailing 6-7, Taranaki having nicked a try underneath the posts. In truth, it was unfortunate for the Lions: their defensive systems had withstood the pounding the hosts had been giving them and indeed, they had turned yet another ball over five metres from their own line. The ball squirted out of the ruck though, and Chris Masoe pounced to wriggle over.

Ultimately, the Lions needed a try that was jammier than a year's supply of Chivers to turn the game in their favour. Five minutes into the second half, Taranaki were pummelling away again; once more, they were getting nowhere, finding only blind alleys and cul de sacs at every turn, a tribute to the Lions' defensive organisation. Inevitably, the ball was eventually turned over, and Murphy whacked it downfield. The sensible option would have been to kick the ball back into Lions' territory, but Chris Woods and Matthew Harvey made a colossal mess of it, trying to work a switch move on their own '22, into a fast-approaching wall of red jerseys. The ball bounced off Woods' chest and, after some ping-pong, re-emerged on the Lions' side. With many of the Taranaki defenders still rumbling back from their attacking exertions, Chris Cusiter looked left, then ran right and passed to Charlie Hodgson, who found

Martin Corry. Hore made a heroic effort to put Corry into touch, but somehow the Englishman kept his legs in the air and managed to plant the ball down in the corner.

It was a devastating blow to Taranaki: their attacking had come up short and, to boot, they'd just conceded a try that could only be described as morale-shattering: from Murphy's right foot clearing the ball to Corry touching it down took less than 30 seconds. Half a minute was all it took for triumph to slip to disaster. The hosts' situation was compounded immediately after the restart, when the Lions gave away their only penalty of the second half. As Hodgson's conversion attempt had been off the mark, a successful penalty attempt from fly-half Sam Young would have brought the 'Naki to within a point. Not only did he miss, but Murphy manufactured a half-break off a poor box-kick from Craig Fevre, and the Lions swept into the home '22. Hore deliberately lay on the wrong side of a ruck, was kicked and yellow-carded for his indiscretion, and, as he made his way off for a ten-minute spell in the sin-bin, Hodgson knocked over the three-pointer. The gap was now 17-7, which left Taranaki needing two scores to win. Once might have been realistic, but two, against an extremely competent Lions' defence, was surely a bridge too far. From a point ahead at the break and a position of control, in less than fifteen minutes, Taranaki found themselves short a talismanic presence up front and a brace of scores adrift.

What followed was a procession as the home side, like the Bay before them, ran out of fuel; only rarely did the Taranaki defence hold up to sustained scrutiny. On 65 minutes, Horgan crossed for the Lions' second try and, six minutes later, Murphy touched down before helping himself to another with five minutes left on the clock. Brendon Watt did touch down for Taranaki with the sound of the full-time hooter ringing around the ground, but that was little more than an irritation for the victors.

The winners on the night individually were Cusiter and Hodgson, with Murphy, Hickie and Horgan combining well out wide, particularly in the second half. Michael Owen had a fabulous game at number eight, showing vision and skill throughout: 'the X-factor', as coach, Gareth Jenkins, put it. Nonetheless, his Test chances are very much in doubt: his wife is due to give birth to their second child and Owen, commendably, is heading home to be by her side. Though he will stay in Wales for only just over a day, and will be unavailable for only one Lions game, the punishing journey will surely sap his energy. Shakespeare's Puck might have been able to put a girdle about the earth in 40 minutes and return to centre stage sprightly and fresh, but the same is hardly true of a gangling Welsh number eight. To fly halfway around the world once is difficult, but to do so twice in a week borders on self-flagellation.

Whatever about Owen quietly slinking off the roster, it seems as if one of the Irish contingent won't be making a serious contribution come Test time. Prop John Hayes, having been twisted and turned every which way by the brutal attentions of the Argentinian pack in Cardiff, received another bad doing from the veteran Slater. He was replaced by Gethin Jenkins less than ten minutes into the second half and, as the gentleman from Bruff lumbered off, it was hard to imagine him playing any great role outside the midweek side, dirt-tracking around the provinces when the test side, potentially containing more than a few of his international colleagues, is resting up elsewhere.

Taranaki: S. Ireland; S. Tagicakibau, M. Stewart, L. Mafi, C. Woods; S. Young, C. Fevre; T. Soqeta, C. Masoe, J. Willis; S. Breman, P. Tito (c); G. Slater, A. Hore, T. Penn.
Subs: B. Watt for Ireland 16, M. Harvey for Tagicakibau h/t, J. Eaton for Breman 64, R. Bryant for Willis 66, J. King for Fevre 67, H. Mitchell for Penn 68.
Yellow cards: A. Hore 53.

Lions: G. Murphy; S. Horgan, W. Greenwood, O. Smith, D. Hickie; C. Hodgson, C. Cusiter; M. Owen, L. Moody, M. Corry (c); D. Grewcock, D. O'Callaghan; J. Hayes, A. Titterrell, G. Rowntree.
Subs: G. Jenkins for Hayes 48, S. Byrne for Titterrell 68, G. Cooper for Cusiter 74.

Referee: K. Deaker (New Zealand).

On every Lions' tour there are only fifteen places up for grabs in the Test team. Generally, there is a split between the side that plays in midweek – known as the dirt-trackers, as they must traipse the highways and byways of the provinces – and that which takes to the field at the weekends. Usually, the bulk of the Test side is selected early in the Tour and plays together on the Saturdays, while those selected in the midweek team try and force their way into the reckoning for weekend selection. Only very rarely will the Test team actually play as an entire XV before the First Test; the fashion is to select that team seven days beforehand and give them a good week of training in the run-up to the start of the Test series.

The Last Great Tour?

This time, it's slightly different. With 45 players – internationals all – in the panel, picking a Test team early in the tour could lead to rifts developing within the playing squad; indeed, some players felt, in 2001, that as the Test team had effectively been selected even before the tour began, they had been treated unfairly and hadn't got a chance to stake their claim. Morale suffered as a result and, to guard against it, Sir Clive Woodward will have to ensure players feel they've had a chance to prove themselves. Thus, while the team that played against the Bay of Plenty on Saturday resembled a shadow Test team, Gordon Bulloch, Matt Stevens, Ronan O'Gara and Mark Cueto would not be considered favourites to line out when the All Blacks are providing the opposition. The only man certain to start in Christchurch is Brian O'Driscoll, while Josh Lewsey, Gareth Thomas, Jonny Wilkinson, Dwayne Peel, Martin Corry, Richard Hill, Paul O'Connell, Gethin Jenkins and Julian White can only play themselves out of that team. Neil Back and Martyn Williams, Shane Byrne and Steve Thompson, Ben Kay and Danny Grewcock are all neck-and-neck at the moment, while, of the rest, Michael Owen, Jason Robinson, Gavin Henson, Shane Horgan, Geordan Murphy, Andy Sheridan and Stephen Jones will be the ones with most cause to hope that at least one outstanding display would put them in contention.

The problem for Woodward is that he only has six games before the First Test: striking a balance between giving all of those players a chance and being able to run the rule over Test contenders, and seeing various combinations – back-row, half-back, back-three, etc – in action will be an extraordinarily difficult task.

Part Three

A Turn for the Worse

MEET THE PRESS TAKE 2

Thursday 9 June 2005, Hamilton

The relationship between the Lions' management and the media corps is deteriorating. The pleasant atmosphere of the Hilton Hotel, where everyone seemed to be accessible and I felt like a cat in a fishmonger's, appears to have vanished. Requests for one-on-one interviews are routinely denied; press conference times change with a suddenness and frequency similar to variations in the wind; 'Campbell' has almost attained the status of a swear word. Everyone is getting the same material, when they are getting any material at all, that is.

The Lions' media team looks lousy and ill-equipped when placed alongside the courteous staff of the NZRU, who always have their phones switched on, always return their calls, always hold their media events as arranged and – this may well be the critical point of difference – gave out a very nice goody-bag to each journalist covering the tour.

This, of course, is only what I'm hearing. The Lions are based in Auckland, which means their media operation is still being run mainly in the Hilton Hotel. I have neither the time, inclination nor petrol money to keep driving north. Meandering through the North Island, stopping here, there and everywhere the mood takes me, seems vastly preferable. If what the rest of the press is complaining about is actually true, my method is vastly preferable; indeed, many of the press conference quotes are distributed via emails which arrive in my inbox sporadically, obviating the need for daily treks in and out of New Zealand's largest city.

I don't know specifically what's going on, but I'm inclined not to agree with the broad thrust of the other journalists' complaints. For a start, journalists will moan about most things. There's a New Zealand joke that runs something like this: how do you know when a planeload of English tourists has touched down in an airport? The whining doesn't stop even after the engines have been turned off. Journalists could well be substituted for English tourists as the butt of that joke. The whining, such as it is, consists of two main charges against the Lions' media team: the organisation is shambolic, with the schedule in a constant, chaotic, state of flux; and there is no exclusive access, which means that everyone is getting the same material.

Certainly, the criticism of the changing schedules seems valid. My inbox is littered with Lions' emails headed 'Change'. But then, such is the chaotic nature of a tour. Players get injured, circumstances change and schedules have to be adjusted at very short notice. In addition, there are at least 50 journalists, print and broadcast, covering the tour at the moment. None of them are in the same place when something happens and the schedule needs to be tweaked; making contact is a logistical nightmare, with the added complication that, if you call the *Daily Mirror* before you call the *Sun*, Tony Roche will be screaming blue murder and, if it's the other way around, Alex Spink will be none-too-pleased. The All Blacks' media operation compares favourably, but then, they haven't been put under pressure yet. And, in any case, it's only two weeks into the Tour: no matter how much planning went into the media side of the Lions' operation, there were bound to be teething problems.

Of course, there's also a cynical response: perhaps Campbell wants it this way. If journalists are running around the place trying to keep up, he's always one step ahead: the journalists spend more time complaining than trying to ferret out stories. Certainly, listening to the press corps moan and moan in New Plymouth last night, one could be forgiven for thinking that, if this were his aim – to perform a gigantic act of misdirection – Campbell has pulled it off with remarkable panache.

There is no cynic's response to the second charge. The reasoning on the Lions' part is simple and two fold. Firstly, with so many journalists covering the Tour, the demands on players for one-on-one interviews would be quite considerable, particularly in terms of time. Woodward is probably of the view that limited time on tour is better spent explaining tactics to the players, not the media. Most journalists, for a one-on-one interview, would like to budget at least one hour. If it's the marketable, quotable Gavin Henson, he could expect a dozen requests a week; again, if one is granted and another is not, that's a nose out of joint and another time-consuming problem for the Lions to deal with, with a mollifying tone, a cup of green tea and the soothing promise of an exclusive.

Secondly, when a player is in a one-on-one session with a journalist, he's more likely to say something that he shouldn't. This can be anything from an inadvertent comment which subsequently bothers the player, to a disclosure of a tactical approach which gives the opposition an advantage, to the ultimate: the sort of material which would take pride of place on the wall of the next dressing room down. Every journalist is attracted to the idea of returning to the office waving, Chamberlain-esque, a piece of paper, with an explosive headline – 'Henson Says He Has Better Hair than Umaga!' – scrawled down in capital letters, and they know little tricks to get players to loosen up. In a 'scrum session' where it's a case of, 'sharpen your elbows, gentlemen' and the journalists muscle their notebook or Dictaphone to the front, it's much less likely that an interviewer and interviewee will build up the sort of rapport that is necessary for the player to relax and feel at ease. If that rapport doesn't develop, there's less risk of a slip of the tongue. There's no sure-fire way of ensuring that players never say something they ought not to, but the restriction on individual interviews is the best possible means of keeping the opposition coaches ammunition-free and individual players without needless worries.

Ultimately, the Lions aren't here to please the media: they're here to win a Test series against the All Blacks, something only one Lions' squad has done before. They will get the media coverage anyway. While most journalists get very similar material, they are all able to put their own particular gloss on it, give it their own particular spin; in a scrum session, they can put their own questions to the players – it may not be particularly glamorous, but they can, in the mêlées that tend to form, pursue a particular agenda and, afterwards, write from a particular angle; two journalists jostling side by side can produce vastly different copy, even with the same material.

Anyway, it's not as if there is a terrifying dearth of stuff to write about: Simon Lewis from the *Irish Examiner* is sending back three pieces a day, the vast majority of which are being used. They may not be the pieces he wishes he were able to file, but, like the rest, in between the grumbling and the moaning, he just gets on with it. One must wonder as well what exactly the Lions want from the media. The strength of their brand isn't going to be badly affected if access to players isn't as good as the journalists would like: the coverage will continue anyway. The Lions are facilitating the press, not the other way around.

Overall, Campbell's strategy has been successful. The players are concentrating on rugby, nobody has said anything they shouldn't and column inches are being filled. Journalists are complaining, but, Campbell would probably say, they always do. And, if they spend their time grumbling, they spend less time causing problems for me. Maybe I'm too cynical, though: it could just be that the Lions are incompetent, unable even to arrange a press conference that starts on time. But then, this is Campbell: incompetence doesn't seem like even the remotest possibility.

There's probably not much the master of the dark arts can do about the New Zealand media. For a start, they don't like Sir Clive all that much. 'Woodward,' wrote Jim Kayes in the *Dominion Post* last week, 'took England from being a rabble that relied on penalties to win Tests to a well-oiled machine that relied on penalties to win the World Cup'. Two things appear to irritate them about the Lions' head coach: the fact that he seems to have a bottomless well of self-belief; and that he won the World Cup playing a style of rugby much less expansive than that preferred by New Zealanders.

And some sections of the media haven't been impressed with the Lions so far, after that stuttering performance against Argentina and their first tour display against the Bay of Plenty, as these excerpts from Gregor Paul's piece in the *Herald on Sunday* suggest: 'So now we know why the Lions have spent all week talking – it seems to be the strongest part of their game ...The Knight of the Realm [Sir Clive Woodward, that is] has assured the Western world the 2005 Lions are the best-prepared in history. It was a massive claim to make before a ball was kicked. It became a hugely dubious one when it emerged in all their meticulous planning they had clearly forgotten to spend any time putting a defensive structure in place ... Maybe [the British and Irish media] have slung the mud at New Zealand's forwards to divert attention from the big tent antics of their backs. Even Brian O'Driscoll looked like taking and giving a pass was a bit beyond him. The back three ran with real energy but then again, so do headless chickens.'

Big Bill's One-Man, One-Act Circus

Friday 10 June 2005, North Harbour Stadium, Albany, Auckland

New Zealand 91
Tries: S. Sivivatu (4), D. Howlett (2), T. Umaga (2), A. Mauger, D. Carter, A. Williams, R. So'oialo, G. Somerville,

A Turn for the Worse

K. Mealamu, M. Muliaina.
Convs: D. Carter (5), A. Mauger (3)

Fiji 0

He led the Haka, and that was the only time he wasn't visibly struggling for breath. He only really caught my eye about mid-way through the first half, when he really started to seriously huff and puff and began to waddle from play to play. 'Big' Bill Cavubati was propping for Fiji on the tighthead side.

The veteran – 'I thought I read about him retiring in 1997', one of the incredulous press corps blurted out – was described by the match programme as 'the world's heaviest-ever Test player'. Apparently, he tipped the pre-match scales at 163 kilos. That's nearly three times my weight, which must make Big Bill close on 30 stone.

Whatever his exact poundage, by the time the twenty-minute mark had passed, he was having serious difficulty in carrying it around the pitch. It was sad to watch a man with a proud history in the game – he had an All Black trial in 1993 and played Super 12 with the Wellington Hurricanes – huff, puff and then just flounder. Every time the ball moved and Bill was forced to readjust, it was almost as if an audible groan rose from his shuddering jowls. As the game wore on, his readjustments became less and less effective and more and more token. At times, it looked like he was operating his own sweeper system: everyone else would run up and try to tackle the All Blacks, but Bill would hang back, just in case. In case what? On one occasion, he was loitering around the '22 when the All Blacks broke through; as Dan Carter knifed towards the line,

Bill came lumbering across, bursting every sinew to catch the flying fly-half. He never got there, only managing to flail a leg outwards in a vain attempt to knock Carter off balance.

Earlier, he'd stood off a maul – he seemed to have a fondness for observing the intricacies of ruck and maul but not participating in them, did Bill – as New Zealand rumbled forward. Byron Kelleher needed no further invitation, sniping around Bill before doing a scissors move with Doug Howlett. Bill again was left floundering, unable to get there.

It was the story of Bill's game – and that of Fiji's. They never quite got there. Up against a ruthlessly efficient All-Blacks' outfit, they never had a chance. Not only were they ruthlessly efficient, but the hosts were focused to a frightening degree. As Carter completed his pre-match kicking routine, the promised 'event' began and fireworks went off around him. With a tremendous bang that had many of the crowd's older members reaching for their angina pills, another explosion sent smoke skyward, belching up between the uprights. Carter was unfazed, calmly stroking the ball home, as if to mock: like fireworks would put an All Black off. This was their first Test of the year, a chance for individuals to lay down markers and an opportunity to show the Lions what they could expect to get in a fortnight's time.

And boy, were they ruthless. The first try was a product of a break by Carter – after an opening six minutes spent soaking up pressure from the visitors – but that description doesn't quite do justice to the brutally clinical nature of the score. The Fijians missed one tackle – just one tackle – and, less than a minute later, were gathered beneath their posts for the first of fifteen such meetings. One missed tackle allowed Carter to break from inside his '22, Richie McCaw and Mils Muliaina carried on; from the resultant ruck, a pop pass found Jerry Collins on the short side, and he slipped the ball away to Carter who cantered in for the try. One missed tackle. Bang, bang, bang. No mercy.

Never mind contending with a hungry set of fifteen All Blacks, things haven't been easy for Fiji in the professional era. To start with, they're starved of funding. Former All Black prop, Brad Johnstone, who coached Fiji and subsequently Italy, wrote in the match programme that, 'Many times I dreamed of what I could do with the talent of Fiji and the money of Italy. As a rough equation, I'd say that Fiji have got six times the talent and Italy have got ten times the finances. Fiji could be such a potent side if they had even a third of that money.' But the rugby community has allowed Fiji to flounder, Big Bill-esque, wandering about with only a vague clue of where to go next, and keenly aware that they don't quite have enough juice in the tank to get there. The International Rugby Board's funding is paltry and the SANZAR nations, South Africa, Australia and New Zealand, have ring-fenced the Tri Nations to keep out the Pacific Islanders and the Argentinians. Wayne Pivac, Fiji's current coach, spoke eloquently about their plight, and the need for more money. But, even after their win in the Sevens World Cup, they have been unable to attract a headline sponsor, critical if they are to progress.

It gets worse: many of their players don't even play for them. Some of the 'corral hoppers' have hopped from Fiji to New Zealand. It must have been particularly galling for the Fijians to watch one of their own, Sitiveni Sivivatu, line up against them tonight and then proceed to score four tries, a record for an All Blacks' Test debutant. With doleful eyes, the Fijians might have pondered what has become a perennial question: how good would we be if we could keep our players? Pivac has made repeated entreaties to prop, Deacon Manu, who plays with the Maori tomorrow night, but, as long as Manu thinks he has a chance of donning the All Black jersey, he's not going to throw his lot in with Fiji.

When Big Bill trudged off at half-time, the last Fijian to leave the field, the scoreboard read New Zealand 50, Fiji 0. That scoreline probably flattered the visitors. Big Bill was eventually substituted early in the second half, his waddling frame an embarrassment that could no longer be tolerated. As he placed his massive bulk on the bench, one half-expected the sub at the other end to be catapulted, Looney Tunes-style, into Auckland Harbour. He wasn't, though, and Big Bill pulled a blanket around himself for comfort.

When the All Blacks were taken off and replaced, they didn't go immediately to the bench; instead, they warmed down on exercise bicycles placed alongside it. Not a luxury available to the stricken Fijians. Mind you, it's not at all clear that Big Bill would have bothered mounting a bicycle, or even if the bicycle would have taken him.

If the Fijians could take any comfort from this trouncing, it was in their commitment. A band of their supporters sat in the stand and cheered and sang all night long. Their players didn't give up either, trying until the very end, even when the situation facing them was cold and bleak. Even Big Bill, in his time on the pitch, never failed to show up for a scrum. No matter how far away he was, without fail, he would jog back to take up his position on the tighthead side. Big Bill may not have had great fitness levels, but he did have great heart. Even in the absence of the resources, money and players needed to compete at the top level, that's worth something.

For the All Blacks, though, this was a largely wasted evening. 'Oh, I think he'll take a lot out of it,' said Graham Henry when asked whether Sir Clive Woodward would learn anything from the demolition job, but it was hard to see how he could. Still, it wasn't totally wasted. In terms of team selection for the First Test, depending on what sort of game Henry wishes to play, Kelleher now looks well ahead of Justin Marshall in the scrum-half race: his distribution is snappier and he allows New Zealand to play a wider game, whereas Marshall prefers a close-in dogfight. Another who laid claim to a jersey was lock, James Ryan, who looked athletic, strong and a good possibility to start alongside the world-class Chris Jack in Christchurch. Carter cemented his place at fly-half, but, worryingly, when he went off at half-time and Aaron Mauger stepped into his position the All Blacks weren't as cohesive; worse, Mauger's goal-kicking was well below-par, at three successful attempts out of seven, so much so that Carter's continued fitness could prove vital. In midfield, Muliaina played the second half at centre, but did little to suggest that he was a possible Test partner for captain, Tana Umaga. Of the newcomers, Sosene Anesi did OK at full-back in the second half, while Derren Witcombe kept up his challenge for at least a place in the squad at hooker. Certainly, if the injured Anton Oliver keeps munching sausages and chips at the rate he did while watching from the stands throughout the second half, he's in with a shout!

One player who now looks almost certain to start the First Test is Sivivatu. His four tries make it impossible to leave him out. The only question is, which winger will feel the axe on the nape of his neck? Howlett continued his rehabilitation tonight,

The Last Great Tour?

Rico Gear, who will play for the Maori tomorrow evening, is the country's form winger, Ma'a Nonu can cover both centre and wing, and Sivavatu's cousin, Joe Rokocoko, has been recovering his form at a Sevens tournament in London.

From a Lions' point of view, this may put the Maori win over Fiji last weekend in some context. Are the Maori all that good? Well, they beat the same Fijian side by two points; the All Blacks beat them by 91. Then again, the Maori played in the stifling heat of Suva, in front of a passionate home crowd, and, during the half-time break, some of the players were as close to death as live men get. Under that baking sun, maybe finishing the game at all was a glorious triumph.

New Zealand: M. Muliaina; D. Howlett, T. Umaga (c), A. Mauger, S. Sivivatu; D. Carter, B. Kelleher; R. So'oialo, R. McCaw, J. Collins; J. Ryan, A. Williams; G. Somerville, D. Witcombe, T. Woodcock.
Subs: S. Anesi for Carter h/t, S. Lauaki for McCaw h/t, K. Mealamu for Witcombe 48, C. Johnstone for Somerville 51, J. Marshall for Kelleher 54, C. Smith for Umaga 56, C. Jack for Williams 58.

Fiji: N. Ligairi; V. Delasau, V. Satala, S. Bai, S. Bobo; N. Little, M. Rauluni (c); S. Koyamaible, A. Ratuva, I. Rawaqa; I. Domolai, A. Matanibukaca; B. Cavubati, V. Gadolo, J. Bale.
Subs: S. Tabua for Matanibukaca 48, J. Railomo for Cavubati 51, J. Qova for Satala 59, J. Rauluni for M. Rauluni 65.

Referee: N. Whitehouse (Wales).

War of Words

Friday 10 June 2005, Auckland

It began in earnest yesterday morning. On every tour; in fact, in the lead-up to every big Test, the opposing coaches lock down and engage with the same aggression they hope their front rows will muster up come match day. The subject, generally, is the refereeing of games: the cheating of X at the line-out; the way Y deliberately slows the ball at the breakdown; X's star prop's habit of 'boring' in the scrum; Y's best defender's use of the shoulder charge to stop his opposite number. And so on, the aim quite a simple one: to influence and intimidate the referee.

In this series, the breakdown will be of great importance and, undoubtedly, the major area of contention. So it was no surprise that Steve Hansen, the All Blacks' assistant coach and the man charged with bettering the Lions up front, fired a shot across their bows in the wake of New Zealand's demolition of Fiji.

'The clear-out area was difficult,' he said tonight, 'with a lot of people flopping over the ball in a manner very similar to the Lions' games, where they look to slow the ball down. Obviously, when you play the All Blacks, the main aim is to slow the game. The Lions are pretty good at it and, hopefully, the referees will be pretty staunch in this area. We want a game of rugby that people can enjoy and if you want that, you can't afford to have people diving off their feet.'

The target wasn't even set up for Hansen: it was an unremarkable question about the areas of the Fiji game that he had been happy with; he went roaming for trouble like a bare-knuckle fighter with a superiority complex.

Expect more of this in the coming weeks. In fact, expect

even more than you might expect; the British and Irish press corps has an obsession that borders on the neurotic with the breakdown, so much so that one might be led to believe that the game of rugby revolves around it and, no matter what, the team that gets the upper hand there will win. It's far from certain that this is the case, no matter how influential the area will be, but it is as certain as certain can be that the word 'breakdown' will be used more often than any other noun in the acres of coverage that, if laid out in a line, could form an ink carpet to the gates of Jade Stadium for the First Test in Christchurch.

While the attempts of both sides to intimidate the Test referees into taking a particular view of various facets of the game always constitute an entertaining battle in their own right, there is that added frisson between Sir Clive 'The Successor' Woodward and Graham 'The Predecessor' Henry. A low-key, though spiteful, war of words between the two men has continued, with Henry recently landing occasional jabs at Woodward's selection of 45 in his touring party, eight more than the former brought down under.

Reacting to the breaking news that Welshman, Ryan Jones, had been called into the touring party as cover for the injured – but not replaced – Simon Taylor, Henry and his other assistant, Wayne Smith, shook their heads. 'How many is that now?' he asked, with an air of incredulity. 'And you guys are complaining about me picking too many players?' he continued, a reference to criticisms that his policy of rotating the All Blacks' squad to deal with the rigour of the international season would 'cheapen' the New Zealand jersey. (Apart from the Test series against the Lions, New Zealand will also play twice against each of Australia and South Africa in the Tri Nations before travelling to Europe in the autumn to face the four home nations individually on consecutive weekends).

There was still more. On Wednesday night, Ian McGeechan had diplomatically ducked a question posed by Stephen Jones of the *Sunday Times*. Jones had wondered what McGeechan's view was of the fact that the touch-judges on duty that night, Steve Walsh and Paul Honiss, had via their microphones, at times made decisions while badly placed to do so. Though McGeechan ducked and weaved with the grace he once displayed as a player, the matter was brought up unilaterally by Woodward at his press briefing the following morning.

'My experience says that sometimes the best referees do not make the best touch judges,' he said. 'Touch judging is an art and I can hear [during the games] what's going on and there's a lot of talk.

'To me the touch judges are there to put the flag up when the ball goes out of play. They're there to watch for foul play behind the ball.'

This statement was then put to Henry for his response. Unsurprisingly it turned out to be a caustic disagreement with Woodward: 'I think the game is complicated enough without one guy having to do it by himself. I think the game is enhanced greatly when there are three people there and you just have to rely on the maturity of the guys with the flags to speak at the appropriate times. The game is very complicated to referee and I think most of them do it pretty well.'

The war of words can now be considered underway, live, on. There will be no backing down.

When Maori Eyes Are Smiling
Game 3: British & Irish Lions V New Zealand Maori
Saturday 11 June 2005, Waikato Stadium, Hamilton

New Zealand Maori 19
Tries: L. MacDonald
Convs: L. McAlister
Pens: D. Hill (2), L. McAlister (2)

British & Irish Lions 13
Tries: B. O'Driscoll
Convs: S. Jones
Pens: S. Jones (2)

'Eh, eh, Phil,' the bald hawker shouted, across a bustling, noisy corner of the University of Auckland campus. 'This guy here's following the Lions.'

'Oh, yeah?' Phil didn't have much else better to do, so he cocked his ear and paid some attention. My bald friend waved a book in the air and smiled a gap-toothed smile. 'He wants to find out how hard it's gonna be!'

The book was Alan Duff's 1992 masterpiece, *Once Were Warriors*, a harrowing story about a Maori family beset by domestic violence, alcohol abuse, incest and suicide. It's a fascinating, poignant tale and, yes, I was wondering how hard it was going to be.

Two of Duff's themes resonated tonight in Hamilton. The first was the notorious Maori shyness, the crippling fear of standing up and performing in front of a crowd, and how, in the family setting, it can be subsumed by the comfort of being with

A Turn for the Worse

one's people. In *Once Were Warriors*, the great opera singer, Kiri Te Kawana, is contrasted with a Maori woman of similar ability who only performs in the local tavern and then, only with the help of a gallon or so of beer. Beth Heke, Duff's central character, watches, thinks, contrasts and concludes that the Maori is often overcome by shyness, preferring the claustrophobia of family and the familiar. On her own, the drunken opera singer would never survive beyond the embrace of her own community but in their bosom she is a star.

The second was the lust for blood and violence. The Maori are a race of warriors, who fought off the first explorers who attempted to land in New Zealand, waged pitched battles with European settlers – the Pakeha – and now, in Duff's sordid world of low-cost social housing, get drunk and fist-fight. In the novel the father, Jake, is a violent brute, useful with his fists in the bar, on the street, or in the bedroom. He is the emperor of Pine Block, like a warrior king of yore: a chief. Jake is a corruption of power, of violence; what happens when the Maori desire for the two is channelled in the wrong direction.

What happens when the Maori desire for the two is channelled in the right direction was illustrated by an incident minutes from the end of tonight's epic game. Jono Gibbes, the Maori captain, had been warrior-like throughout; it was said that, almost crippled by a chronic foot injury, he was barely fit to play and, as he lay on the ground with time running out, stretching what looked like cramp in his legs, it appeared as if the sceptics were right: Jono was crocked. But then he sprung back to life. Lions centre, Gordon D'Arcy, tried to snipe around the blindside and his arcing run took out three defenders before he straightened up and attempted to run forward into space, a potentially game-saving move. He had the misfortune to run into Gibbes. Not only did he run into him, but he bounced back, to the sound of a collective, 'Ooooo' rolling around the Waikato Stadium. When danger loomed, the flanker shot to his feet – oblivious to pain – as a warrior should, and did his duty, in the bosom of his team-mates and the hundreds of thousands of watching Maori.

Warrior qualities were evident as well in the display of Leon MacDonald, the full-back and scorer of what proved to be a crucial second-half try. Receiving the ball five metres from the line, MacDonald twisted, turned, fended and muscled his way past no fewer than five Lions' defenders before reaching out and planting the ball for the game's critical score.

As for shyness? The New Zealand Maori is a family. Some of the players appear far from pure Maori. Paul Tito, the Taranaki lock who lined out against Fiji, is ginger-haired, but he qualifies because he is at least one-sixteenth Maori and he can trace his *whakapapa*, the genealogical line of descent from a Maori chief. Once you have a *whakapapa*, you are as much a Maori as the olive-skinned Rua Tipoki, their gallant centre.

'You're in other teams and they say, you have to wear this for breakfast, this for lunch and this for dinner but in the Maori team, you can wear what you want,' Tipoki said afterwards, explaining what makes the New Zealand Maori special.

'They just give you a lot more freedom, but when it's time to perform, on the field, and at training, they make sure you step up and do your job. Other than that, you just look after yourself off the field. It's just real ... *whanau*, that's the Maori word for family and that's what the thing's all about; looking after each other, helping each other.

A Turn for the Worse

'It's a real family atmosphere. We have sing-songs on the bus when we're driving from "a" to "b". After the game, we do haka and sing-songs in the training shed. It's really a fantastic atmosphere.'

'The Maori is a special team,' MacDonald said. 'We do a lot of things differently from any other team that I've been involved with. There's a lot of people who've worn the jersey before us and done it with a lot of pride. It's great to be part of because it does your family proud as well. We're only together for a week and a half, but we get really tight in that week and a half.

'There is something special about the jersey too. It's really the jersey of all the people from your family. It's got a lot of history and a lot of *mana* [a Maori word, meaning respect] about it, which is important for us. We're very proud to play for it.'

From family traditions, the Maori draw strength. From their warrior traditions, they draw pride. Shyness disappears and, on the pitch, their warrior qualities are channelled to great effect, not to where they can damage both the warrior and the Maori community, but to where they can wreak havoc on the enemy.

Tipoki, I discovered later, may be the man in the squad best placed to explain what being a Maori means, but he might not represent the most wholesome example either. A number of years ago he was ruled out of action for his club, North Harbour, after breaking bones in both his hands. He and two team-mates told the club that there had been a gym accident involving a twenty kilogram weight, but it in fact turned out that Tipoki had done the damage while fighting in a festival rugby match.

Throughout the game, as the Maori threw themselves into Lions with seemingly no respect for their own bodies or mortality, the words of Ian McGeechan came thundering back. This is their only chance to play against the Lions. Couple that with the fervour that pulling on the Maori jersey can inspire and there grows a sense that the Lions were playing against more than mere mortals tonight.

'This jersey,' said Carlos Spencer, with elation still hanging in the air, and his hand beating the crest on his Maori shirt, 'I respect it more than the All Black jersey.' How could the Lions possibly compete with that?

And, as if all that wasn't enough, there was still more to spur the Maoris. Hika Reid, the former All Black hooker and another to proudly don the jersey of the Maori, entered hospital a few days ago to receive chemotherapy, having been diagnosed with leukaemia at the age of 47.

'There wasn't much said,' was Gibbes' response when he was asked what effect that bad news had. 'It was about the team first tonight. It's there alright though: you know it has an influence, but nothing much was said about it. It was around the team, even though not a lot was said.'

More, more, more. This was Spencer's last game in the jersey before heading north, to English club Northampton. But more importantly, it was also the last game for coach Matt Te Pou, who, over more than a decade in his role, has almost assumed the status of legend amongst the players.

'He's been amazing for the Maori team,' said Tipoki, with a joyful, preacher's glint in his eye. 'There have been times when the New Zealand Union has talked about cutting the team, but because of the success he's had against international teams, that hasn't happened.

'He's such an astute man and he carries so much ... *mana*.' Then, Tipoki fixed me with a stare as laced with passion as his voice. 'You know what that word is?' *Mana* is a Maori word – without a true English equivalent – which, loosely translated, means, 'respect', though that translation doesn't quite do justice to the meaning it has to Maoris, in whose language it is a strange polyglot of authority, tradition, respect and ancestry. 'He carries so much mana and respect from the boys and he speaks straight to you. He doesn't try to bullshit you or anything and the boys just give him so much respect.'

Te Pou has significant status in the Maori community as well. On an Internet messageboard I happened to drift across during the week, someone was seeking help in tracing their *whakapapa* to a location near where Te Pou lives and someone else had replied by supplying Te Pou's home phone number. Ring him, the messenger said, he'll be happy to help. Now, the iconic figure of Te Pou is shuffling off the coaching coil and that, along with everything else, created a deep well of emotion from which the Maoris could drink their fill of inspiration before tonight's encounter.

But, for all that, the post-match press conferences were calm affairs. The singing had died down. And the truth may be more prosaic.

'Well, we were up for playing the Lions,' MacDonald explained. 'And then, it was Matt's last game, Carlos is heading away, there was Hika Reid, so there were other factors. But mainly, it was the Lions and we just wanted a crack at them. That was our goal and we felt we had the team to beat them.'

In truth, the Lions had not looked, against Bay of Plenty and Taranaki, like a team set to rampage unbeaten through their provincial games. They had struggled against the ferocity of the challenge presented by teams of proud part-timers playing for the badge on their jersey and, maybe, just maybe, a place in history. Now, they were up against the New Zealand Maori, a XV composed entirely of Super 12 players, and, in Spencer, MacDonald, Carl Hayman, Gibbes, Caleb Ralph and Marty Holah, seasoned internationals. Like the Bay and the 'Naki, they would play with plenty of pride; unlike the Bay and the 'Naki, they weren't going to run out of steam.

It turned out that Gibbes' half-time message was simple: 'I just said that the other New Zealand teams so far had given the Lions a good run for 40 but they'd never backed up the second 40. I said to our pack and to the rest of the team, if we kept going for the whole 40, kept asking the question, then we were gonna be there or thereabouts. That proved to be the case.'

His back-row colleague – a proud Maori with a name that wouldn't raise eyebrows in the Scottish Highlands – Angus MacDonald, confirmed this: 'We'd seen the Bay of Plenty and Taranaki have a crack at them and the call was, go for 80. That was the call well before we got to the field and it was reiterated at half-time.'

While the Lions' coaches were happy to accept that they'd been beaten by a better side and, in the words of Sir Clive Woodward, it would have been an 'injustice' if they had stolen it at the end, the message from Eddie O'Sullivan was, again, more prose than poetry: 'I don't know what the stats are, but I reckon we played 75 to 80 per cent of that game in our own third of the pitch. And, you're not going to win games from that quarter.

'We couldn't give ourselves enough control to establish field position and that was the root of our problems tonight. We struggled to get control. It's something we've talked about, but we haven't managed to get it yet. It was sloppy at the breakdown, we couldn't clear the ball quick enough, and there were a lot of problems in that area. And we didn't really give our half backs a platform to kick us out of our third of the pitch. That was our biggest difficulty tonight.'

When the Lions' vice-captain, Paul O'Connell, showed up later on, showered and thoughtful, he elaborated: 'At times, maybe we were working a bit hard on defence and not putting as many numbers as them into the ruck. Maybe that cost us a little bit. At times, it looked like we had ball won in rucks and they were able to drive us off it. They were putting more men into it.

'We're working on a lot of things, we're trying to get a lot of things right, whereas, every team playing us, it's a cup final for them. We were beaten in a lot of areas tonight, line-out, break-down, aggression. But I don't think that will happen again on this tour.'

For the Lions, it's now a case of building on the disap-pointment. 'We realise that a game like that makes or breaks us,' said captain Brian O'Driscoll. 'We just have to keep tight together. I'm sure there are going to be comments thrown around in the media that we're not up to it, not up to the chal-lenge, but we've got to believe in our own talent, our own abil-ity and regroup.

'We're going to take the hurt from this game and make sure we don't feel it again.'

As it was, a moment of magic from O'Driscoll almost meant that there would have been no hurt at all. The Maoris dominat-ed possession and territory, punishing every skewed line kick and pressurising the Lions remorselessly. It was 6-6 at the break, which didn't quite do justice to the power of the Maori performance. Willed on by an as-ever passionate crowd, they pinned the Lions down with ferocious tackling – two Lions went to the blood bin for stitching in the opening 40 – powerful running, and exceptional work at the breakdown, particularly through Holah. The Lions couldn't compose any patterns of their own, struggling to retain the ball in the face of what amounted to an onslaught and losing prop Andrew Sheridan, yellow-carded for a wild swing at Maori centre Luke McAlister; then again, the situation against Taranaki and the Bay of Plenty had been similar at half-time.

On this occasion, though, there was no respite. Spencer, as planned, came off the bench two minutes after the restart, replacing the solid but unspectacular Dave Hill. He sparked the back-line into life and, on 57 minutes, a well-worked move saw Spencer play in MacDonald, who somehow forced his way over for the try. McAlister had already kicked a penalty and now he added a conversion to put the Maori well ahead. Indiscipline from D'Arcy gave his opposite number the chance to tack on another three points and, with less than a quarter of an hour to go, the Maori led 19-6.

Yet the Lions might still have sneaked a victory they manifestly did not deserve. Terrified of defeat, they threw themselves into attack, abandoning their play-book and running the ball from deep. O'Driscoll squeezed over, skipping past McAlister with six minutes to go and Jones nailed the conversion to close the gap. One converted try would have brought the Lions victory and, had Josh Lewsey not been obstructed late on as he ran in support of number eight, Michael Owen, they might have pulled it off. But the referee and touchjudge – ironically, in the wake of the week's controversy – didn't see, or simply ignored, the incident, and, more rightly than wrongly, heroism, bravery and courage became the story.

'To be honest, I'm not going to complain about that,' Woodward replied when asked about the foul on his full-back. 'I think we lost fair and square tonight and I'd much rather concentrate on that. I think the better team won and, if anything, the scoreline in the end actually flattered us. If we had snuck a win, I think it would not have reflected the game. We have to look in a lot more detail at what happened and why we lost and go from there.'

Maoris: L. MacDonald; R. Gear, R. Tipoki, L. McAlister, C. Ralph; D. Hill, P. Weepu; A. MacDonald, M. Holah, J. Gibbes (c); S. Hohneck, R. Filipo; C. Hayman, C. Flynn, D. Manu. *Subs*: C. Spencer for Hill 42, G. Feek for Manu 52, D. Braid for Filipo 72.

Lions: J. Lewsey; T. Shanklin, B. O'Driscoll (c), G. D'Arcy, S. Williams; S. Jones, M. Dawson; M. Owen, M. Williams, R. Hill; P. O'Connell, S. Shaw; J. White, S. Thompson, A. Sheridan. *Subs*: G. Jenkins for Sheridan 48, S. Byrne for Thompson 72.

Yellow cards: Sheridan 38.
Referee: S. Walsh (New Zealand).

The streets of Hamilton were paved with staggering revellers once the stadium sent them into the night. There was no escaping the joy the town took in the Maori victory.

'Who-ah, mate, I can't let you in wearing a tracksuit,' said the heavy-set Maori on bouncer duty outside one of the town's less busy-looking establishments. He had the girth of me, several times over, and an apologetic tone. A bouncer? Apologetic? Anything was possible tonight, with joy all around the way love is in bad pop songs.

'Ah, come on. I'm Irish, I'm harmless and I'm only here for one night ...'

After a moment's pause, romance won: 'Go on then.' He almost chuckled.

Inside, I quickly realised this was not the sort of tavern I prefer. The barmaids, attractive and all as they were, were selling many, many more bottles of water than beer. The patrons' eyes lolled in the gloom, their bodies sinuous, the way a river slowly winds and twists through a gorge, as techno music filled the room. Somehow, in my tracksuit pants and runners, I'd managed to land in pill-head central, Hamilton. Feeling quite pleased with myself, if only for the novelty value, I sat back with my beer, crossed my legs and had some fun observing the water-sippers, remembering some comedian's observation about ecstasy being such a dangerous drug, it makes white people think they can dance.

Before too long though, I discovered that rugby had seeped beneath the door of this place too. A Rastafarian took a seat beside me, eyes and jaw rolling in perfect harmony. 'Were you at the game, maaaan?' he asked, employing the strange sixth sense New Zealanders have which allows them to pick out a rugby supporter.

'Sure was, my friend. Wasn't it something?'

'Yeah, maaaan. It was waaaay cooool.'

And then he clasped my hand to his, looked into my eyes, and sashayed gracefully into the night.

No room at the inn

Sunday 12 June 2005, Hamilton

This morning, Graham Henry announced a 26-man squad for the series against the Lions. There will be raised eyebrows and narrowed eyes back home. Joe Rokocoko, scorer of seventeen Test tries in twelve games in 2003, has been omitted: he drops to the Junior All Blacks' squad. He's joined there by Marty Holah, despite his heroic efforts against the Lions last night and despite the fact that there is only one specialist openside flanker, albeit the great Richie McCaw, named in the squad.

Another of last night's heroes – perhaps, the hero – Jono Gibbes, gets the booby prize of 'training with the squad'. He's covering for the Canterbury Crusaders' number eight Mose Tuiali'i, who is struggling with a pinched nerve in his back. Also in this bracket is hooker Derren Witcombe, back-up for the sausage 'n chip munching Anton Oliver.

There are no prizes for guessing that Rokocoko's elimination is at the expense of his cousin, Sitiveni Sivivatu, who was guaranteed a place after his performances in the final trial and against Fiji saw him touch down six times. James Ryan's sterling work in those two games sees him included as well, while there's also a berth for Sione Lauaki.

Another talking point is the absence of any specialist fly-half and goal-kicker to cover Dan Carter. In both areas the only cover will come from Leon MacDonald, a full-back, and Aaron Mauger, mainly a centre. As Mauger's efforts with the boot on Friday night proved, he is no front-line Test goalkicker, and, in a pinch, MacDonald might not do either. If Carter has an attack of the yips, there could be trouble; he's a confident young man but he really has never experienced the intensity that he'll experience against the Lions: an awful lot will rest on his shoulders.

All Blacks' Squad:

Backs:

Mils Muliaina, full-back/wing/centre, Auckland, Auckland Blues, 26 caps, 70 points

Leon MacDonald, full-back/wing/centre/fly-half, Canterbury, Canterbury Crusaders, 26, 105

Rico Gear, wing, Nelson Bays, Canterbury Crusaders, 2, 5

Doug Howlett, wing, Auckland, Auckland Blues, 46, 180

Sitiveni Sivivatu, wing, Waikato, Waikato Chiefs, 1, 4

Tana Umaga, centre, Wellington, Wellington Hurricanes, 64, 160 (captain)

Aaron Mauger, centre/fly-half, Canterbury, Canterbury Crusaders, 24, 57

Conrad Smith, centre, Wellington, Wellington Hurricanes, 3, 5

Ma'a Nonu, centre/wing, Wellington, Wellington Hurricanes, 7, 10

Dan Carter, fly-half, Canterbury, Canterbury Crusaders, 18, 247

Byron Kelleher, scrum-half, Waikato, Waikato Chiefs, 33, 25

Justin Marshall, scrum-half, Canterbury, Canterbury Crusaders, 78, 120

Forwards:

Rodney So'oialo, number eight/flanker, Wellington, Wellington Hurricanes, 10, 20

Mose Tuiali'i, number eight/flanker, Canterbury, Canterbury Crusaders, 5, 5

A Turn for the Worse

Richie McCaw, flanker, Canterbury, Canterbury Crusaders, 27, 15

Jerry Collins, number eight/flanker, Wellington, Wellington Hurricanes, 23, 5

Sione Lauaki, number eight/flanker, Waikato, Waikato Chiefs, 1, 0

Chris Jack, second-row, Canterbury, Canterbury Crusaders, 37, 15

Ali Williams, second-row, Auckland, Auckland Blues, 21, 10

James Ryan, second-row, Otago, Otago Highlanders, 1, 0

Carl Hayman, prop, Otago, Otago Highlanders, 17, 0

Greg Somerville, prop, Canterbury, Canterbury Crusaders, 43, 5

Campbell Johnstone, prop, Canterbury, Canterbury Crusaders, 1, 0

Tony Woodcock, prop, North Harbour, Auckland Blues, 7, 0

Keven Mealamu, hooker, Auckland, Auckland Blues, 23, 15

Anton Oliver, hooker, Otago, Otago Highlanders, 43, 10.

Apart from that show of strength, there was more bad news for the Lions. Simon Taylor, the classy Scottish back-row forward, has finally been ruled out of the rest of the tour. Like Dallaglio, he too was invalided out of Australia four years ago. 'Obviously I am massively disappointed that my tour has ended this way,' he said.

It is just an unfortunate coincidence that this is my second tour to end like this, I thought that I had a lot to offer this time round, especially having fought so hard to come back from injury over the past season.

The Last Great Tour?

It is frustrating as I had been involved this week in full training sessions and my rehab had gone well but you have to be philosophical about these things, move on, concentrate on getting right. It is not a long-term injury but with only a few weeks left of the Lions' tour there are just no guarantees that it would be right in time.

Still, he was able to sound an optimistic note and wish all the best to Ryan Jones, who is now a fully-fledged replacement: 'I still think that this group of players, despite last night's result, have the opportunity to be successful in the Test series – and good luck to Ryan for when he joins the tour from today. In the meantime I just have to focus on getting back for the start of the season over the next few weeks.'

Part Four

A Turn for the Better

An Historic Cabbage Patch

Sunday 12 June 2005, Tihoi

'Oh, I played with him.'

'Really?'

'He was a scrawny lad when he came over. Bit soft.'

'Really?'

'Yeah. Typical moaning Pom. But we hardened him up.'

'Yeah?'

'Took him on a pig hunt one day. He broke his arse.' Gales of laughter rippled the tops of a couple of mugs of Waikato Draught.

'A pig hunt?'

'Yeah. With dogs. You hunt wild boar. Well, we caught it anyway, and threw it on his back. Made him carry it the whole way back.'

'Like an initiation ceremony?'

'Yeah, something like that.'

'Hey,' came another voice, 'the pitch he used to play on is down the road.'

'Yeah, go to the top of the hill, turn right, and it's about two ks down on your left.'

'It's a gravel path though, so you might want to be careful.'

''Specially in that.' A finger pointed beyond the grimy window at my campervan.

'Anyway, you'll see a sign by the fence. "Martin Johnson Stadium". You'll see the goalposts too.'

'And the swedes.' More chuckles and, in the mugs, further froth disturbance.

Swedes? One could only wonder. Tihoi is a lonely little outpost, like so many lonely little outposts in this vast country, situated on the road between Taumarunui and Turangi. It's off the beaten track. And, it's off the beaten track where Martin Johnson, the titanic English second-row forward, who twice captained the Lions and later lifted the World Cup, played for a season.

The pitch is overgrown now, hidden away. As you round the last corner, two sets of rusty goalposts prop themselves against the view, a hill to the left, a mound to the right.

'Martin Johnson Stadium', a plain white plaque proudly proclaims. It lists Johnson's achievements too and makes very sure to mention the time he wore the 'crested fern' on the All Black jersey: while here, he played for the New Zealand Colts. It's been a while since the stadium saw action though: in place of stud marks and whitewash is a field of crop: swedes, as the lads, between chuckles, had put it.

Out here, in the middle of nowhere, Johnson once rose into the sky and plucked lineout ball after lineout ball. Out here, in the middle of nowhere, Johnson turned from a scrawny boy into a burly man, such a great leader that, it is whispered, Sir Clive Woodward tried and tried to convince him to tour one last time.

'He married that girl from up the road.'

'Yeah, that's right,' added another patron, as if some distant memory had suddenly been jogged.

I knew that Martin Johnson Stadium was out here somewhere, in the vast wilderness that is the centre of New Zealand's North Island, and I knew, vaguely, of some place called the Tihoi Trading Post, a bar-cum-shop-cum-post-office-cum-God-knew-what that wasn't far from where I wanted to go. In any event, Tihoi was a little dot on the map, and, exactly where Tihoi was marked, the Tihoi Trading Post showed up, an unassuming building with an oak tree stretching out in front of it and a few of the battered, mud-coated pick-ups favoured by the country's legions of sheep farmers parked on the gravel in front.

As with everywhere else, the people were friendly.

'How are you?' I was asked, within a minute of ordering a coffee. It turned out that one of the ten people in the bar that Sunday afternoon had played with Johnson. They don't play that much any more though. Too old and too wise.

'We've more of a social team.'

'We play the sheep shaggers versus the cow tippers,' chipped in his work and drinking colleague from the next stool. I couldn't quite summon up the courage to ask how the teams are selected.

'Naw, he was a good player, Martin, bloody good.'

It turned out that one of the locals had just returned from Ireland. He brought two Irish girls back with him too.

'Boy can they drink,' piped up the lady of the house, the

first one who had enquired as to my well-being. 'Well, one of them can. There's a big one and a skinny one. The skinny one couldn't drink that much, but the big one? Whoo. Shot after shot after shot. She'd drink anyone under any table.'

It was good to see the homeland's reputation wasn't suffering.

'Wait there, I'll give 'im a call, see if they're around.'

'Ah,' I put my hands up, as apologetically as I could, 'don't go to any trouble'. I sensed a long night ahead in the Tihoi Trading Post if the Irish girls materialised and I was forced to drink their health. But before I could do anything, the phone had been raised and my hostess was talking with their host.

Mercifully, the girls had gone on a day trip to nearby Taupo.

'They're not back yet,' she reported, with the weary sigh of the disappointed matchmaker.

The trading post had seen about four campervan-loads of Lions' supporters wondering after the health of Martin Johnson Stadium. 'There was a piece in the paper too,' sighed the owner, of an article in the *Herald on Sunday*, 'but we expected more people'.

Still, there's hope yet. Martin Johnson is due in New Zealand with his friends, and, down in Tihoi, they're hopeful of a visit. A game would be nice, but, as George, the warrior who toiled alongside him rightly said, 'It'd be a job to get that pitch ready'.

The Desert Road

Monday 13 June 2005, Tongariro National Park

As State Highway One winds its way south, through the forests and empty green fields around Hamilton, snaking around the volcanic valleys of Rotorua, and onwards towards Wellington at the North Island's southernmost tip, it makes its way into the little town of Turangi, near the Tongariro National Park.

Here, three volcanoes dominate the landscape: Kakaramea, Tihia and Pihanga. The Tongariro Crossing is a five-hour trek by foot, across the top of the trio; the Desert Highways, which encircle it, are almost as arduous behind the wheel. The incline goes from murderous to begin, to steep, to sharp, as it begins to level out, not much less than 10,000 feet above sea level. The climb begins on a road surrounded by lush, subtropical greenery, but by the time the plateau is reached, high above, desolation and biting cold are the traveller's only companions.

On long, bare stretches of road, the landscape yawns for miles on either side, acres upon acres of gorse turned a depressing red by the wind and cold, as if the green had, buffeted for years, laid down arms and rusted over. And there, rising like humps of magnesium out of the desert, are Tongariro's three snow-covered peaks.

Oddly, though its existence is indicative of the New Zealander's urge to live normally in conditions that are anything but normal, there is a golf course in the tourist town of Whakapapa, which looks for all the world, like the only links course situated thousands of feet above sea level – an oasis of normality in the desert.

The Headquarters of the Verb

Tuesday 14 June 2005, James Cook Grand Chancellor Hotel, Wellington

On the sixteenth storey of the James Cook Grand Chancellor, hooker, Gordon Bulloch, was fielding questions. Has the intensity in training gone up, Gordon, since the defeat to the Maori?

'What do you think?' he replied, gesturing to a freshly-stitched cut above his eye.

'On Saturday night, I think we were a wee bit soft at times and a little bit less aggressive than we could have been. We've challenged ourselves and the coaches have challenged us to bring it up a notch, so I think you'll see that in the next few games.' John Hayes, it turned out, was to be blamed for the cut eye, but it was only a minor incident. At least the Lions are responding to the failures of Saturday night.

Bulloch, having led Scotland into battle against the SAN-ZAR nations more than once over the past few years, is also well placed to talk about the quality of forward play that the Lions have encountered on tour so far. There have been rumblings over the past few years that, in the Super 12 environment, the emphasis slips away from rugged forward play – something encouraged in the bearpit of the northern hemisphere's Heineken Cup – and that, as a result, New Zealand, Australia and South Africa are all vulnerable up front. So far, that hasn't been the case though.

'No, I think the standard of forward play has been very impressive from the three teams we've played. Obviously, we have to be more clinical around the breakdown: they're getting hands on our ball on the floor, stealing our ball and putting a lot of pressure on us. We've been working on that a lot this week;

it's taken us a bit of time to get up to pace on that and what the referees have been calling, when we're allowed to go for the ball, when we're not allowed to go for the ball. We've really got to raise the stakes now and bring our aggression levels up to meet the Kiwis.

'If you watch any of the Super 12 or New Zealand games in recent years, they've always been very competitive in scrums and line-outs. You would never have seen them as being hugely destructive at scrum or line-out time, but they have been effective. From that point of view, we know exactly what we're up against and we've still got a week and a half to the First Test, another week to raise our performance levels in those key areas.'

Which is where getting kicked in the head by John Hayes comes in.

This time, the media access really was a scrum. A handful of players drifted around; Bulloch, Simon Easterby and Dwayne Peel were all mobbed in turn. It was a relief to leave and experience what someone once described as 'the world headquarters of the verb ... a city of action' up close.

In a bar near the hotel, I pitched up with a copy of *New Zealand Rugby News*, an excellent glossy magazine that had, inevitably, the three Tests as its focus.

'You're interested in the rugby, mate?' came a voice from my elbow.

'Yeah. Here for the tour.'

'Oh, you're Irish, right?' The owner of the voice was a youngish, bespectacled gentleman, in a pinstripe suit.

'Yeah. Good guess.'

'Well, I'd a one-in-four chance, eh?'

The Last Great Tour?

So began a wide-ranging twenty-minute discussion on the merits of the northern hemisphere game, the restructuring of New Zealand's provincial rugby competition (my correspondent's team, Hawkes Bay, will ply their trade in an expanded Division One of the NPC next year), the Celtic League, the paucity of International Rugby Board funding for the Pacific Nations, and even the Bangladeshi cricketers' recent shock win over Australia.

It was only after 20 minutes that we thought to introduce ourselves. Sure, why pause for introductions? Why waste time that could be spent talking about rugby? Kindred spirits – here, having rugby in common qualifies two spirits as kindred – meet by chance at a bar? Such luck, not to be sniffed at. Christ, he even turned away the people he had come in with. 'I've met the most interesting guy.' And with that unwarranted flattery and a wave of his hand, the companion was gone, his focus back on me and the world of professional rugby.

My correspondent, it soon turned out, far from being a professional observer of the game, was Scott Dennison, the press officer for one of New Zealand's smaller political parties, the libertarian ACT.

'Ah, those guys!' I should have known, from the brief but violent and vigorous shaking of his head during our discussion of the IRB.

'It depends,' I had said, 'on whether you think a vast, centralised bureaucracy is the best way to administer this sort of funding.' And then came the head shake.

Not only had we rugby in common, but a love of Hayekian free market economics too and so, via several more pints and a conversation which segued effortlessly into politics, a visit to the country's Parliamentary offices followed, and I left with a sneak preview of the billboard campaign ACT will be waging over the next few weeks, and a 'Bush-Cheney '04' campaign sticker to put on the back of my campervan. (If nothing else, it will be interesting to see if it dissuades people from making conversation). Again, the quiet, unassuming kindness of the New Zealand stranger, and the willingness to make firm friends of passing acquaintances, was on view, mixed with that strange intensity with which every native follows the game of rugby permeating even the houses of Parliament. Oh, and I'm of course invited to dinner in the week of the Second Test.

'I'll be in touch.'

Unfortunately, the less pleasant side of the New Zealand drinker was on view later this evening. In Molly Malone's bar on Courtenay Place – 'There's bound to be a party there,' Scott had said – I ran into a native who, from nowhere, began to pour a torrent of abuse down on a beleaguered barmaid. He was short, squat and looked naturally unpleasant.

I had tried to help him communicate his order. 'I think he wants the Steinlager in bottles.' The Good Samaritan was fixed with a glower.

'Mind your own fucking business, mate.' Silly me. In a crowded bar back home, a spot of light interpretative work or the lending of a helping hand can lead to the formation of life-long friendships.

'Sorry, boy, only trying to help.' And I turned away, own drink safely in tow, only to hear a shower of f-words directed at the barmaid.

'Hey, give her a break. She just doesn't understand you. Here, let me help.'

'Whaddid I tell ya? Mind your own fucking business, eh?'

'Alright, boy, take it easy.' But by now, there were veins a-popping all over his head and neck. While with five or six bottles clutched in his paws, serious physical violence wasn't on the cards, he looked like the sort of guy who'd harbour a grudge long enough to send me face first into a urinal if he got the chance later on.

'Fucking Paddy.' That was just about enough.

'Go on away, boy.' A simultaneous contemptuous flick of the hand and head, delivered in the Cork fashion – handed down from generation to generation – that says, 'I'm bored of ya now. Get outta my face'. The poor New Zealander was flummoxed. Just as well, considering that, even with the help of a chainsaw, I couldn't fight my way out of a wet paper bag.

'What the fuck do you know anyway?'

'Go on away boy.' Repeat step one. I leaned back on the bar. He glowered. I relaxed, he glowered some more. 'Go on away, boy.' By the end, he was reduced to snarling at me, muttering 'Fucking Paddy' under his breath. A minor victory for pacifism was chalked down when he trundled away, but, temporarily, the headquarters of the verb became the headquarters of the swearword and a black mark was registered against the natives.

All they care about is rugby sometimes
Wednesday 15 June 2005, Paekakariki

Just outside Wellington is a little town called Paekakariki. It's notable for a few things: there's a railway museum and there's a beautiful public park. But, to the New Zealand mind, only one thing matters: it's the home of the great Christian Cullen, holder of the record for tries scored in the All Black jersey now plying his trade in Ireland, with Munster. There were no life-sized statues of the full-back lying anywhere unfortunately, and, despite a good, long drive around, I couldn't find the local rugby pitch.

In fact, the most interesting person I bumped into didn't even care about rugby.

'Oh, I don't follow it,' said the Englishman behind the counter of a second-hand bookshop in the town. 'But everyone else does. All they care about is rugby sometimes, you know. When the All Blacks are winning, everyone's happy, and when they lose, everyone's going around depressed. It's a bit unhealthy, I think'.

It might be unhealthy, but it's an atmosphere that's been pretty good at producing remarkable rugby teams.

Game 4: British & Irish Lions V Wellington
Wednesday 15 June 2005, Westpac Stadium, Wellington

Wellington 6
Pens: J. Gopperth (2)

British and Irish Lions 23
Tries: G. Thomas
Pens: J. Wilkinson (6)

The *Dominion Post*, Wellington's daily newspaper, will describe the Lions as 'bumbling' tomorrow and that opinion isn't likely to be an isolated one after this performance. Again, the Lions were unconvincing in victory, and an already unconvinced New Zealand media will remain, well, unconvinced. The public won't be too bothered either, with just over a week to go to the First Test. To the ranks of the unconvinced can now be added the British and Irish media and many of the Lions' fans will also be harbouring doubts. Once more, the visitors needed a late try to seal victory, having introduced a succession of international-class substitutes against a Wellington side deprived of all but one of its All Black contingent: Ma'a Nonu was the only international released from camp for this encounter.

Even before tonight's display there were ominous signs: empty seats dotted the stadium outsiders call 'the Cake Tin' but Wellingtonians know as 'the Colosseum'. A wind that drove the rain into the stands in downward sheets didn't help – as Brian O'Driscoll quipped afterwards, 'Tonight, the ball was like a bar of soap out there and the wind, well, I haven't seen a wind swirl like that since I last played in Lansdowne Road' – but the over-whelming feeling, as the crowd squelched out afterwards, was of being underwhelmed.

But there were signs, to my eye at least, that the Lions, tonight fielding what looked like a shadow Test team, are moving in the right direction. They want to play a particular type of game, which involves holding the ball for long periods, moving through phase after phase after phase, waiting and waiting for space to appear, or for the opposition to concede penalties. This strategy can be derided as attritional human chess, but it was this sort of attritional human chess which won the 2003 World Cup for Sir Clive and his team. The problem is that Woodward had years to develop his 2003 team; with the Lions, he has to shoehorn a similar programme of development into several weeks.

Nonetheless, there is clearly a discernible pattern of play on display: the Lions break up into different pods, maybe two or three at a time, the idea being that Pod 1 wins the ball on the right, moves it to the left to Pod 2, and so on. The problem is that the players don't know each other well enough yet. Throughout the tour, and again tonight, space has opened up and a player has made a break. Even though the burst looks spectacular, in fact it can be terribly damaging to the team: there may be only one or two players in support while, 40 yards away, five or six players wait for the next phase of play, the next chapter in the play book. Suddenly, with only a couple of red jerseys sharp enough to arrive in support, the Lions are outnumbered at the breakdown and one of a number of things happens: the ball is simply lost or a penalty conceded; the ball is won but untidily; or the ball is won, but, the play book having been ripped up, chaos ensues. In Woodward's 2003 England vintage, individual bursts were not as damaging, probably because the players knew each other and knew when a team-mate was likely to make a forward change. Then, they could anticipate where the breakdown would be and get there in time to support him. The Lions have not developed that understanding yet; then again, they are not far away from doing so, and on more than one occasion this evening, a Lions' team-mate did anticipate a break and were able to support him.

As a result, though the sceptics might have greeted his sanguine words with snorts of disdain, it was no real surprise to me that midweek coach Ian McGeechan, professed himself reasonably happy. 'I was very pleased with the control of the game tonight,' he said. 'I thought the pack was good and, at times, we were very close to some significant scores. There are still things that we have to work on – the players know that – but I think this was a significant step forward in terms of what we want to do in our setpiece, contact area, and support work.'

Later, when talking about the difficulty of playing in such poor conditions, McGeechan elaborated: 'I don't think the weather was conducive to strong back play. One of the problems with a wet pitch and a wet ball and it raining is that you probably lose about a second for what you want to do. I think doing the same things in dry conditions with dry hands, we probably would have got players free. We felt there were occasions on which we were, really, only one pass away from some significant plays.

'It's back to the challenge of the Lions: players have to learn to play with each other. You've got to do it on the pitch, not just the training park and I think that's where we're starting to see some, I think, significant steps forward.'

There was optimism as well from one of the senior players. Martin Corry, tonight's vice-captain and a veteran of the 2001 tour to Australia, also professed himself pleased with the Lions' progress.

'Maybe in the first few games we've played too much as individuals and not as a unit. I think it's an ongoing thing. Three weeks ago, we all turned up from different walks of life, different clubs, different countries and what we're going through is a gelling process. Things can't just click. We can't expect that: it just doesn't happen. How I feel is, once we've ticked the big boxes, then we can start to look at the little things, the intricacies, and that's what's happened now.'

A Turn for the Better

'I think that's all down to reaction,' thought Simon Easterby. 'We've got some great individual players, who can sniff a gap, and it's up to the support then to get with him when he gets to the deck. You've just got to react and we're all good enough players to do that. You've got to expect the unexpected with the quality of player we have here, especially in the backs.

'Wellington wouldn't be as strong a side as the Maori, I think that's plain to see, but I think we took a step forward in the contact area, the way we got to rucks and cleaned out.'

Softly-spoken prop, Julian White, was of the same view: 'It's about being in a group and getting used to different players. We haven't had the same fifteen for two games consecutively yet, so it takes some time to get it together.'

Of course, as McGeechan suggested, it's unlikely that the exact Test XV will make it onto the field together before the First Test, which means the coaches are placing massive reliance on getting things working smoothly on the training ground. That is quite a risk but, as McGeechan also pointed out, 'I think we're one game short leading into the First Test'.

Another problem for the Lions is that maybe the reliance on the pod system is fundamentally flawed. There was an illustration of why 21 minutes into the game. The Lions had been in possession but when a break into space meant the pod system foundered, they were unable to recycle the ball, though they were awarded a scrum, from which Wilkinson moved it left to O'Driscoll, who was tackled. The first two men to hit the ruck, to try and move the Wellington players away from the ball, were Gareth Thomas and Gavin Henson: the blue jerseys were moved not an inch and, again, play broke down. While Thomas and Henson struggled to free the ball, Neil Back, the Lions' openside flanker, nominally the man who secures possession in such situations, was waiting near the scene of the scrum for the ball to be moved back across the pitch. He was in Pod 2, waiting for the next page in the manual. With the best will in the world, and the best weight training, Thomas and Henson will not be able to secure the ball as quickly as Back and Easterby. When they come to face the All Blacks, they will find Richie McCaw, the best openside in world rugby, and Rodney So'oialo, another breakdown specialist, trying to muscle into every ruck. It's at least a sobering thought, if not a potentially fatal flaw, especially when added to the tourists' difficulty in coming to terms with New Zealand aggression, technique and refereeing interpretation at the breakdown.

Indeed, some of the Lions' most impressive rugby tonight came after they ripped up the play book. When Stephen Jones entered the fray with twenty minutes left on the clock and Jonny Wilkinson moved to inside centre – where, it has been suggested, he may start in the First Test – the visitors played a much wider, more fluid game, and were able to gain good momentum; and when you're going forward, it doesn't matter as much who's clearing a ruck. When the game became more broken, though, the Lions obviously couldn't have as much control – at one stage, there were no line-outs for nearly ten minutes – and couldn't strangle a Wellington side who themselves were more than happy to run the ball. Nonetheless, with four minutes on the clock, Thomas put the game beyond doubt, seizing on a Wellington handling error, kicking ahead and touching down.

For all the progress the Lions appeared to make, the final scoreline flattered them somewhat. Wellington's insistence on keeping the ball in hand told against them in the end – in the conditions, handling errors were inevitable, and, with the Lions content to kick the ball into the corners, the home team put themselves under too much pressure. Perhaps the game's vital score, a try for Lions' prop Gethin Jenkins, was a result of this pressure: the Lions took good line-out ball, Dwayne Peel made a break, Corry was in support and he passed to Jenkins, who strolled over from inside the '22. Had Jimmy Gopperth, the Wellington fly-half, been as good at kicking the ball as he was at passing it – if, in other words, he had been more pragmatic and cynical – the outcome might have been different. As McGeechan alluded to, trying to play a wide game when the ball has taken on the physical qualities of a leaking can of industrial-strength lubricant is very, very difficult.

'We were a little naïve I think, in attack,' Gopperth's coach, John Plumtree, duly acknowledged. 'We played far too much rugby in what we call the yardage area. We probably overworked our forwards. We wanted to play rugby tonight: we knew we'd have to score tries to win, but as it turned out, we had to mix it up a bit and I don't think we kicked enough in the first half.'

Or, indeed, the second half!

'That was disappointing. We spoke about it, but I think a lot of it could come down to the fact that we're a very young side in certain positions, and that's how you react to pressure. Maybe we didn't react in the right way. I just felt for the pack a little bit that we had a lot of lateral running and when we got behind them in the last twenty and got some quick ball, we didn't really get the benefit of it.'

The tale of the evening was of the Lions grinding out a victory against a Wellington side that, had they been a bit more hard-nosed, could have been closer than they were. Had the rest of their All Blacks – Jerry Collins, So'oialo, Tana Umaga and Conrad Smith – been available for selection, who knows what the result might have been.

Aside from that second of two sobering thoughts, there were other worries for the Lions' management, foremost among them a patchy display from Jonny Wilkinson. On several occasions, he sent passes skidding along the ground, some of his line kicking was poor and he missed a number of shots at goal. He looked decidedly fragile as half-time approached, and the Wellington number seven, Ben Herring, appeared to sense vulnerability; Wilkinson must have been relieved that Herring was forced to retire injured at the interval and he wasn't as hounded in the second period. Indeed, when he moved to centre, the Lions enjoyed their best period, which, incidentally, is bad news for Henson, who at times showed nice touches, but never looked like a foil for O'Driscoll; given that, as captain, O'Driscoll's name is carved onto the teamsheet, he will be partnered in the centre by the player thought best-equipped to complement him. Wilkinson's performance at twelve may see the Welshman edged out of contention, with Stephen Jones slotting in at fly-half to continue his partnership with Dwayne Peel, his international team-mate.

Another conundrum is presented by Neil Back's performance, which may have moved him ahead of Martyn Williams in the pecking order. Williams suffered against the Maori, while Back scurried around the pitch like a man ten years his junior tonight. Of course the problem is that Back doesn't have the same instincts as Williams in open play, something which was apparent after just five minutes: the Lions had made a break down the left touchline and Back arrived in support; though he had a man inside him, he didn't make the pass and set up a ruck instead. It seemed like just the sort of situation in which Williams would have lubricated the attack and maintained its pace, as he did so effectively for Wales in the Six Nations.

A solid line-out, in which Shane Byrne's throwing – an ace in his hand which may trump the claims of his hooking rival, Steve Thompson – defied the miserable weather, was probably the highlight of the Lions' evening. Only two throws went astray and Byrne's international team-mate, Simon Easterby, had a fine game jumping at the tail. So, all in all, while the New Zealanders, and even some of the British and Irish, may sneer, McGeechan was entitled to the smile that a sense of optimism had stretched across his face. Is it possible though to get a Test team in place and playing before the First Test? No one could be better placed to answer that question than Ian 'Mr Lions' McGeechan, who toured twice with the Lions and has coached them on three previous occasions in an association that has now planned tour decades.

'From experience, I don't think you can. What you need is to make sure that you've got units that are working together and you've seen different options so you can put that together in Test week. That's one of the challenges of the Lions: if you do it any earlier, then you're not giving players a fair chance to show what they can do. You prepare for that First Test the week before with the combination you've come to. It's about the balance; I think we're one game short leading into the First Test, which is a bit more pressure. The extra game you play on a tour is helpful sometimes, but I'm quite confident that we'll have some significant combinations put together.'

Wellington: S. Paku; L. Fa'atau, M. Nonu, T. Tu'ipulotu, R. Kinikinilau; J. Gopperth, P. Weepu; T. Waldrom, B. Herring, K. Ormsby; L. Andrews, R. Filipo; T. Fairbrother, M. Schwalger, J. McDonnell (c).

Subs: K. Thompson for Herring h/t, L. Mahony for Schwalger 59, C. James for Kinikinilau 67, J. Purdie for Filipo 71, R. Flutey for Weepu 73, J. Schwalger for Fairbrother 76, T. Ellison for Tu'ipulotu 76.

Lions: J. Lewsey; G. Thomas, B. O'Driscoll (c), G. Henson, J. Robinson; J. Wilkinson, D. Peel; M. Corry, N. Back, S. Easterby; B. Kay, D. Grewcock; J. White, S. Byrne, G. Jenkins.

Subs: S. Jones for Henson 62, S. Horgan for Lewsey 68, M. Stevens for White 72, C. Cusiter for Peel 72.

Referee: P. Honiss (New Zealand).

The Entente Cordiale
Thursday 16 June 2005, Wellington

So much for Sir Clive tending towards the mushroom farmer school of media management (keep 'em in the dark and feed 'em manure): 'It's part of the players' job, media, and they understand that.' Upstairs at the Intercontinental Hotel, an entente cordiale was beginning between the Lions and the assembled press corps. At a media briefing before last night's game, Mick Cleary, rugby correspondent of the Daily Telegraph, who doubles as current chair of the Rugby Writers' Association, addressed the room. Apparently, there had been a 'crisis meeting' between Cleary and Stephen Jones of the Sunday Times – representing the interests of the Fourth Estate – and the Lions' management. There, the concerns of the journalists about the chaotic schedule and minimal player access – the fact that only a handful of players from Wednesday night's starting line-up had been available for interview the day before the game was unlikely to have lightened the media's mood – were relayed.

'Clive,' reported Cleary, 'said he was "staggered" to find out that there were any difficulties'. It was a theme that continued to play itself out this morning, where, as part of what Cleary, tongue-in-cheek, called 'this new era of glasnost', the players and substitutes from last night's game were all available for interview. First though, dressed in a tracksuit and shirt, Woodward spoke to the three dozen or so journalists who had braved the early rise. But, before speaking, he asked for all recorders to be switched off and notebooks to be temporarily decommissioned. A photographer who dared to take a quick snap was politely told to lay down his camera.

For the most part, Woodward's few words – and it's only fair not to quote him at length; I only recall the events at all to make a broader point – were a re-hash of what Cleary had imparted last night. Clearly though he was 'staggered' that the press corps was so unhappy. But perhaps the most interesting revelation was that he was amazed no one had come to him and said, 'Clive, there's a problem'.

Therein lay the rub. Having layered the Lions with so many managers and media advisors, Sir Clive had insulated himself, accidentally it seems, from direct contact with the press. Journalists' requests for this, that or the other went to Louisa or Alastair, as did whatever whinges there were – these evidently weren't communicated upwards – and nobody thought to broach the matter directly with Woodward and Bill Beaumont until the complaints had reached a crescendo. Indeed, so staggered was the head coach, he urged that if anyone had any issues they should seek him out for a few words over a beer. The picture that emerged during this short briefing was one of a man who was genuinely surprised to find that there were problems; indeed, being charitable, the picture that emerged was of a man who was slightly embarrassed by the whole situation.

The absence of Campbell might also have had something to do with the change. He returned to the UK earlier in the week to tend to other matters and, as his spectral presence wasn't skulking around, perhaps the media suddenly felt emboldened. The master of the dark arts was elsewhere, and, hardly coincidentally, the Lions began to suffer heavy casualties on the media front.

When Cleary announced the 'new era of glasnost' last night, there were cynical mutters from the audience. 'Wait 'til he sees tomorrow's papers ...' Sure enough, the training ground accident that led to Gordon Bulloch having a wound stitched closed had escalated into full-scale violence. 'CIVIL WAR' screamed the back page of one UK daily: 'Lions bust-up'; 'Lions in punch-up'; and 'Lions have a ruck ... with each other' also made the back pages. A combination of irritation at the amorphous schedule, frustration at the lack of access to players and the absence of Campbell, whose brooding presence alone may have quelled some of the dissent within the assembled ranks of the media, or at least urged them to run the 'Civil War' story by him before printing it, had finally bubbled over.

The fact that it became a story at all was remarkable. The

injury to Bulloch actually occurred at an open training session and was witnessed by a Scottish writer, Andrew Innes (the other journalists were away on a wine tour at the time; Andrew had also wanted to go, but, unaware that there are two Holiday Inns in Christchurch, went to the wrong one and waited in vain). Then Bulloch was wheeled out to speak to the press on Tuesday – hardly evidence of a cover-up; indeed, he spoke freely of the incident and brushed it off. That it did become back-page news just shows how frustrated and irritated the press corps had become, as if they wanted to goad the Lions' management into a response. Also unhelpful was the fact that the journalists felt they were being kept in the dark on injury news: Andy Sheridan was clearly limping on his way to the sin-bin on Saturday night but his failure to reappear was, officially, a tactical switch, odd considering that Sheridan had been the best prop on display; and rumours were abounding that a stomach bug accounted for Brian O'Driscoll's subdued performance.

Whatever about the training-ground bust-up goading the press into action, the prompting of Messrs Jones and Cleary certainly did the trick and as Woodward finished his little speech – urging a bit more decorum in their overly-aggressive Dictaphone wielding on the part of the media as a *quid pro quo* for the improved access – the players dutifully filed in, joining Martin Corry, who had sat impassively in the corner while his head coach ran through his soliloquy. And sure enough, from Gethin Jenkins to Josh Lewsey, all the players sat down at tables, relaxed and ready for questions. So much for my cynicism then: to my eye, Woodward keenly wants to accommodate the media. This is as good a way as any.

The raft of bad news stories didn't end with the fight that

wasn't though. The Lions, it emerged last night, have tweaked their community activity schedule. Well, fairly severely tweaked: the rumour doing the rounds was that the activity had been cancelled.

'It's been rescheduled, not cancelled, to get quality time for the players,' Ian McGeechan had explained in response. 'They've had some pretty long days. An example would be last week, when some of them were out on the training park at eight in the morning and not back in the hotel until two the following morning.'

This morning Beaumont elaborated: 'We thought we needed a change. Like all things, after doing it for a few weeks, we looked again at it. We're still absolutely committed to doing the community work and I think we've been outstanding at doing it.

'Yesterday for example I was in Wellington and went to a number of schools and got a first-class reception. I took three players with me, went to seven schools. I think the work and the Maori receptions have been great and I think the players have enjoyed it. But now that we're getting near the Test week, it's a very, very long day for the players, so what we've done is change it to the day after. The big advantage of that is the players who were playing can attend, which means that the youngsters can meet the players who were playing against their local side.'

Though the last line smacks of, at best, making a virtue out of necessity and at worst, of spin, the fact that the community work has been tampered with brings to mind the conversation I had with Martin Corry back in Auckland. 'Let's face facts,' he said, 'we're rugby players and we want to be focusing on what happens at the weekend.' It's a view that Beaumont agreed with.

'Players do need to get out of the playing environment and

get on with meeting the people. But ultimately, we will be judged as a rugby team and we will not compromise our rugby. We'll find out whether or not we got the balance right.'

Right now the outlook is positive. The players all looked relaxed and happy, confident in their own minds that progress is being made. Even Jonny Wilkinson, who was surrounded by the biggest posse of reporters and who, by his own high standards, performed below par last night, looks calm. Of the rest, Julian White, Danny Grewcock and Ben Kay were only too happy to have a chat about the set piece. Well, it wasn't much of a chat, seeing as the scrum was reasonably solid and the Lions coughed up only two line-out balls. One was stolen and the other was a mistake.

'The ball that got overthrown was just Munch [Shane Byrne] not being used to the way I was signalling and I was up in the air a little bit longer than he would have liked,' explained Kay. All in all, not much to chat about, though that little story does illustrate how close the line between success and failure can be at this level and how difficult it is to mould fifteen players into a playing XV in just a few weeks. Anyway, 30 minutes later the players began to file towards the bus, bound for the airport and then for Christchurch. The journalists were happy too, with quotes a-plenty tucked away in Dictaphones and notebooks. The entente cordiale was underway.

One more bad news story emerged during the week as well. The security erected around, and inside, the Intercontinental didn't do much to help the Lions' image. Yellow barriers lined the entrance to the hotel, with burly security men posted on the doors. Entry was restricted to guests and, even then, they were warned not to photograph or converse with the players. On the way into the press conference this morning I was stopped three times to have my credentials checked.

Perhaps the strongest denunciation of all this came from the *Guardian*'s Rob Kitson, one of the most mild-mannered members of the press corps:

'Not content with erecting screens around the squad's training grounds, the management's Greta Garbo tendencies are now so advanced that non-playing guests in the hotel have been issued with a stern notice warning them not to bother passing squad members.

'There are crash barriers outside and a security guard verifies the identity of new arrivals before they get anywhere near the check-in desk. Yesterday, a Lions' supporter keen to take a photograph of some team members in the lobby was warned he risked having his camera confiscated. Autograph hunters are equally frowned upon. At this rate Kiwis will not be alone in cheering the home team once the Test series starts.'

The truth, it turns out, is more prosaic: the hotel management took the security measures of their own volition. It's quite understandable too: unlike the Hilton in Auckland, sheltered slightly away from the madding crowd, the Intercontinental is uncomfortably close to the drinking establishments frequented by the travelling supporters; reluctant to risk the embarrassment of inebriated fans slobbering all over tired and cranky players, the hotel's management has erred on the side of caution. Nonetheless, the heavy-handed nature of this caution is not calculated to win hearts and minds and, read alongside the reduction in community activity and the crisis in media relations, it tells a tale of a bad news week for the Lions. Funny that all happened when Alastair wasn't around.

Windy Wellington

Thursday 16 June 2005, Picton

It's clear now, having watched 80 minutes of wind and rain rival last night's rugby for the crowd's attention, and having spent an evening battered by coastal gusts blowing in low from the harbour, why they call it 'Windy Wellington'. It was almost a relief to be boarding a ferry to the South Island, even though, in this hemisphere, travelling south increases the risk of snow, not that of sun.

Even allowing for the wind of the past few days, it's not like the crossing will be particularly dangerous; it certainly won't be weighed down by Lions' supporters. While an estimated 20,000 will roll into Wellington by the time the Test series comes around, the crowds have not yet materialised. Getting a booking for the ferry wasn't difficult at all; a week ago, there was still plenty of space. Also, many of the marquees erected around the city centre and on the waterfront were quiet this week, although it was slightly busier last night. But it is down south, to the resort town of Queenstown, home of bungee jumps and tandem skydiving, and to Christchurch, venue for the First Test, that the fans will flock.

Part Five

Down to the Real Business

SHUTTING UP SHOP

Friday 17 June, 2005, Amberley

Predictably, the Lions' decision to 'reschedule' their community activity has garnered significant coverage in the New Zealand press. Even more predictably, it's all negative.

'In this part of the world,' the Otago coach, Wayne Graham, is quoted as telling *The Press*, 'it's not how we like to do things and it seems a long way from real life in Otago and especially in Otago country.

'From that point of view it's very disappointing and my memories of touring were very much about mingling with people and that was a big part of what we were about ... I guess in the year 2005, professional rugby might have changed to such an extent where you lock yourself in a hotel and prepare yourself for your next game. I think it's a shame.'

Russell Gray, the Otago union's chief executive, went even

further: 'Otago isn't likely to be the only province rejected by the Lions – they are expected to continue their policy of ignoring the regions for the remainder of the tour'.

The 'ignoring the regions' jibe is particularly galling: nobody asked the Lions to schedule community activity in the first place; they could very easily have come to New Zealand and stayed in their hotel rooms for six weeks; indeed, they could have refused point blank to travel to places like Hamilton, New Plymouth, Dunedin and Invercargill, preferring to focus instead on the Test matches. But for Sir Clive Woodward's insistence on making this 'the last great Lions' tour', Graham and Gray wouldn't have anything at all to complain about; hell, they'd currently be in camp preparing for the provincial championship.

It's not as if the players dislike going out and meeting people: the handful who turned up in Stratford a week ago gave freely and happily of their time. And, as Gordon Bulloch said earlier this week, 'The guys have enjoyed it. When you're away for eight weeks, the last thing you want to see is the same four walls of your hotel room'.

However, Graham and Gray, being the enemy, for this weekend anyway, are entitled to seek psychological advantage wherever they might find it. If these sly little digs unsettle the Lions then bully for Otago. And, to be fair to those who had visits to them cancelled, for the most part, they have kept schtum, and only murmurs of disappointment have reached the papers. In a little coffee shop in Amberley, a town from which the scenic route to Christchurch veers off the main highway, the waiter, a former player, was sympathetic as he handed over an espresso con panne.

'It's the Test results that matter, isn't it?'

The Last Great Tour?

The rescheduling has affected a handful of groups. Dunedin's 'Little Sisters of the Poor' rest home and Alexandra Rugby Club will not be graced by the Lions' presence this afternoon; and, next Tuesday, Southland Boys' High School and Southland Hospital will be Lion-free zones. Instead, the players will meet local children and teenagers on the Sunday and Wednesday mornings before their chartered flights return them to their Christchurch base. So, semantically at least, it's a rescheduling rather than a cancellation, but whatever about the semiotics, and however understandable it all is, it's a blow to Woodward's aim to bring the Lions to the furthest-flung corners of New Zealand. If the defeat to the Maori was the first blow to 'the last of the great tours', this is the first body blow.

Leafing through the papers – having spent most of yesterday in transit – it became clear that Graham has also placed himself in the front line in the war of words.

Apart from his curt words about the community activity issue, the Otago coach has also attacked the Lions' scrummaging – 'their game at scrum time is all about disruption and they will pull every trick they know to try and disrupt your scrum'; their behaviour at the breakdown – 'at the contact area they have developed ways to disrupt or steal your ball ... they seem to be able to leave their feet, which is something I thought was outside the laws of the game ... [but] once they go to ground they just lie there and try and disrupt things'; their penchant for talking to referees – 'it's been an eye opener about how much the Lions' playing fifteen tries to manipulate the decisions. Those not involved in the contact area are suggesting to the referee what should be decided ... there's a lot of yap about what should be happening and what shouldn't be happening'; and, naturally, what is by now the old canard of the size of the Lions' squad – 'There must be a lot of people in the camp who are thinking, "What are we here for?"' Once again, a provincial coach finds himself co-opted into the offensive against the Lions; one more sign of how New Zealand tends to see itself as a whole, fighting against an invading army.

Most of this battle is conducted by the media, of course. Their disdain for the Lions has been apparent, either implicitly or explicitly, in virtually every paragraph written since the touring party touched down. As Alastair Campbell put it this week in a newspaper column in the London *Times*, the New Zealand media sees itself as a 'sixteenth man'.

The absence of Campbell this week has been accompanied, as noted yesterday, by a serious decline in the Lions' already low media stock. Security, community visits and training ground bust-ups have dominated the headlines. One can't help wondering again if things might have been different had the great man been around. It's notable that Bill Beaumont's post-dinner address after the Wellington game, in which he complained that the All Blacks' management team's refusal to release international players for the provincial matches damages the concept of the Lions' tour, has garnered little or no attention from the New Zealand media, or, for that matter, from the British and Irish press. It is a legitimate complaint and indeed one that reflects well on the Lions: rather than licking their wounds after the thumping from the Maoris, they're looking for more punishment, even if, a cynic might well point out, they know that these comments won't lead to, say, James Ryan suddenly being released to lock the Otago scrum tomorrow.

Home, Sweet Home
Friday 17 June, 2005, Timaru

Having spent three weeks in New Zealand, it has become distressingly clear that, despite being 12,000 miles away, I might as well be travelling around Ireland.

But for the constant, unyielding friendliness of those working in the hospitality industry – there are none of the occasional scowls, or, for that matter, high prices, that disfigure Ireland's; instead, an unrelenting helpfulness and quality produce which is easy on the wallet – it's just like home, with the GAA replaced by rugby.

Every two-bit township boasts a pair of rugby goalposts. Sometimes they look for all the world like a pair of telephone poles placed close together, but pity the man who laughs: as I found in Whangamonoma, rugby has all the passionate, tribal qualities of the GAA, and here, like home, there is no slight like a slight on the parish.

The country towns – places like Foxton and Amberley – seem like the twins of places like Buttevant and Durrow, there to be passed through, inviting only the occasional stop for food and water. Auckland, for its sprawl and the fact that it houses over a quarter of the country's population, might as well be called Dublin, and the disorientingly winding streets of Wellington bring to mind a Cork with trams. The city towns in between conjure up a feeling of déja-vu also: tonight's stop, Timaru, could be Kilkenny. Nearby, the slightly larger university city of Dunedin is reputed to be of such dimension as to make it a fitting first cousin for Galway or Limerick.

The landscape – acres of green dotted by sheep and cows stretching to horizons dominated by mountains – is familiar too, though the New Zealand landscape assumes an almost magical quality in places, and her mountains stretch higher into the air. 'I was in Ireland once,' one native told me, 'and how come your mountains are all shaved off at the top?'

New Zealanders are proud of their country's role in fighting for king and empire. In Wanganui I stayed on Somme Parade; in Takapuna in Auckland, Anzac Street bears the name under which New Zealanders fought; on the side even of the Forgotten World Highway was a Memorial Hall, dedicated, as was Victoria Park in Stratford, to those who gave their lives in conflict. The country draws strength from the deeds of the past; while Ireland hardly recognises its people's role in the Great War we too draw sustenance from the past. We may not have Somme Parade, but we have Pearse Street and Connolly Station, plaques which commemorate famous ambushes and roadside displays which laud those who fought, died and killed for Ireland.

The roads are, sadly, all too similar. While generally of a higher quality – probably because much of this country's population seems to spend its time working in road crews of one sort or another – they are disfigured by the crosses (flashes of bleached white) which appear like bones in the ditches with shocking regularity. Again, like home, they tend to gather like tiny roadside graveyards near right turns, blind corners and sharp bends. Most are just white skeletons against a backdrop of green but, to others, fresh flowers cling, every petal a wail for a lost son, daughter, brother or sister. They even drive on the same side of the road as us.

***

The Last Great Tour?

I first met Huw Richards of the *Financial Times* on the media bus to the All Blacks V Fiji.

'That's not the Southampton *Evening Echo*?' he leaned across the seat to ask, curiosity aroused by the name on my credentials.

'No, no,' I replied with a laugh. 'The Cork version. They very kindly sent a cover letter for me, even though I'm doing no work for them!'

'Yes, I didn't think the Southampton *Evening Echo's* budget would quite stretch to sending someone to New Zealand. I'm Huw Richards, by the way.'

It turned out that Huw, too, was traipsing around in a campervan. Well, his second campervan, the first having been rear-ended on State Highway One as he attempted to make his way to Napier. Instead, he made the close acquaintance of the bumper of a rather large gravel truck. Soon afterwards, he spilled Coke on his laptop, and by now found himself hauling a rental model around the country.

Happily, by the time our paths crossed in Timaru, he was in some sort of equilibrium and we wandered into the town for a drink. While almost everything else about New Zealand is similar to Ireland, the natives' relationship with alcohol is markedly different.

Generally, the New Zealanders don't drink as much as the Irish, the pub not being, for the most part, the social hub that it is back home. When they do attempt to drink as much as the tourists the consequences are dire. By the time I was wandering Hamilton looking for a tipple after the Maori game, it was only eleven o'clock but already the Kiwis were stumbling about the streets.

Down to the Real Business

Even this evening, a dry, mild Friday night with the clock ticking towards eleven, Timaru was deathly quiet. Only teenagers roaming around the town centre, and a loud guitar band in a pub with strobe lighting – 'I've always had the most terrible aversion to pubs with strobe lighting,' Huw had said, urging me onwards – broke the silence. This was hardly surprising: it is the middle of winter and, from Turangi to Timaru, New Zealand slips gladly into the darkness after night falls and shuts down after six o'clock.

And then, all of a sudden, we stumbled upon something. We were close to the edge of the town centre and, having spied no premises which we fancied, things were looking bleak. Until, all at once, a neon sign peeped around a corner.

'Ah, look, the Clarence Hotel,' I said. 'We should be able to get a drink in there. Might even see Bono.'

Even allowing for the biker bar in New Plymouth – the one with the topless barmaids – and the Craic Shack's skirt night in Auckland, this was my most remarkable New Zealand drinking experience yet. All the patrons, including a sulking, sour barmaid smoked, in direct contravention of the country's no smoking laws. Our entrance swelled the crowd to ten. Every other person there, with the possible exception of the not-so-friendly barmaid, was drunk. Not drunk in the slightly-tipsy-wobbly-but-happy sense, but drunk in the barely-able-to-talk sense. Huw and I, even though we were two exotic strangers, barely merited a glance, never mind a discussion. There wasn't even a mutter behind our backs. It was only when we were halfway through our second beers that one of the regulars lurched towards us and grasped me by the arm.

'Are you guys from the radio, or something? You look like

149

journalists.' At least, I'm pretty sure that's what he was trying to say.

'No! No! No! Eh, we're just tourists.'

Eventually we did make it out of the Clarence Hotel. While, back in Ireland, there are drunks a-plenty, they're usually lost in the crowd; I've never been in a pub where they constituted exactly 100 per cent of the clientele.

Game 5: British & Irish Lions V Otago
Saturday 18 June, 2005, Carisbrook, Dunedin

Otago 19
Tries: B. Lee
Convs: N. Evans
Pens: N. Evans (4)

British & Irish Lions 30
Tries: W. Greenwood, R. Jones, S. Williams
Convs: C. Hodgson (3)
Pens: C. Hodgson (3)

When the Lions played in Carisbrook in 1983, Allan Hewson, the New Zealand full-back, wore mittens and Stu Wilson, the legendary winger, donned plastic bags over his socks. Ollie Campbell, the Irish fly-half, wondered what the hell was going on, until he turned blue, long before even the half-time whistle.

The 'House of Pain' in Dunedin was a graveyard for that Lions' team, and has been a graveyard for many Lions' teams down through the years. Apart from Auckland, Otago is the province that has inflicted most defeats on touring Lions' teams. This afternoon, the TAB – New Zealand's chain of over-the-counter betting shops – had the hosts at around 4/1 to win.

'Good odds, considering, aren't they?' On the way into the town, two of the local clubs' Colts' (Under-20) sides were in action on a sun-drenched pitch by the side of the road. Pulling in to stretch my legs, I wandered over and fell into conversation with two of the locals.

'Bloody right, mate. I've money down.' I was tempted to throw a few quid on Otago myself. Their record against the Lions was one reason, their ferocious forward play another. The art of rucking was pioneered by an Otago coach called Vic Cavanagh and, on the evidence of the Colts' game, is still in wide practice in the area. The fact that their back row boasted Josh Blackie and Craig Newby, both of whom played at openside flanker in the All Blacks' final trial a few weeks ago, which threatened the visitors with endless problems in recycling the ball, was the clincher: if they could stop the Lions from developing continuity, Otago would be in with a chance, and, driven on by history and thoughts of the great deeds of the past, could well win.

Then again, the weather was good – no mittens or plastic bags tonight – and the Lions had showed against Wellington that they were moving in the right direction. Against an Otago side, *pace* Bill Beaumont, shorn of its internationals – Anton Oliver injured and James Ryan and Carl Hayman on All Blacks' duty – a defeat would have been a surprise, even allowing for the weight of history.

As it turned out, history was slightly disappointing. Carisbrook is a rickety old place: like Lansdowne Road, the stands seem to have been thrown in on an *ad hoc* basis; when the singers began bellowing out the 'Lions Song' prior to kick-off, the microphone wasn't working; and the scoreboard spent some time on the blink midway through the first half. The over-all impression was of a creaking relic: even the Mexican waves that lapped the stadium seemed arthritic. Then again, such are the joys of a proper Lions' tour and, had there been an upset rather than another uninspiring win for the tourists, the old ground would have been rocking, and this would be a paean to tradition rather than a whinge.

The introduction of heavy artillery off the bench in the last quarter again contributed more than its fair share to the final score, the Lions finishing Otago off with a try fifteen minutes from the end. 'I wasn't on the field, but they looked pretty big from where I was sitting,' said Wayne Graham of the impact of Thompson, Sheridan, Grewcock *et al*, seasoned internationals each. 'But that's the beauty of a touring side, to have interna-tional firepower off the bench. We had two or three guys walk-ing into the changing room after who it would have been nice to take off at that point.'

There were other problems for Otago. Nick Evans, he too of Possibles V Probables, Napier, 3 June, fame, had a decent match at number ten, looking menacing with the ball in his hand, but, like Jimmy Gopperth on Wednesday night, failing to kick it effectively. Without a big, relieving boot, someone to turn down the heat when under pressure, or launch huge touch find-ers over the Lions' heads to pin the tourists down in their own half, the provincial teams will always struggle. Whatever else about the style of play encouraged in the home nations, it pro-duces fly-halves who are exceptionally good at kicking offen-sively, to put their side on the front foot, and defensively, to relieve pressure. Only against the Maori, when the Lions had little or no control of the ruck and, as a consequence, little or no control of the ball with which to kick it, was this weapon neutralised. So, once more, it had a huge effect on proceedings.

In general, the Lions played poorly and it represented a step back from the performance against Wellington, with very few players pushing themselves into Test contention. 'Andy Robinson said something interesting to me on Friday, which makes a change,' Will Greenwood said afterwards, holding court in the media room. 'He said that in 1989, with Donal's Doughnuts [Irish second-row, Donal Lenihan, was the captain of the midweek team on that Tour of Australia] one of the things they did was to force as many players as possible from the perceived midweek team into the perceived Test team. We spoke about that before the game. Some have pencilled in names already and it was our job to take the baton from Wednesday night and try and push as many forward into the hat as possible.'

He later remarked that, 'A lot of guys put their hands up tonight', which was commendable loyalty from the vice-captain for the evening but flew in the face of what had actually transpired: another stumble to victory. In the first half they were desperately poor and were very lucky to go in level at the interval. There were, strangely, a raft of forward passes in the opening period and that, allied to a general lack of cohesion, made it look as if the Lions were trying too hard, with the promise of a Test place looming large and fifteen would-be heroes attempting to perform miracles which would inspire their team-mates to higher feats.

'Lions eat Kiwis for breakfast, lunch and dinner,' one of the supporters' banners read, but on the basis of their first half display, these Lions would have been lucky to make it to the buffet.

The visitors did manage a handful of incisive attacks, which yielded two penalties for Charlie Hodgson. These merely cancelled out two early strikes from Evans though and the first try of the evening went to the hosts. Off slow ruck ball, centre Neil Brew broke through the tackle of Denis Hickie and then Hodgson, before popping the ball to scrum-half Danny Lee. The Lions' equaliser – on the stroke of half-time – came in unusual circumstances. They had been awarded a penalty close to the touchline on the left-hand side of the pitch and Hodgson shaped to kick for touch; instead, he turned and launched the ball crossfield, where Greenwood was lurking. The bounce, and a mix-up in the Otago defence, proved favourable and the vice-captain touched down. Hodgson converted and it was 13-13.

'That was the crucial point of the game,' sighed Graham afterwards. 'To go in 13-6 up would have been psychologically huge.'

Even though Evans lashed over another penalty within three minutes of the restart, it was one-way traffic in the second half. Aided by the introduction of five replacements around the hour mark, the Lions, inspired by Ryan Jones, who had a tremendous game at number eight – although a few penalties blotted his scorecard somewhat – and the dancing feet of his fellow countryman, Shane Williams, enjoyed a territorial edge throughout the second half. Nonetheless, the Lions were far from convincing and, even with the heavy artillery removed from the bench, locked and loaded, it took two moments of genius from the Welsh duo to swing the game decisively in favour of the tourists.

After 52 minutes the pair combined, Williams balleting

infield to create space and set up Jones, who burst over for the try. Then, after Hodgson and Evans exchanged penalties, Williams himself touched down. This time, Jones was the inspiration, taking a quick tap penalty, which turned into a rapid recycle of the breakdown. When it was whipped out, substitute Ollie Smith and Greenwood handled exceptionally, Geordan Murphy came thundering up from full-back, and his pass gave Williams the room he needed to notch the game's clinching score.

In another – not to labour the point – none-too-convincing display, the Lions weren't helped by a recurrence of their problems at the breakdown. Time and again Lyndon Bray's whistle sounded when the Lions went into contact. Scrum! But this meant that, whenever they did manage to get the ball clear, avoiding yet another scrum, the tourists were playing with slow ball, making it difficult to test the Otago defensive system.

Bizarrely, post-match, the discussion didn't centre around the Lions' efficiency in the area, but rather, whether or not their tactics were legal. The debate was sparked by Newby, the Otago captain: 'The Lions cheated like buggery. I think they've been under a lot of pressure about the breakdown. I think it might be unfair pressure – we didn't see it as a weakness of theirs going into this game – but I think they attacked our ball and they got away with it.'

His coach chimed in: 'I think they are allowed to come in from the side and when they get their bodies in there it can be hard to play the game at speed. I think that's probably a deliberate tactic they use to keep the game at their pace. I think they like to play the game at their speed, a game based on wearing down the opposition, getting into an attacking position and scoring points. I'm not saying there's anything wrong with that tactic, but it's the way they play the game.'

It smacked of a continuation of the nationwide campaign to focus on a particular aspect of the Lions' game, making them and the officials paranoid about what's going on. This time, it backfired somewhat. Ian McGeechan's response, when asked what he thought of allegations of cheating, was to say, 'I think that means we're competitive in that area now!' which disarmed the critics but also deflected any further questioning.

In any case, with the First Test rapidly approaching, the focus shifted rapidly to Sir Clive Woodward. 'Really, I'm not going to put out any of my Test players in the Southland game on Tuesday,' he said. 'That's been my plan from the start, but the people who play in the Southland match still have every chance of being involved in the Second Test, or even the First Test, because you do get knocks and injuries and things happen. I just think, behind the scenes, the buzz is fantastic. This test series will be won or lost by 45 players, it's as simple as that'.

So, one foolish questioner wondered, what could we read into the selection, due to be announced tomorrow, of that team to travel to Invercargill – somewhere close to the end of the world?

'Well, if you're good at maths, if I pick 22, that leaves 23 who are not going to Southland, so you'll be pretty close.' Picking those 22 should not be too difficult: despite Greenwood's contention that more than one of tonight's combatants painted themselves into the selection picture, it looks as if most of them will be packing emergency supplies of thermal underwear for a trip to the very bottom of the South Island: Brian Moore, the former England and Lions' hooker, now a BBC commentator, likened Invercargill, in a pre-tour documentary, to Chernobyl.

Sitting at the top table tonight were not the regular

Down to the Real Business

Saturday coaches, Eddie O'Sullivan and Andy Robinson, but their midweek equivalents. This too was part of the plan: 'They've [O'Sullivan and Robinson] been able to work on the New Zealand team for quite some time now to be honest and this gives them a few extra days. We won't be taking any of the Test squad down to Southland.'

Those worried that the Lions may struggle because the eventual Test team may not have played together – in fact, they almost certainly won't have played together as a unit – were given an insight into Woodward's thinking on the matter: 'You can do a lot in training when you've the numbers we've got. You can play against each other and get the timings right. The biggest thing is getting our best players in that 22 and being fresh.' So behind the red fences at the Onewa Domain and elsewhere, big things have been happening. Hopefully for the head coach that will be enough.

His opposite number tonight was also bullish about the Lions' prospects, despite the barrage of criticism he subjected them to during the week. 'I think we've a lot more to see from this Lions' team,' Graham said. 'I think they're only building up. I wouldn't read too much into what we've seen up to now; I think they've got a lot left in the cupboard.

'I think the All Blacks will look to play a game of momentum and the question is, will they be able to clear ball quick enough to create that momentum and play the game at pace? If it becomes a kicking, forward battle, it'll come down to whose drop-kickers and goal-kickers are better. There'll be a contest next week alright.'

While Graham was bullish, Woodward was positively buoyant. 'I've got a warm feeling about this,' he began, later adding that, 'It's going to be a fantastic week. Those of you at home, if you catch this, get a plane down here. I've just got a feeling that something special is happening. Don't miss it.'

Otago: G. Horton; H. Pedersen, N. Brew, S. Mapusua, M. Saunders; N. Evans, D. Lee; G. Webb, J. Blackie, C. Newby (c); T. Donnelly, F. Levi; C. Dunlea, J. MacDonald, C. Hoeft.
Subs: J. Shoemark for Brew 47, J. Aldworth for Dunlea 52, J. Vercoe for MacDonald 62, C. Smylie for Lee 75.

Lions: G. Murphy; D. Hickie, W. Greenwood, G. D'Arcy, S. Williams; C. Hodgson, C. Cusiter; R. Jones, M. Williams, S. Easterby; D. O'Callaghan, S. Shaw; M. Stevens, G. Bulloch (c), G. Rowntree.
Subs: O. Smith for D'Arcy 52, M. Dawson for Cusiter 61, A. Sheridan for Rowntree 62, S. Thomson for Bulloch 62, R. O'Gara for Hodgson 70, M. Owen for Jones 77.

Referee: L. Bray (New Zealand)

'There are worse things,' I thought to myself, as big Dai cradled me in his arms. I'd bumped into Tucker and Justin again, this time with Dai, the one who sweats profusely, in tow. The button on Justin's digital camera was close to being worn away not long after the press conference; they'd spent the time since the final whistle loitering around Carisbrook's draughty arcades, having their picture taken with, amongst others, Carl Hoeft, Ryan Jones' parents, Ryan Jones, Geordan Murphy and even Sir Clive Woodward himself.

Down to the Real Business

''E was a gentleman, Sir Clive,' said Tucker, proudly. 'Dai was going to take the photo and Clive said, "Hang on a minute, he won't be in the photo then". So we got a security guard to take it. You know what else he said?'

'What?'

'He goes, "Your boy went well tonight, didn't he?" about Ryan Jones.' Well, that's a definite pointer towards next weekend. Maybe the boss wasn't too concerned about the penalty count, or maybe I had miscalculated. Either way, a place at least in next weekend's squad was beginning to look secure for the number eight-cum-flanker.

Hence, Dai's next question: ''Ooo would you 'ave in the back row then?'

Dai, who is about the same size as Jones, had, of course, a Welsh flag draped over his broad shoulders.

'Well, it'd have to be Ryan Jones, Michael Owen and Martyn Williams, wouldn't it?' Three Welshmen.

As soon as my selection registered, Dai guffawed, bellowed, 'Good man', and I got the cradling treatment. In reality, only Jones looks like making the Test squad, but I squirmed away and wriggled out of the House of Pain.

I blundered on through the night; in fact, I was drowning my sorrows, having been embarrassed by Will Greenwood at the press conference. I had noticed that the centre had, at one stage in the second half, thrown his arms upwards, as if in triumph after the referee had awarded a scrum in the Lions' favour. Foolishly – Greenwood is one of the wittier members of the touring party – I took it upon myself to question him on his gesture. Mercifully, there were no cameras present.

'I think what you'll find is that I was delighted with Charlie's

[Hodgson] call for the scrum,' he replied, rather cryptically, and was greeted by a few nervous giggles. 'We'd wanted to move a call for a while and it had nothing to do with the scrum decision. Charlie'd called a move and I was very excited about it.' Cue gales of laughter from the rest of the room and cue scarlet spreading on the cheeks of one particular smart arse. So, I felt entitled to have a few drinks.

Of the venues the tour has taken in so far, Dunedin boasts the most impressive nightlife, as befits a university city. In the town centre lies the Octagon which, by eleven in the evening, was packed with revellers, Lions' fans and 'Scarfies', the student supporters of Otago. In the afternoon a live band entertained the masses in the afternoon, food stalls sent spices and aromas wafting onto the air, where they mingled with good-natured banter, and the crowd milled around. By the time the clock moved towards midnight, the scene was the same, only for the smell of spilt beer holding sway over that of satay chicken and hotdogs and the crowd not quite displaying the same elegance – or balance – in its milling.

I eventually ended up, through sheer luck, in the same club being patronised by members of the Lions' team that had ground out the win over Otago earlier in the evening. The name of the premises escapes me, or more correctly, it escaped my blurred vision when I stumbled in at three in the morning. Most of the Lions were all blazered-up and in a presentable condition, though a certain Welshman was slumped on the bar counter, and one of the backroom staff was dancing with a woman who didn't, from a close distance, look much like his wife.

Shane Williams, the dancing winger, was pinned down by a group of cooing Welsh girls, and it looked as good a time as any to go and talk about Tucker and Brynaman.

'I met a fella in a bar in Auckland who said he used drink with your dad in a place called Brynaman,' I slurred, Williams only paying any attention – I being slightly less attractive than a doe-eyed brunette with Welsh flags painted on her cheeks – when the name of his home village had been dropped.

'Oh aye, Brynaman. That's where I'm from, mate.'

'He said he used drink with your old man. He said he's a bit bigger than you are.'

'Aye, he is aye,' he giggled.

'Can't quite sidestep like you can?'

'Sidestep? 'E can't even step!'

Greenwood was there too, but, in the interests of not having my press credentials revoked, I elected not to throw a half-empty Steinlager at him.

The First Final Cut
Sunday 19 June 2005, Christchurch

Tomorrow will all be about Henson. He doesn't play again until Tuesday night, but this Monday will belong to Henson. The Welsh centre, the one even those who know nothing about rugby know everything about – the guy with the shaved legs, permatan, dyed hair, and celebrity girlfriend – will play against Southland in Invercargill, which all but rules him out of Saturday's First Test, Sir Clive Woodward having made it clear last night that, barring injuries, those who play this week will not face the All Blacks.

Henson's omission is the biggest surprise. Graham Rowntree, praised by Gareth Jenkins after his display last night, earns a place in the Test squad, as do Shane Williams, Ryan Jones and Will Greenwood. But Greenwood's inclusion is the second-biggest surprise, particularly as he has effectively been picked ahead of Henson. While he was a steady hand on the tiller last night, and turned in a barn-storming press conference performance, it is hard to conceive of him starting against New Zealand. Even though this writer harbours serious doubts about the permatanned one's Test-level credentials, Henson surely offers more of a threat from the bench than the ageing Englishman.

Whatever about that gripe, there is obviously a certain logic to leaving Henson out: otherwise, to state the obvious, Woodward would have picked him. However, he has partnered Brian O'Driscoll twice on tour and on neither occasion has the pair looked like a convincing international partnership. Henson's lateral running lines, while they work exceptionally well for Wales and have on occasion looked good on this tour, have yet to bring the best out of O'Driscoll and, given that the captain is an automatic pick at outside centre, the head coach's decision is far from nonsensical.

There is the further complication of Jonny Wilkinson's twenty minutes at inside centre on Wednesday night, during which period the Lions played their best rugby of the evening. It had been whispered that he may start there, alongside O'Driscoll, in Christchurch, and now it looks a distinct possibility. Wilkinson was always likely to be in the Test side, his goalkicking alone giving him an advantage over every other member of the touring party. Of the remainder of the 23 not on duty in Invercargill only Shane Horgan, though primarily a winger for Ireland and on his tour outings so far, and Greenwood could realistically expect to don the number twelve jersey on Saturday.

Unfortunately for the Lions the squad that will do battle against the All Blacks looks depressingly familiar: with a mere handful of differences, and allowing for injuries, it is the squad that most people would have picked before the touring party left Heathrow. Only Ryan Jones, with his powerful display against Otago, can be said to have played his way into the reckoning. There have been very few outstanding individual performances and virtually none from what would be viewed as the midweek side. Of those who will traipse further south on Tuesday, only Henson and Chris Cusiter could justifiably claim to be disappointed to miss out on the Test squad, with maybe Gordon Bulloch, Charlie Hodgson and Mark Cueto close behind them in the queue; Tom Shanklin has impressed on tour but his niggling knee injury has effectively ruled him out of contention; likewise, Andy Sheridan has been struggling with an ankle problem. There lies the Lions' problem: no one is clambering onto the top of the team bus and bellowing 'Pick Me! Pick Me!' at anyone who will listen. And when you contrast that situation with the embarrassment of riches from which the All Blacks can choose, it's worrying.

What the Lions' Test squad does have going for it is experience. Twelve of the thirteen Englishmen picked are World Cup winners and the other, 34 year-old Rowntree, is the holder of plenty of other medals. They know what it's like to succeed at the highest level, most of them having faced down New Zealand in Wellington in 2003 before going on to bring the William Webb Ellis trophy for its first four-year stint in Europe. That is where Woodward has put his faith – indeed, it was the main reason he cited to Henson for leaving him out – but it's not as if anyone else was offering him a compelling alternative.

Nonetheless, Henson declared himself 'gutted' at the decision.

'When Clive read out the team for the Southland game I was absolutely devastated,' he said. 'It was really hard to take in because I thought I had a chance of making the Test side, or at least the 22, so to be told I wasn't involved came as such a shock. I take my game very seriously and this will take me a while to get over.

'I had a proper chat with Clive and he told me he doesn't have a problem with the way I'm playing and he said he just wanted to go with experience for the Test. There are 45 players on tour and the coaches have to make the decisions in the end. I understand that.

'It's a bit like when I got left out of the World Cup. Back then I felt really low. I don't want that to happen again and luckily there are three Tests. You just don't know what will happen. All I can do is try to play well. I have a point to prove. I want to show everyone what I am capable of. Right now I'm just gutted.'

Woodward chose not to broach the Henson question, preferring to speak of the selection in broader terms: 'We have a strong squad, and the strength of the side picked for Southland shows that.

'I have made clear that the players selected for Southland will not feature in the First Test, but that does not mean they do not have the opportunity to play in the Second and Third Tests. That is underlined by the history of Lions' tours down the years. I want these players to keep challenging for Test places as the tour goes on by their performance on Tuesday.

'Another lesson of Lions' tours is that, where they have

been successful, it has been when the unity of the squad has been strong. If we win the test series, it will not just be a win for the players out on the pitch, but for the whole squad. All 45 have all been fantastic in helping to create the environment we need to win.'

'I have been on many tours,' Ian McGeechan added, 'as a player and coach, and when we have won, the people to thank have often as not been the people who did not play in tests but who helped create a winning environment for those who did.

'This is a terrific group of players and they have worked very hard to create that winning environment. What is more, there will be players selected for Southland who without doubt will feature in future tests. The mood in the squad is very positive. The excitement is growing. The next step is to win against Southland.'

Still, tomorrow will all be about Henson.

Lions' Team V Southland: G. Murphy; M. Cueto, O. Smith, G. Henson, D. Hickie; R. O'Gara, G. Cooper; M. Owen (c), M. Williams, L. Moody; D. O'Callaghan, S. Shaw; J. Hayes, A. Titterrell, M. Stevens.
Subs: G. Bulloch, A. Sheridan, S. Easterby, C. Cusiter, C. Hodgson, T. Shanklin, G. D'Arcy.

Lions' *de facto* First Test squad: J. Robinson, J. Lewsey, S. Williams, G. Thomas, B. O'Driscoll, S. Horgan, W. Greenwood, J. Wilkinson, S. Jones, D. Peel, M. Dawson, M. Corry, R. Jones, N. Back, R. Hill, P. O'Connell, D. Grewcock, B. Kay, J. White, G. Rowntree, G. Jenkins, S. Thompson, S. Byrne.

It is nice to see that Gareth Cooper is getting a game. A spoof 'Missing Person' poster has been whizzing around the internet, with a picture of the Welsh scrum-half on it. 'Gareth, from Bridgend,' the text reads, 'flew to New Zealand with some friends on May 27, but very little has been seen of him since his arrival. He was last seen playing nine minutes of rugby against Taranaki but has now well and truly disappeared … If you have any information on the whereabouts or well-being of Gareth please contact your local police station.'

Still, Woodward made it clear back in Auckland that some players wouldn't get much game time: he hoped that, even if they didn't, they still would learn enough to ensure that they didn't regret spending their summer in New Zealand, rather than the Canaries. 'I want to maximise the benefits to all four countries,' he explained, and it would be simplistic to say that, just because an individual hasn't got much game time his tour was wasted.

The Gold Coast
Monday, 20 June 20, Alexandra

The Desert Road encircling the volcanoes of Tongariro might have been spectacular, the Forgotten World Highway's trek through the Tangarakau Gorge memorable, but they both pale by comparison to the road from Alexandra to Queenstown, along the South Island's Gold Coast.

This morning in Alexandra, a small town between Queenstown and Dunedin, it was freezing. The ground was close to iced over and a cold mist clung to cement and skin alike.

'Ah, it'll come right,' said the campsite owner, with typical

Down to the Real Business

Kiwi optimism: cheerful and unconcerned. What he meant was, the fog would probably lift, but, if it didn't, what the hell, there's always tomorrow. Of course, it didn't necessarily bode well for an unwieldy campervan travelling along winding, mountaintop roads and even though Invercargill isn't the world's most attractive destination – in fact, it's pretty much the world's last destination, short of travelling to the Antarctic – the game against Southland was looming and the last place I wanted to be was marooned somewhere between there and here.

So I ploughed onwards into a mist so thick that the sideview mirrors struggled to pick out the rest of the vehicle, the headlights seemed to be operating on energy saver bulbs, and even the roadside was swallowed up by the gloom. Welcome to June, southern hemisphere-style.

And then, as if a curtain had been raised, it did 'come right'. A rising sun swept the fog away as I rounded a bend and found myself transfixed by the Gold Coast. It was no wonder that nineteenth-century prospectors were drawn here in their thousands: the mountains towering over the road on each side seem to be daubed with streaks of gold, as if a golden dye had come spilling down from their peaks; even the river running through the valleys looks tinged with yellow.

Only yesterday, the lush green plains of Canterbury had stretched for miles around; today, on a road winding a torturous trail through the midst of the Southern Alps, New Zealand was a different country. Perhaps it's no wonder that the population unites around a rugby team: in a country of such diverse landscapes, maybe the people need something, if only a sports team, to be common and permanent.

Goodbye Merths, Hello Michael
Monday 20 June 2005, Arthur's Pass

As the road from Alexandra continued to wind its way into Queenstown, all the radio stations began cutting to the same story: not that Gavin Henson had been dropped out of the Lions' First Test reckoning, but that New Zealander Michael Campbell was on the verge of winning the US Open golf tournament. All the radio stations cut to the news, some taking live commentary, all of them breathless, informing listeners that a New Zealander, for the first time in 40 years, was going to win a major golf title. At least it moved Henson, whose omission dominated the sports pages today, out of the spotlight.

Later in the evening, having spent an afternoon trekking around Queenstown, I was quenching my thirst in a bar in nearby Arthur's Pass. On the television a music channel played, with the sound turned down. Nobody paid any attention. But as soon as digital watches began beeping to announce the arrival of six o'clock, curious eyes started turning towards the television.

'Hey, turn on the news, wouldya?' someone asked the barmaid.

It must have been an unusual request: the barmaid fumbled for a moment and had to summon help from a co-worker before the channel was changed and Campbell's smiling face flashed up on the screen. The bar fell into total silence, broken only by the sound of swallowing, as the anchor told of how the Maori had held off the field to win one of golf's most prestigious competitions. As the news moved through the rest of the day's events, it lost the crowd's attention and the silence was displaced by a happy murmur, as the patrons lauded the achievement of one of their own. In a small country like New Zealand any triumph on a global scale is a cause for celebration and delight. After all, the only praise a man can get which is higher than the rapturous silence of a group of drinkers is the raucous cheering of thousands.

Another New Zealander who has probably experienced both in the course of his career is the great All Black fly-half Andrew Mehrtens, to whom no less than a leading editorial in *The Press*, one of the country's three major broadsheet dailies, was devoted today. Of course, *The Press* is also the newspaper which operates out of Christchurch, Mehrtens' home town; nonetheless, the fact that he pushed a debate on carbon taxes into second place shows how seriously the Kiwis take their rugby.

As, indeed does the tone and content of the editorial, which began: 'When Cantabrians were asked in a poll a few years back to name the three things that best represented the province, the winners were the Port Hills, Christchurch Cathedral and Andrew Mehrtens.

'The results were hardly surprising. After all, Mehrtens has been as essential a feature of the landscape over the last thirteen years as the hills that shelter the city and the cathedral at its heart ... His career has been outstanding not just for its longevity and the dominance of his position, but also his continuing influence on the world game and the way he has inspired a generation of young players.' Like I said, they take rugby pretty seriously here.

The reason for the editorial and the plentiful column inches devoted to Mehrtens over the weekend is that on Friday the great man announced he had signed a two-year contract with the Harlequins club in London.

The praise, which came from all quarters, was close to deafening. Canterbury coach Aussie McLean: 'Like the great Michael Jordan, if "Mehrts" was in your team you had a pretty good chance of winning. For as many as six years he has been critical to the winning and losing of games. Off the field he is also a fantastic talisman for Canterbury rugby.'

Canterbury chief executive Hamish Riach: 'Whether he's been wearing the red and black of Canterbury and the Crusaders or the All Black jersey, "Mehrts" has influenced the results of games he has appeared in at every level of New Zealand rugby ...

All Black coach, Graham Henry: 'Andrew has been a world-class player and was probably the best number ten in the world in the late-1990s. Over the last decade he has been one of our foremost All Blacks and a great character'.

As one shuffles off, another strides on. Happy is the land with heroes.

Soaking it Up

Tuesday 21 June 2005, Queenstown
'So, will you travel down?'

'I've got about five minutes to make up my mind,' the Welshman replied.

'But that pint is three-quarters full.'

'Yes it is. I don't think I'll bother, to be honest. It's cold enough here.' He wasn't talking about finishing his pint.

'Yeah. Whaddya make of Henson?'

A grunt.

Down to the Real Business

It was just after twelve in Pogue Mathone's pub in Queenstown, yet another Irish bar which this time, boasted – and how miraculous this is for an Irish bar in New Zealand, most of which are about as Irish as Joe Rokocoko – an Irish barman, from Ballincollig in Cork.

The Welshman was one of hundreds of Lions' fans who have pitched up in Queenstown. Whatever about Dunedin being a lively nightspot, this town, a backpackers' mecca, is renowned. Apart from the sky-diving, luge, bungy jump (it's not 'bungee' here, I was frostily informed), jet boats, shot-over-flights, helicopter rides – you name it, Queenstown's got it – for which it's famed, the narrow pedestrianised streets in the town centre gave off a hum of activity even early in the morning. It was hard to conceive of any of these bars closing before ten in the evening. Certainly, with a large contingent of thirsty travelling fans here, there was a giant, dollar-shaped incentive to prop open the eyelids and keep the cash register ticking over.

I suspect that the Welshman nursing his pint of Guinness may have travelled down the street for something to eat later in the day, but few are the chances that he made the three-hour journey to Invercargill. Many others will have stayed put too: this Lions' tour, for the fans, is as much about travelling around the country, having a good time and seeing the sights, as it is about watching 30 men chase an oval-shaped ball around a green rectangle. And, God knows, there are few enough sights in Invercargill; the opportunity of watching the Lions' midweek side play one of the more mediocre New Zealand provinces doesn't add a whole lot either. All the better to soak up the atmosphere here and conserve energy for the First Test on Saturday.

That snide comment about Irish bars can't go undeveloped either: while nearly every major town here and, without doubt, every city, boasts several bars masquerading as 'Irish', there is nothing, apart from the over-application of green paint, to mark them out as different from 'New Zealand bars'. Irish bar staff are few and far between, as are Irish customers: a cynic would say that the concept of the Irish bar is used only to capitalise on New Zealanders' love of Guinness. Signs advertising the Dublin-brewed stout abound, even on the walls of bars which don't proclaim themselves 'Irish', and, in some bars, etched onto a plaque on the wall are the names of those who have drunk enough Guinness in a week-long period to join the 'hundred-pint club'. Guinness is the only multinational beer available on tap down here: there is no Heineken or Carlsberg; even Fosters stays on the other side of the Tasman Strait. Auckland, Wellington, Christchurch and Dunedin are all home to breweries and, from plenty of the smaller towns between them, other beverages are shipped out. That Guinness is able to break into this market at all is heady praise; indeed, even headier because in more than place I've seen it pulled in a single pour.

Game 6: British & Irish Lions V Southland

Tuesday 21 June 2005, Rugby Park Stadium, Invercargill

Southland 16
Tries: H. T-Pole
Convs: R. Apanui
Pens: R. Apanui (3)

Down to the Real Business

Lions 26
Tries: G. Henson (2)
Convs: R. O'Gara (2)
Pens: R. O'Gara (4)

'Welcome to Invercargill, the Arsehole of the World', proclaims an official sign, no less, on the way into the city. Mick Jagger christened Invercargill thus; if nothing else the natives have a sense of humour. Indeed they had a poke at Brian Moore yesterday too. When the Lions' team arrived off the plane in the local airport, they were greeted by a welcoming committee dressed in luminous protective gear.

'Brian Moore was totally wrong,' I said to a newsagent. 'This place is much nicer than Chernobyl.' This was a white lie: I've never been to Chernobyl but I imagine it is somewhat bleaker than Invercargill, even if the latter does resemble a giant industrial estate, with far too many empty units.

'Why, thank you.' The lady behind the counter beamed, her smile and tone indicating that she was delighted to receive the compliment. 'You're very kind.'

In the opening ten minutes of tonight's game, it looked as if the natives were going to be most accommodating on the pitch as well. The night was mild – 'Thank God', murmured the travelling fans – there was little dew on either grass or ball and it looked as if the tourists might get the fillip of a comprehensive, morale-boosting win before the First Test.

Sure enough, the Lions played some of the best, most expansive rugby of this tour in the opening minutes, getting through the phases with ease, fly-half Ronan O'Gara's sumptuous deliveries getting the ball wide quickly and stretching the

Southland defence. A try from Gavin Henson – who else? – after twelve minutes, when he powered over from close range, gave the Lions a ten-point cushion. Happy days: it looked like the tourists were going to get that timely fillip.

Then, the wheels came off. 'The first ten minutes was easy and we felt we were on for a good night,' O'Gara said. 'These were probably the best conditions we've had in New Zealand to play rugby in, but after ten minutes, we lost our shape, took our foot off the pedal and thought they were there for the taking. They made it difficult for us and we didn't help ourselves by turning the ball over too many times and giving away too many penalties. We addressed the issue at half-time. The coaches gave us a bollocking and we deserved it.'

The management concurred. 'We started particularly well, maybe too well,' was Gareth Jenkins' assessment, 'and if you're looking at the overall performance from our point of view, you'd say we became far too individual far too early in the game. What they've done is fronted particularly well, they got in us, got amongst us and have taken advantage of us not having the cohesion in our performance. We've made hard work of that performance'.

It's much more important, Jenkins said, to get points on the board, get a lead and subdue the provincial teams. Then, play some rugby: 'When we went out, we really felt that, to play these type of games, to put in a good performance, we've to limit the game to start, and hopefully, in the later period of the game, we try to expand it and loosen it. And having scored a good try and gone ten points into the lead, we decided in the first fifteen minutes we were going to play a catch-up game. It wasn't planned, that's for sure.'

Down to the Real Business

'Unlike the other games,' sighed a disappointed Ian McGeechan, 'where we built momentum and got stronger as the game went on, we allowed Southland a lot of easy possession tonight, which encouraged them. They, quite rightly, felt in the game until the end, where, if we had done things tidily, the outcome would have been somewhat different.'

Once again, the breakdown was at the root of the Lions' problems. With the ball whizzing, sevens-style, across the pitch with dizzying regularity, it was difficult for the tourists to get numbers to the rucks.

'The breakdown became a bit of a mess, with players coming in from different directions,' said McGeechan. 'You then get a less structured game because you get players coming from different angles. Probably, we found space too early and didn't use it well because we didn't build on it. Because of the extra room we found tonight, we probably tried to score from first phase rather than build momentum. That's when you get the errors and a lot of the turnovers that hurt our game.'

Southland coach and former All Black full-back, Simon Culhane, agreed that the game was very loose: 'It probably started at the breakdown: there were bodies flopping everywhere, the ball was popping out and that probably contributed to it.'

Although they were much the better side, and dominated that first period in terms of possession and territory, the Lions led by only seven points, 10-3, at the interval. Had they got on the scoreboard again early in the second half, stretching their lead to a decent size, things might have ended differently. It wasn't to be: instead, Southland got a vital score within ten minutes of the restart. That levelled the sides and thereafter the Lions were never more than two scores clear, meaning that the hosts could always harbour hopes of coming out on top, and the tourists would be forced to play a dour, territorial game to, once more, bore the opposition into submission. So much for that timely fillip.

The introduction of Tom Shanklin helped the Lions to build some momentum and, within five minutes of his arrival on the pitch, Henson had crossed for a second try, Shanklin having made the hard yards off a line-out. From then until the end, both try lines were never in serious danger of being crossed and O'Gara, despite being roundly booed by the home crowd every time he elected to kick for goal, secured the win with a string of three-pointers. It was quite a climb-down for the visitors: in the opening period, a succession of penalties had been kicked into the corner, in the hope of scoring enough tries to finish the game off before the 40 minute mark.

That ploy failed, so by far the most interesting aspect of the second half was the rumour sweeping the ground that Shane Williams and Shane Horgan were sitting in the stands, fuelling speculation that both might be doubtful for Saturday's game. Sadly the truth was more prosaic and McGeechan put a stop to the grinding of the rumour mill: 'We've extra players who come down in case someone gets injured in the warm-up or gets ill. We've done that for all the games.'

Once more, there were few individual performances worth shouting from the rooftops about. Donncha O'Callaghan probably edged his way into contention for a spot in the squad for the Second Test, but inevitably the focus was on the two tries notched by Henson.

Culhane was certainly impressed: 'He was good, yeah, took his tries well. He's very strong with ball in hand, stronger than I thought he would be. He's a good player.'

Of course, it was little use in convincing an opposition coach of his talents. Happily, McGeechan seemed to concur with Culhane's assessment: 'He took his tries well and he did a lot of good things ... There's parts of his game that we still want to improve and there are some parts that work really well.'

When quizzed on what parts of his game exactly, the coach was slightly evasive: 'You're just talking about sense of play. Positioning, repositioning, working off others, others working off him, and it's just looking at all those aspects. To me the essence of a Lions' tour is that you try to grow and improve players in this environment with good people around them. He's doing a lot of good things and there are some other things that we think we can work on.'

The man of the moment was wheeled out in person afterwards, the brooding presence of Alastair Campbell, who returned from the UK a few days ago, very much in the background.

'I haven't got a clue,' a sulky-looking Henson replied when asked had he been told why he was overlooked for the Test squad. 'I feel I'm playing quite well at the moment. The first game, I played 60 minutes and felt happy with myself. The second game, I thought I was good, thought my game was getting better, so I thought everything was going well. It's nice to play 80 minutes tonight and I just feel that I'm getting more and more confident with these players ... I just love playing rugby, so it wasn't a case of it being hard to get up for the game or anything like that. It's great to be playing, simple as that.'

A lighter moment was to follow. Phil Edwards of Sky Sports, referring implicitly to the visit to Wellington of Charlotte Church, Henson's girlfriend, wondered if off-field exertions had taken their toll. 'That's a stupid question,' the centre answered, glowering, much to the amusement of all concerned. Even the three team-mates sharing the top table with him failed to contain their laughter.

As ever though the ethos of a Lions' tour, bringing with it the focus on a group rather than on individuals, was to the fore for McGeechan: 'There's obviously disappointment for the players but I have to say, since Sunday, I've been impressed with their attitude, just working towards tonight's game. We know we haven't had much preparation because we only got back from Dunedin and Saturday's game and it was important that some of them trained twice on Monday to help with the [Test side's] preparation. The squad will go back and train tomorrow as well, in preparation for the Test match; it's been a big ask of them to which they've responded well.'

Flanker Lewis Moody agreed: 'It was a superhuman effort from some of the players to play on Saturday and front up again tonight with training twice yesterday and tomorrow as well. Since the Test team's been announced, it's been a massive effort all round. Yes we're frustrated, but it's been a good effort from the boys, really.'

'They've been travelling and playing for the last week now,' McGeechan continued, 'but I take my hat off to them: no questions, no complaints and that's what I think builds you and lets you win in the long term.'

'I think the most important thing tonight was to win,' Jenkins commented and, while that's an unarguable point, it would have been nice had they won in style this evening. As it is, it's on the back of another in an unbroken line of unconvincing performances that the Lions will enter the Test series.

Down to the Real Business

Southland: J. Wilson; M. Harrison, B. Milne, F. Muliaina, W. Lotawa; R Apanui, J. Cowan; P. Miller, H. T-Pole, H. Tamariki; D. Quate, H MacDonald; A. Dempsey, J. Rutledge, C. Dermody (c).

Subs: J. Wright for Miller 40, D. Hall for Rutledge 59, P. Te Whare for Milne 63.

Lions: G. Murphy; M. Cueto, O. Smith, G. Henson, D. Hickie; R. O'Gara, G. Cooper; M. Owen (c), M. Williams, L. Moody; D. O'Callaghan, S. Shaw; J. Hayes, A. Titterrell, M. Stevens.

Subs: A. Sheridan for Stevens h/t, G. Bulloch for Titterrell 50, T. Shanklin for Smith 50, C. Cusiter for Cooper 50, S. Easterby for Owen 68, G. D'Arcy for Murphy 75.

Referee: K. Deaker (New Zealand)

Part Six

Enter the All Blacks

GOODBYE TO ALL THAT

Wednesday 22 June 2005, Ranfurly Shield Challenge, Jade Stadium, Christchurch

Canterbury 67
Tries: A. Pelenise (3), J. Nutbrown (3), G. Naoupu, C. McIntyre, S. Yates, B. Nowell, M. Tito
Convs: A. Mehrtens (6)

Marlborough 3
Pens: S. Howe

And so Andrew Mehrtens' career has turned full circle. He announced himself on the New Zealand rugby scene in 1994 when he kicked a penalty to ensure that the Ranfurly Shield, one of the country's oldest, most prestigious trophies, stayed in the hands of his province, Canterbury. Today, while the current generation of All Blacks spoke to the media about how much they were looking forward to taking on the Lions, Mehrtens was warming up for his last game on home soil before moving to London.

The Ranfurly Shield, played for by all the provinces affiliated to the NZRU, was first presented to Auckland, in 1902 and first played for in 1904. The holders defend the 'log o' wood' every year, in a series of challenge games. Previously a complicated system, which even the most sophisticated computers struggled to figure out, was used to grant pretenders a shot at the Shield. The ownership of the trophy could, and still can, change a number of times over the course of a season. With the National Provincial Championship now dominant, in terms of provincial rugby, all the holder's home games in that competition count as Shield defences, and victory sees the 'log o' wood' travel from the losing province to the victorious one. But to keep in touch with tradition – so important in New Zealand – every year, there must be seven defences of the Shield and so, some Second Division teams are given a chance to challenge the holders. This year, first up to challenge is Marlborough, fifth in the second tier in 2004.

In truth though it wasn't a challenge in the true meaning of the word. As well as Mehrtens, Canterbury, even in the absence of five Junior All Blacks and nine members of the senior international squad, could call on former New Zealand captain, Rueben Thorne, up and coming centre Steve Yates, and other highly-rated performers like Jamie Nutbrown and Sam Broomhall. They even had the luxury of naming a former All Black prop, Greg Feek, amongst the reserves for today's game. There is no comparison, and Mehrtens' farewell turned into a victory parade.

The Last Great Tour?

It was not by any means a vintage performance from him, though with only touches of genius illuminating the occasion. More impressive than his display was the size of the crowd. Despite the game kicking off at just after three o'clock on a Wednesday afternoon, over 10,000 paid in to bid 'Mehrts' adieu. That alone shows how strong the game is in this country, but the survival of the Ranfurly Shield concept, still sailing blithely through the stormy waters of professionalism, tells a story too. How many people, I was moved to wonder, attended the last Munster Senior Cup final?

Here it is All Blacks, province, club and it will ever be thus, in the same way that American Marines, fanatical look in their eyes, will bellow, 'God, Country, Corps'. Beside his name in the programme, High School Old Boys is listed as Mehrtens' club. From there, he progressed to become a Cantabrian, donning the black and red of his province in the NPC and, when it was inaugurated in 1996, the Super 12. He starred for the Canterbury Crusaders and then he became an All Black. And still, some Saturdays, All Blacks, beaten and battered in the Super 12 and Tri Nations, line out in club games up and down the country, at a level of competition that remains vibrant and healthy. Old traditions – like the Ranfurly Shield challenges and the Deans Cup they play for in Whangamonoma – are the glue which keeps the game together and binds the country as one. It is indeed a fitting way for a true great to depart.

Canterbury: M. Wells; B. Allen, S. Yates, C. McIntyre, A. Pelenise; A. Mehrtens, J. Nutbrown; S. Broomhall, H. Hopgood, R. Thorne (c); C. Clarke, G. Naoupu; M. Tito, T. Kopelani, W. Crockett.

Marlborough: M. Campbell; A. Smith, S. Gibbons, N. Peipi, O. Temo; S. Howe, A. Large; L. McGlone (c), G. Love, R. Love; W. de Waal, M. Bosman; T. Moran, M. Stewart, A. Norton.

Referee: B. Lawrence (New Zealand)

Warm Feelings and Camaraderie
Wednesday 22 June, Christchurch Town Hall
'Boom, boom', went the sound system.

'What the ...?' went the press corps.

On two large screens either side of the top table in Christchurch Town Hall, brief, live-action pictures of the Lions selected to play on Saturday flashed up on screen, one after the other. Jason Robinson through to Gethin Jenkins and on to the subs. Flanked by Eddie O'Sullivan and Andy Robinson, the two men spared the trip to Dunedin the better to let them prepare for the First Test, Sir Clive Woodward sat, impassive but exuding a glow that said, 'Look at this! Look at the lengths I've gone to! Didn't I tell you all this is the best-prepared Lions' team ever?'

As the clips began to roll, the 22 players filed in. About 150 media people, between television, radio and print, sat in the middle of the room, thumbs a-twiddling, questions at the ready. There is a heavy air of cynicism in the press corps now. The Lions' head coach has described every game as 'fantastic'; the tour is a 'great occasion'; he's 'delighted' to be in Dunedin or wherever; every player has been 'outstanding'; it's a 'special group of players'. It's not so much the fact that he's using these words and phrases, more the regularity with which they're

employed. It's come to the stage where, before press conferences, the journalists wonder which will come first: X had an
'outstanding game', or, 'it was a fantastic game tonight', or, the
favourite: 'it was another great occasion'.

But before we could even get that far, the wheels repeated
last night's performance and came flying off. As the players sat
down, slightly bemused by the warlike music pounding out of
the speakers and the flashy editing unfolding on the screens in
front of them – the sort of entrance more appropriate to a
heavyweight champion of the world – it turned out that there
weren't enough chairs. The 2005 Lions might be the best-prepared of all time but it looked like the preparation hadn't
extended to learning how to count. Yet, no matter how well-prepared a team is, it still has to be capable of making decisions
on the spot, of showing leadership, strength in adversity. So
they squeezed up and someone, Paul O'Connell, I think, was
able to perch himself on the edge.

So, things began. 'Can we have the first question from the
floor, please?' asked Louisa Cheetham, the Lions' media manager. Inevitably, the topic of Henson was broached. Jonny
Wilkinson had been selected to start wearing twelve, with
Stephen Jones inside him at number ten. Jason Robinson won
the full-back berth but, apart from those two, there was nothing
approaching a surprise. Jenkins, Byrne, who threw so well in the
rain against Wellington, White, O'Connell, Kay, Hill, Back, Corry,
Peel, Jones, Lewsey, Wilkinson, O'Driscoll, Thomas and
Robinson. Shane Williams was number 23, missing out on a
bench spot to Shane Horgan. But never mind that: time again to
bring up the Henson question.

'Gavin Henson's had an outstanding tour,' said Woodward,

cueing a few chuckles from the audience. 'I think he's incredibly unlucky not to be involved. He's done nothing wrong at all; it's just a very competitive environment.'

Those of the media blessed with excellent lateral vision then caught something out of the corner of their eyes. Alastair Campbell's tracksuit pants were pulled down. None other than a giggling O'Connell was immediately pinned as the culprit; when you're ginger, six-feet-five and about eighteen stone, it's hard to be inconspicuous.

Throughout the proceedings, some of the players sat impassively: Jonny Wilkinson's face betrayed no emotion, though his selection was the one which was questioned at most length. Why Wilkinson over Henson? Woodward, of course, had to be diplomatic: he couldn't say, 'Because I'm not sure that Stephen Jones' goalkicking will be able to handle the pressure'. And that is the reason: Wilkinson's goals won the World Cup for England, and saw them win countless times in pressure situations; Jones, while he was the pivot in Wales' Six Nations success this year, missed what might have been a crucial kick early in the deciding game against Ireland, and also had an off day with the boot against England earlier in the season. That, incidentally, was the day that Henson wrote himself into rugby folklore with a mammoth, winning penalty late on. Jones is a good kicker but he's not in Wilkinson's league, was what the coach couldn't say for fear of damaging the former's morale.

If Wilkinson as he focused on the questions being asked indirectly of him was inscrutable, the rest were at ease and relaxed. Some whispered amongst themselves; a few winked at journalists they know; others sat and listened patiently.

The other slightly controversial pick being Robinson,

Woodward also had to explain his reasoning. Was the decision to select him, thereby excluding Williams, who had dazzled with Wales and played superbly against Otago, based on reputation, of which Robinson has plenty, or form, of which he currently has rather less?

'A little bit of both, I think. You've got to go on what you're seeing, but also you've got to go on what you know, about how players perform under pressure. It's a big pressure match on Saturday night.'

And we're back to this word: pressure. After the Otago game, referring to the First Test, he used it seven or eight times in one sentence. Clearly he thinks that, with the backbone of the side that won the 2003 World Cup, albeit minus two of that team's most influential members, Martin Johnson and Lawrence Dallaglio, the Lions will be able to handle the pressure. The unspoken inference is that New Zealand won't. There is some basis for this: in the last World Cup, having cut quite a dash up to that point, they collapsed in the semi-final, coming undone against an Australian team that had been lucky to beat Ireland in their final group match; to boot, the last All Black team to win anything of note was Laurie Mains' 1993 vintage, which beat the Lions. In 1995, 1999 and, of course, 2003, New Zealand have failed. Maybe Woodward is right.

Whatever about being right on the question of the opposition's ability to perform under pressure, what about the fact that six of the Lions' team selected have played only one game on tour?

'You've got to go with what you've got,' was Woodward's reply to that searching inquiry, from Gerry Thornley of *The Irish Times*. 'When I send Brian and the team out on Saturday, I want them to be the best prepared, to be rested and fresh. I think that's what you need if you're on tour in this part of the world. When you're playing a fixture like this you have to start with your freshest team. We've had to strike a balance between that and giving guys a game. I think we've achieved that and I'm really looking forward to Saturday night.'

Clearly he still has that warm feeling. Despite the stuttering performances, I'm inclined to share it. There were enough signs against Wellington to suggest that the Lions have been developing the sort of cohesion that would allow them to impose themselves on the All Blacks. If they can get a platform up front, win their line-outs and assert themselves in the scrummage, with Jones and Wilkinson bombing balls down-field and the latter kicking his goals, victory ought to be within their grasp. Of course, much depends on what's been happening behind closed doors on the training ground. Sir Clive has been close to the action and if he feels confident enough to proclaim that he has a warm feeling, taunt New Zealand about not being able to handle pressure, and invite anyone who's got the plane fare to come down and experience 'something special', that has to count for something. Otherwise, the man is setting himself up for a gigantic fall.

What do his players think? If there isn't togetherness off the pitch, it's unlikely that there will be togetherness on it. What's the spirit like in the camp?

'It's different to Munster,' said Paul O'Connell, 'where we've all known each other for years. You come over here and there's 45 players and 30 staff to have to get to know. And I think, in fairness, everyone has been making a conscious effort to be open minded. It's been great; I've really enjoyed it. If we'd lost a few more games, there might have been a bit of consternation, but we've got momentum going now and we're building up nicely to the First Test. Everyone's very positive.'

Sitting all alone in the corner of the room was Graham Rowntree, a man who's seen more than most of this squad. The veteran Leicester prop toured with the Lions in 1997 and since then has experienced the highs of winning European Cups with his club, and the lows of being left out of Woodward's World Cup squad. Is there confidence within the camp?

'Mate, if you're not confident, you might as well go home. There's a real strength there.'

Is there camaraderie? How does it compare to previous tours?

'I wasn't on the 2001 Lions' tour, but, from the stories you hear from other guys, this is on a different planet: everything about it. And it's the desire to do well, to do well against the All Blacks, to beat these guys. In this rugby-mad country. They're almost blinded by commentators telling them how good the All Blacks are. They think they will win and any visiting team is crap.'

It must help too to have old hands like Rowntree around the place. Is he the sort of old sage to whom people come to for advice?

'No. I don't think ... not openly. I'd chat to anyone, but I don't want to be some old bastard, boring people, trying to take them under my wing. I don't want to be like that. Not condescending or anything like that.'

But if they asked for advice, he'd give it, right?

'Of course I would. But I don't think anyone here needs it.'

There was a steely confidence about Rowntree, as one might expect from an old warrior who has toiled at the coalface for so long. And some of his words, about taking one's chances, should resonate deeply in the lead up to a game as big as this one.

'It's like anything in life: you have to take your chance. I don't want to get too deep, but you just have to take your chance. I mean, I'll never get to tour like this again. This Lions' tour is the last long tour, and there's a lot that can happen. It's the last chance for me to tour like this, so you've got to put it together, you've got to take your chance.

'You should never give up. Through my setbacks, missing out on the World Cup, for example, I've never lost faith in what I was doing. I'm not saying I'm any kind of a hero, but I've never had enough reasons not to attempt some kind of a comeback in my career.'

If his team-mates can marry that relentless focus to the camaraderie that exists within the camp, Woodward might just be right about 'something special' being on the cards.

They'll be up against a formidable All Blacks' side, however. Leon MacDonald's performance in the Maori shirt sees him preferred to Mils Muliaina at full-back, and the more combative Justin Marshall displaces Byron Kelleher, who started against Fiji, at scrum-half. On tour form so far it's hard to see too many of the Lions doing much displacing of the incumbents were they too eligible for All Black selection. Still, when the pressure's ratcheted up, who knows what will happen?

New Zealand: L. MacDonald; D. Howlett, T. Umaga (c), A. Mauger, S. Sivivatu; D. Carter, J. Marshall; R. So'oialo, R. McCaw, J. Collins; A. Williams, C. Jack; C. Hayman, K. Mealamu, T. Woodcock.

Subs: D. Witcombe, G. Somerville, J. Gibbes, S. Lauaki, B. Kelleher, M. Muliaina, R. Gear.

Lions: J. Robinson; J. Lewsey, B. O'Driscoll (c), J. Wilkinson, G. Thomas; S. Jones, D. Peel; M. Corry, N. Back, R. Hill; B Kay, P. O'Connell; J. White, S. Byrne, G. Jenkins.
Subs: S. Thompson, G. Rowntree, D. Grewcock, R. Jones, M. Dawson, W. Greenwood, S. Horgan.

A Pair of Partners in Crime, a Trio Really
Thursday 23 June 2005, Christchurch

The reason for my mad dash from Invercargill to Christchurch yesterday – an eight-hour drive which, to take in the Ranfurly Shield, involved leaving at six in the morning – was this morning's job. Doing the whole trip in one day was unavoidable, so I decided to make the best of it and treat myself to a double of Mehrtens' farewell and the tourists' press conference. I was also motivated by the fact that the Lions were laying on a journalists drinks and canapés session last night though obviously, being a serious professional and not a student on the piss 12,000 miles from home, I was travelling north primarily for the important things.

I did, however, miss out on a special night in the Marist clubhouse near Rugby Park Stadium in Invercargill. It was there that Lions prop, John Hayes, spent some time playing, and the atmosphere was excellent. Apart, that is, from one incident recounted to me by Liam Heagney of *Ireland on Sunday*.

'There was this Dublin lad in the jacks, he asked two fellas where they were from and when they said "Limerick", he started mouthing off about how only scumbags come from Limerick and that sort of stuff. And to make matters worse, he was wearing a Dublin GAA jersey. Anyway they made him come out and apologise in front of the whole bar. It was either that, or they'd take him outside!'

A pity I missed that.

This morning's job involved driving out to Christchurch Airport and collecting a partner in crime, Oisín Langan from Newstalk 106. I love Oisín dearly – I am sharing a very confined space with him for the next two-and-a-half weeks – but am more motivated by the fact that he's paying over a grand for the privilege of sharing said confined space for the next two-and-a-half weeks.

First stop in town was an electrical store, for adapters and other things you need to send radio broadcast material 12,000 across the world. This, apparently, is the sort of thing for which you can't rely on a carrier pigeon or, even in extreme circumstances, DHL.

Christchurch's streets were so quiet and dreary that Oisín, a native of Ardmore in County Waterford, found fond memories of his childhood being rekindled.

'It's like 1980s Dungarvan.'

Even by the time downtown Christchurch approached what most other cities call rush hour much of the city continued to resemble an abbey in which over 300,000 monks had taken a vow of silence. Wide streets were empty, devoid of traffic. Red jerseys were few and far between; most, presumably, had opted to stay in Queenstown where there is nightlife as opposed to day death.

The Last Great Tour?

Things thankfully were a bit livelier in the Town Square, under the shadow of Christchurch Cathedral. Lions' replica shirts a-plenty milled around the open-air stalls, and there were players a-plenty drifting around the streets. Donncha O'Callaghan and Paul O'Connell had the misfortune to wander into our path.

'How's it goin' lads?' bellowed Oisín and we paired off, he to O'Callaghan, me to O'Connell.

'Much hassle off the fans?' I asked O'Connell.

'Yerrah, not really.' I told him the story from Napier, of the New Zealand triallists enjoying their drinks in peace and quiet – except for the interventions from Tucker and Justin – as if a forcefield repelled all those who would disturb them.

'Yeah, the Kiwis don't bother you that much. It's our own crowd who'd be giving you hassle!'

In a nearby Starbucks there was a sighting of two of the All Blacks. Richie McCaw, who has been suffering from a back strain – which necessitated an emergency call up for Marty Holah, who did his bit to destroy the Lions while wearing the Maori jersey – and Greg Somerville happily posed for photographs; almost inevitably, it was Lions' fans who were doing the asking.

At first glance, it seemed remarkable that, with just over 48 hours to go before the First Test, the players could be so relaxed. Then again, what else would they do? Sit knitting in their hotel rooms? Write endless postcards to distant relatives? Perch themselves in the hotel bar putting away bottle after bottle of Steinlager, with the help of a few Wild Turkey chasers? Of course they have to get out and about. And, as experienced professionals, they're hardly going to be on edge. It's not remarkable that they're relaxed, but perhaps it is remarkable that, unlike this country, the players aren't consumed by the game. If New Zealand were an international player, or there were an international player with New Zealand's psyche, he'd spend most of his time sitting on the edge of his bed, teeth grinding, brooding on what might have been and what must be, next time.

The country is almost certain to be brooding over the tweak in McCaw's back. According to Graham Henry, it isn't likely to threaten his participation: 'Richie has come through the hardest part of the training week and is good to go. Marty's presence is insurance just in case Richie's back should worsen unexpectedly. All the signs are that his back will be fine, but backs can be a little unpredictable so we've taken this extra step.'

'My experience is that I can play and train with this niggle and it usually comes right after a few days,' said McCaw. 'But in case it does something unusual, it's good for the team to be ready.'

If McCaw were to miss out, he would be a huge loss: he is, by some distance, the best openside flanker in the world, and one of only a select few who could honestly contest for the title of 'World's Greatest Player'. Even though Holah is also exceptionally talented – he would, almost certainly, start for the Lions were he British or Irish – McCaw failing to line out would be a massive boost for the Lions. Luckily for New Zealand, it looks like that won't come to pass.

***

Happily, Christchurch City Council isn't so consumed by the game and overcome by worry at the state of Richie McCaw's back that its officials haven't managed to put facilities in place for the travelling supporters. A secure car park is available, a ten-minute walk away from the hubbub of the town square. 'Lions Enclosure', roars the sign, with another, smaller one beneath it reading, 'Do not attempt to feed or place fingers through the wire'. When we got inside, parked and jumped out of the vehicle, a six-foot Maori security guard beamed a smile at us, extended his hand, and, in the manner of a Baptist preacher beginning a sermon, said, 'Welcome to New Zealand'. Once again, the country's hospitality is proved exceptional.

***

Once night fell, it was time to hit the town, fingers firmly crossed in case it turned out to be as quiet by night as by day.

'The only way to get over jetlag Oisín is to drink your way through it.'

'OK.' Little resistance there.

Even though Oisín, bless him, fell by the wayside early in the evening, by then I was in the company of two men who would more than make up for his premature departure. Ian McDermott was in school at the same time as me and is studying Finance in University College Cork. At the moment, he's on a round-the-world trip with his father, Mahon, a retired accountant. One might think that two accountants would be poor company. Far from it. I could hardly put my hand in my pocket all evening, partly because I was holding two drinks at a time but mainly because of the generosity of my new companions. Ian and I staggered on to a nightclub, Mahon having retired to their hotel to place his daily phone call to his wife, and, by the time I collapsed into bed at about half-three in the morning, I was the subject of an invite to a reception featuring two former Lions, Fran Cotton and Derek Quinnell, at the McDermotts' hotel.

Even though the city isn't packed to the gills with travelling supporters – tickets are not difficult to come by; indeed, there have been empty seats at every provincial game since Hamilton – the atmosphere is still special. In yet another Irish bar tonight, the premises erupted into song shortly before mid-night, the Welsh leading the rest through 'Bread of Heaven' and 'Land of my Fathers'; on the stage, a band banged away in vain.

Gentlemen All Round

Friday 24 June 2005, Christchurch

'You should have seen it,' Mahon was saying. He and Ian are staying in the same hotel as the team and, before we went upstairs to enjoy the company of Fran and Derek, we sat at the bar having a quiet drink.

Apparently earlier, Sir Clive and his wife, both looking a touch tired and drawn, arrived back in the lobby, on the way to their hotel room for some much-needed kip; but not if the Lions' supporters could have anything to do with it.

'It was unbelievable,' Mahon continued. 'He must have been stopped four times as he went across the lobby. With his poor wife.'

'What happened? Did he elbow his way through?'

'No. Not at all! He spoke to each person individually, took the time to talk to them and thank them. And when all that was done, he got in the lift with his wife.'

The Last Great Tour?

'A gentleman?' The words of Tucker, Dai and Justin – ''E's a gentleman' – were ringing in my ears.

'A gentleman is right. Only word for him.'

Increasingly, I've been impressed by the way the Lions' management conduct themselves. On Wednesday night, at the free drinks and canapés, the coaches and staff mingled freely with the invited British and Irish media. Bill Beaumont and Mick Cleary made speeches. One segment in particular of Beaumont's was memorable. 'I spoke at a dinner in Hove Rugby Club some time ago and I saw on the wall that M. Cleary was club captain for a number of years in the 1980s, so it is a great honour to be able to introduce Mr Mick Cleary, chairman of the Rugby Writers Association.' Not only was Beaumont's remark witty, it was also laced with humility – remember, apart from being the tour manager, he's the chairman of the Lions' Committee, a former international and successful businessman – which reflected well on him, just as Woodward's afternoon treatment of the fans reflected well on him. Something else about the head coach bears mentioning as well: when I spoke to Gordon D'Arcy back in Auckland, Woodward's name came up. D'Arcy almost said, 'Sir Clive ...' but, as soon as the first 's' was on his tongue, he swallowed it and just said, 'Clive'. Clearly, the players were under orders not to call him 'Sir'. Another tick mark for the knight. Gentlemen all round.

Fran Cotton turned out to be a nice chap too. He and Quinnell worked the room like old pros and, even when Mahon cornered the former England and Lions' prop with, 'Are you Fran Cotton?' he wasn't caught off guard.

'I certainly am,' came the reply. 'Are you from Ireland?'

'Oh yes, we are.'

Enter the All Blacks

And so began an anecdote which involved one of his former opposite numbers, Irish prop, Phil O'Callaghan, and the word 'gorilla'. Then, he was gone. But when we went to bed at least we could say we'd met Fran Cotton and Derek Quinnell. But as I had been in the toilet when Derek Quinnell was pinned down, I could only say that I met Fran Cotton.

Whatever about Sir Clive being a gentleman, he made another, eve-of-Test attempt to rattle the hosts. In a television interview, he repeatedly referred to the pressure of tomorrow night:

'I just look at it [media coverage of New Zealand rugby] and smile. The pressure that it must put on players and coaches here is intense. Everyone is talking about it [rugby] from the radio shows and newspapers, with some of it pretty informed comment and some of it, you just have to smile.

'The pressure on players and coaches is huge. It is everywhere similar to how football is back home. Sometimes when you build up so, so much, the pressure to deliver is extreme. It is a great word, pressure because you know some people thrive on it and sometimes some people think they thrive on it and when it really comes they are not as good as they think. That is why I am pleased with the Lions' team. We have very good people who have won World Cups. The Welsh last year in the Grand Slam really delivered. They played 40 minutes in Paris which I think is the best 40 minutes of rugby I have ever seen. Pressure was really on a few of the players and Stephen Jones, [Dwayne] Peel and Gareth Thomas just went like that. That was when I knew that the Welsh revival was really on ...

'I just think that you are at your best when the pressure is at its greatest and that is the true definition of champion sports-people. It is about playing under pressure as the importance of this game is huge.

'We have been down to your country ten times and lost nine so I am not putting us under pressure for that because we are not expected to win. I can understand why because you have to throw a team together last minute and they are all different. They have their quirks, their strengths, weaknesses, especially the English. To get them in a room and know you are going into a very hostile environment is a challenge.

'It is different, it is unique. I think romantic is a good word because it's romantic what we are trying to do in a way, because common sense says we should not win because we are up against the most professional team in the world in New Zealand. They have fantastic players and top coaches and they are a team. They have been developing as a team and we have just thrown this together.

'But I know I am here with a very well-prepared team and the best players from four countries and I think we have half a chance.'

Bring on tomorrow!

Singing in the Rain
Game 7: British & Irish Lions V New Zealand, First Test
Saturday 25 June 2005, Jade Stadium, Christchurch

New Zealand 21
Tries: A. Williams, S. Sivivatu

Enter the All Blacks

Convs: D. Carter
Pens: D. Carter (3)

British & Irish Lions 3
Pens: J. Wilkinson

Suddenly, Christchurch turned from drab and dreary to in-yer-face and oppressive. The morning dawned fine, sunlight piercing through the curtains, but it was no portent of what was to come. By midday, the temperature had fallen and by three o'clock black clouds were scurrying across the sky. Black, black, everywhere.

As one of the historic tram rides that tour the city made its way through the streets, All Blacks' fans appeared at every corner. The merest flash of red from the tram was enough to send them into paroxysms: 'All Blacks! All Blacks! All Blacks!' they chanted, again and again and again. The New Zealand landscape can change from quiet, laid-back and accommodating one minute to ugly, intimidating and aggressive the next; so too the population. The niceties had been put to one side: there was a Test match to win. There had been glimpses before of how seriously New Zealanders take the fortunes of the All Blacks. Nothing quite like this though. Black, black everywhere.

But a few hours before kick-off, the rain began to lash down on Christchurch, and, mindful of Sir Clive's 'warm feeling', confidence began coursing through my veins. The 7/2 odds on a Lions' win seemed extraordinarily generous. In the wind and rain anything could happen; most importantly, the ludicrously-talented All Black back-line might not happen. If the Lions' game plan was to strangle the opposition up front and rely on Jonny

Wilkinson to kick the penalties, they couldn't have asked for better conditions.

At the venue the Lions' supporters were in ebullient mood. The turn out wasn't quite as remarkable as that in Australia four years ago, when Martin Johnson was able to gather his team-mates together before the kick-off and tell them that they might as well have been playing at home, but it was an impressive show of strength from the travelling hordes. Though there was more black than red, and the eight Cantabrian members of the New Zealand line up were cheered heartily when the teams were read out, the chants of 'Lions! Lions! Lions!' in the build up carried up into the night air and out onto the drenched streets alongside Jade Stadium.

The roars reached a crescendo when Brian O'Driscoll led his side onto the pitch, but their volume diminished away to almost nothing by the time Joel Jutge blew his half-time whistle.

O'Driscoll, having led his troops in an unusual response to the Haka, the traditional war dance conducted prior to battle by the All Blacks, was carted off the field with just over a minute on the clock. Richard Hill limped out of the proceedings after seventeen. By then, Paul O'Connell was in the sinbin and the Lions were 6-0 down. Soon after O'Connell returned, the All Blacks struck for the first try: Ali Williams grabbed another of the visitors' malfunctioning line-outs and charged over the try-line from fifteen metres out. The Lions could hardly win a line-out: they only claimed four in the first half, two of which were 'Hail Mary' throws which missed the assembled jumpers and lifters altogether.

That Williams try though was a critical score. Bizarrely, it came from a Lions' penalty on the New Zealand ten-metre line.

Enter the All Blacks

For reasons best known to himself, Stephen Jones attempted the ploy which had worked so well against Otago and aimed a kick crossfield at Josh Lewsey. Quite apart from the fact that Lewsey, all alone and marked by some of the All Blacks' most dangerous runners, wasn't exactly bellowing for the ball, it was an appalling decision. Just when the Lions needed some respite and some field position, they had been handed the opportunity to kick the ball deep into New Zealand territory and put some pressure on the hosts. Instead they handed it back. Inevitably Lewsey failed to claim the ball, and the All Blacks poured upfield, their relentless advance only coming to a halt when Leon MacDonald was bundled into touch inside the '22. Shane Byrne's throw went directly into Williams' grasp and the second-row trundled over to make it 11-0.

There were throaty roars from the red-shirted fans when Byrne made a break down the touchline, but most of the cheers were plaintive, rather than hearty. Byrne himself summed up the first half when, after another line-out had misfired, he muttered, in tones of disbelief, 'fucking hell', close enough to the referee for his microphone to pick it up. Then, with five minutes to go before the break, only a last-ditch effort by Gareth Thomas denied Sitiveni Sivivatu. On two other occasions, the All Black winger was denied by the video referee when Jutge couldn't tell whether or not he had touched down legitimately.

Apart from that Byrne break, and a chargedown by Martin Corry, there was absolutely nothing for the Lions to sing about. But, for all that, despite having been comprehensively outplayed, they trailed by only eleven points. After the pummelling they had received, it was a more-than-manageable deficit. And so, when they returned to the field for the second half, the fans were close to full voice again. If only their heroes could score first.

If only. Just another 'if' to hang over the history of this Lions' Tour. Dan Carter, in tandem with Aaron Mauger, orchestrating affairs masterfully, kicked a penalty after three minutes to stretch the lead to 14-0. Then came the killer blow. Appropriately it was a try for the ages.

Off a scrum towards the right of midfield in their own half, New Zealand attacked. Justin Marshall took a few steps to the left before feeding Carter. He passed to Mauger, who half broke the tackle of Stephen Jones. Half a moment was all Mauger needed to pop the ball to his captain, Tana Umaga, who burst through in support. Umaga found himself in the clear but, with the rain sheeting down, and Josh Lewsey – moved from wing to full-back after Jason Robinson suffered a nightmare first half – to beat, his options appeared to be diminishing fast.

From the stands, Sivivatu could be spotted, free and in space on the left touchline, but at least 30 yards separated he and Umaga. The captain surely couldn't sling out that sort of a pass, could he? Not in these conditions, right? Wrong. With peripheral vision that bordered on the supernatural, Umaga picked out his team-mate and whipped the ball straight into his chest.

Thirty metres from the line and closing, Sivivatu needed no second invitation. He strode powerfully forward, to face down Lewsey. The Englishman, waiting for cover, in the form of Wilkinson, to arrive, showed him the outside right up until the point that Sivivatu decided to go inside. Lewsey fell sprawling to the ground, Wilkinson dived desperately, only to find himself clutching at thin air, and they both watched from the sodden deck as Sivivatu touched down.

Enter the All Blacks

Scrum-half Dwayne Peel must have been the most deject-ed Lion as they trudged back under the posts. It was his unfor-tunate error that gave New Zealand the scrum from which they launched the decisive attack. The Lions had been awarded a penalty and Peel, as he does to such great effect for Llanelli and Wales, elected to take it quickly and run at the opposition; this time, however, the ball fell forward from his grasp, the chance was lost, and an excellent decision was turned by his-tory into an awful one. If only. Carter converted, it was 21-0, and, even with more than half an hour to go there was no doubt about who was going to win. Black, black, everywhere. 'In those conditions,' said a dejected Will Greenwood, the replacement for O'Driscoll, 'you want it to be a three- or six-point game. Once it gets out to eleven, fourteen points, you really have to chase the game and it's very difficult.'

A chorus of 'Lions! Lions! Lions!' attempted to rally the tourists, but it was an impossible task and the supporters sensed it: the chorus didn't quite deserve exclamation marks this time. New Zealand sat back for the remainder of the game, inviting the Lions to attack them. In the wet weather it was vir-tually impossible to put any sort of width on the ball, and the series of crash, bang, wallop manoeuvres that the Lions con-jured up never stretched the hosts. Worse again, with the rain belting down, the All Blacks knew that the visitors would find it difficult to get the ball wide quickly. So the wingers were able to sit back, which prevented the Lions from kicking the ball in behind them and gaining field position. With their line-out – a notional strength – still in a state of disintegration and their scrum – another notional strength – being shunted this way and that, they lacked a platform to perform even the most basic functions, never mind anything more complicated. Even chasing the game was beyond them. Only a Wilkinson penalty, kicked after 55 minutes when they trailed by 21 points, salvaged some pride but the fact that the Lions opted to kick, rather than risk losing another line-out in pursuing the try they so desperately needed, showed how shell-shocked they had been.

It was a shipwreck of a performance, not helped by the loss of four key men: Malcolm O'Kelly, the Irish line-out specialist, was the first to fall, leaving the tour before it even began; then, Lawrence Dallaglio, the battle-hardened former captain of England, felt his ankle give way in the first quarter against the Bay of Plenty; O'Driscoll, the captain and would-be talisman; and Hill, like Dallaglio, battle-hardened and experienced. Perhaps that quartet, inspirational and experienced in equal measure, could have steered the ship away from the rocks. If only.

'We'll put our hands up and say we were all poor out there tonight,' said Martin Corry, who took over as captain. 'If you're a member of the British and Irish Lions, you want to have fond memories. Today isn't one of them.'

If there was consolation to take from the defeat, it was that, had the conditions been dry, the score might have been double what it was. Similarly, had the All Blacks played any meaningful Test match in the build up, the margin might have been a multiple of eighteen. 'They were right!' replied Graham Henry when he was asked what he had to say to those who had described his team as 'undercooked'. 'We were undercooked. We only had one game together as an All Blacks' team. We were undercooked and I think we'll improve.'

His assistant, backs' coach Wayne Smith, said the tight-five was the 'basis for the win, really', and it was hard to argue with his assessment. The second-row pairing of Chris Jack and Ali Williams was simply magnificent, in all aspects of the game. They destroyed the Lions' line-out, helped, of course, by the fact that there was little there to destroy in the first place, but more than that, they bullied their opponents. Paul O'Connell, who had been a contender for the Lions' captaincy, came off well and truly second best against Jack, now clearly the best lock forward in the world. His partner was mightily impressive too, not just for the try he scored but for the way he rose to the occasion; many in New Zealand had doubted his Test credentials, but Williams proved them all badly wrong.

'They were never in doubt in my mind,' said forwards' coach, Steve Hansen, of those credentials. 'I've said before that he could be one of the stars of this series.'

But it is wrong to single out individuals. The performance of the three-man unit in front of Jack and Williams was monumental. The much-vaunted Lions' tight-five was outclassed in every facet of the game. Hansen didn't gloat though: 'We felt that their tight-five was something they thought was a strength and, like any strength, you've got to attack it and take it off them. That's what we've tried to do. We've got to go and repeat the performance.'

By the time Woodward faced the press, the New Zealand media was in full sneer mode.

'What happened to the warm feeling you had, Clive?'

'Well, it was pretty cold out there tonight,' he replied, with disarming humility, before accepting the blame for the defeat and admitting a 'bad night', but calling for 'cool heads'.

Inevitably, someone asked whether or not the result was

down to New Zealand's greater ability to handle the pressure Woodward had spoken about so often over the past week. Inevitably the question was ducked.

His assistant, Andy Robinson, whose brief is the line-out, held his hands up too: 'I think we were completely outplayed. At times, we got our communication wrong and didn't get people in the air, on a number of other occasions, New Zealand read our movements very well and got jumpers in the air. I certainly hold my hands up and take responsibility for that. We have to work on that this week. It's a major disappointment, and also that we didn't put much pressure on them. Their line-out functioned well and that was a platform for them to win the game.'

'Just a few mistakes early on,' began O'Connell's assessment, 'a few missed calls, and the bad start just got worse as it went on. But we have to look forward, we have a few good line-out operators in the team. Every line-out has a day like that, so we just have to look forward and work hard preparing for next week.'

The body language of the players as they trooped out of the dressing room told its own story. Ryan Jones, who had come in as a substitute for Hill, exuded none of the confidence and effervescence with which he had regaled the press after his powerful display in Dunedin. In the bowels of Jade Stadium, with a semi-circle of Dictaphones like a succession of wreaths laid in front of him, his bowed head and cowed expression suggested a man who had been recently bereaved.

Greenwood too gave off the air of a shell-shocked man. 'It's time to stick together now,' he said, glazed eyes drifting towards an unknown spot somewhere between the floor and the top of the skirting board. 'It's not going to be easy but we have to make sure we do. People can't be forming cliques and slipping off into groups of their own. We all have to front up. We all have to ask some hard questions. And those questions will be asked. We know that a performance like that was unacceptable.' If only they had been able to win some quality possession, the Lions might have made it a contest. But that's another if only.

Even allowing for the collapse of their set piece, the Lions looked like amateurs against professionals. The handling, pace and sheer physical power of the All Blacks, even in the foul conditions, rendered a colossal gulf between the sides. The skill deficit the visitors are suffering from was most evident in the forwards: every member of the New Zealand pack, apart from being big and strong, is able to carry and pass the ball and step off either foot.

There was some respite for them in Henry's response to a questioner who wondered whether the Lions would be able to regroup after the defeat: 'Oh, for sure. They've got a lot of top-quality players: they'll come back.'

But already there were signs that the post-match analyses are going to be dominated by something else. When O'Driscoll suffered the injury that forced him out of the game, a group of Lions' fans nearby were clearly enraged by something that had happened. Umaga, who had apparently been close to the incident, refused to comment on what had occurred, fuelling speculation that something untoward had taken place.

Then, when asked what his captain's condition was, the Lions' head coach stoked the fires: 'He's not good. It took them 25 minutes to get his shoulder back in: it was a very bad dislocation and I haven't seen what happened. Richard Smith [the Lions' legal expert], who handles these things, is trying to get tapes from broadcasters, who tend to be, for some reason, quite slow in providing all the angles. I spoke to a few people who did see it and I want to see all the tapes.'

Woodward wouldn't comment any further, but his demeanour left those watching in no doubt: the O'Driscoll injury, which was in any case bound to cast a pall over the coverage of the game, would now come to dominate it. Black, black, everywhere.

New Zealand: L. MacDonald; D. Howlett, T. Umaga (c), A. Mauger, S. Sivivatu; D. Carter, J. Marshall; R. So'oialo, R. McCaw, J. Collins; A. Williams, C. Jack; C. Hayman, K. Mealamu, T. Woodcock.
Subs: G. Somerville for Woodcock 67, B. Kelleher for Marshall 67, M. Muliaina for MacDonald 68, R. Gear for Umaga 74, D. Witcombe for Mealamu 74, S. Lauaki for Collins 76.

Lions: J. Robinson; J. Lewsey, B. O'Driscoll (c), J. Wilkinson, G. Thomas; S. Jones, D. Peel; M. Corry, N. Back, R. Hill; B. Kay, P. O'Connell; J. White, S. Byrne, G. Jenkins.
Subs: W. Greenwood for O'Driscoll 2, R. Jones for Hill 17, S. Thompson for Byrne 56, S. Horgan for Robinson 56, D. Grewcock for Kay 56, M. Dawson for Peel 72.

Yellow Cards: P. O'Connell (12)
Referee: J. Jutge (France)

Spears, Smears and Terrace-top Theatre

Sunday 26 June 2005, Wellington

'He has,' announced a breathless text message from Will Downey, a radio colleague of Oisín's, 'a new angle on the O'Driscoll incident.'

'Well that settles it. We're going to this bloody press conference then.'

The Lions, for some reason – a conspiracy against unfit journalists, probably – are hosting all their media events in Wellington in the James Cook Grand Chancellor Hotel which, unless you know which way to go, involves a climb up the sort of sheer cliff wall at which even hardened mountaineers would turn up their noses. We didn't know which way to go. But we felt if there was a new angle, we were duty-bound to make our way up the endless steps which lead to the hotel.

Controversy over the O'Driscoll incident has been raging all day long. Television pictures have shown that Keven Mealamu and Tana Umaga upended the Lions' skipper in a ruck early on in the game. In rugby speak, it was a spear tackle, so called because the victim is thrust down at the ground like a spear being stuck into soil – or a prone victim. It's dangerous and illegal. And, to make matters considerably worse, Umaga didn't even extend the courtesy of enquiring after the health of his opposite number; it was left to scrum-half Justin Marshall to offer a sympathetic pat on O'Driscoll's back as the Irishman left the field. But, first things first. For a start, Gareth Thomas has been named as the new captain.

'Gareth Thomas is an outstanding player and a natural leader,' said Sir Clive Woodward after a meeting with the players this morning. 'After last night's match we are going to need big characters out there who can dig deep and show real fight and courage. Gareth is such a character. We did not play as well as we could or should have last night but I am in no doubt we can beat New Zealand. Gareth's leadership will be central to meeting that challenge.'

Thomas himself was honoured to be named as captain, albeit in circumstances which were rapidly moving from disappointing to suspicious. 'The whole squad is devastated for Brian. He is a great player and a great bloke, and to lose him as our captain is a big blow. The fact that he was put out of the game in the way that he was will fire every single one of us to get out there and do better in the Second and Third Tests than we did last night.

'Brian would be the first to say we have to get over the disappointment of losing him in those dreadful circumstances, and get on with the job of preparing for Tuesday's match and then the Second Test.

'It is an unbelievable honour for me to be named captain for the rest of the tour. And the New Zealanders better understand I will be around a lot longer than a couple of minutes. This is a squad of great players with a lot of fight in them and we are going to put the disappointment behind us and show the world what we are made of.

'It was fantastic being chosen for the Lions' tour in the first place. To be captain is beyond any dreams I ever had as a kid'.

The Lions' injured captain went to the lengths of issuing a statement from his hospital bed:

I am in no doubt whatever that it was deliberate foul play,

a double spearing. It was a cheap shot which has put me out of the tour. But the truth is it could have been an awful lot worse because they could have quite easily broken my neck. I was turned upside down, in the air and speared into the ground.

I tackled one of their players and then a ruck formed. I was pushing against Jerry Collins and two guys came in, they had a leg each, I got turned around in the air and speared into the ground. I knew straight away that it was serious. I had this searing pain that just wouldn't go away. I have never had a dislocated shoulder before so I did not know that is what it was but I knew instantly that I was out of the game.

I can hardly believe that I put so much into this and just got over a minute of play in a Test match. I have worked so hard for so long to get to this and to have it taken away by such a cheap shot leaves a really nasty feeling. I am really shocked that Umaga did that ...

It is very hard to describe any emotion at the moment. I just cannot put it into words. I am angry because it was such a cheap shot. It was one of the most dangerous things that you can do in our game. It is why spear tackling is banned.

On the airwaves, the controversy had raged all day. This morning, it became clear that Mealamu and Umaga had not been cited by the South African citing commissioner. It doesn't help that the citing procedure is somewhat arcane: the commissioner sits in a room and watches a video of the game and can independently cite players for foul play. More often though the respective teams complain of particular incidents which have upset them. The citing commissioner then reviews the footage and decides whether or not there is a case to answer. If there is a case to answer a judicial committee investigates the matter and, if a player is found guilty, levies an appropriate penalty. In this case, the commissioner has now returned to South Africa, having decided that Umaga and Mealamu do not have a case to answer; instead, he has cited Danny Grewcock, the substitute Lions' second-row, for an alleged bite on the finger of Mealamu. The hearing into that incident began this morning and, by the time Woodward opened this evening's press conference, an outcome was imminent.

What then would the Lions' head coach be showing us now? Considering that there was now absolutely no chance that either of the players allegedly involved in the incident can suffer any disciplinary action, he must have unearthed some extremely damaging footage.

By the time, breathless and sweaty, we reached the sixteenth floor the event was just about to get underway. And what theatre it turned out to be. Woodward stood in front of a large television monitor, pointer in hand, like a schoolteacher running through a geography video. Journalists were packed into the room; never mind standing room only, this was breathing room at best.

As the clip began to roll – we knew it was going to roll because Woodward told the guy with the remote control, 'If you could just start it rolling' – more than 100 necks craned, eyes squinting at the monitor. In slow motion, the footage began. O'Driscoll was in a ruck when Umaga and Mealamu arrived on the scene. They grabbed O'Driscoll and hoisted him into the air, at which point, as that camera was beginning to pan away, the view changed. O'Driscoll was upended in the air and, as that camera too began to move away, the two All Blacks left him drop into a heap on the ground, landing heavily on his shoulder.

'Phew', exclaimed the press corps, exhaling as one. Murmurs swept through the room as the tape ran again and again. Thomas, the new captain, could be seen on the video haranguing the touch judge and protesting vehemently. 'I was standing next to the linesman and I could hear him say, "Leave him alone, leave him alone, the ball is gone",' he explained. 'The whole play continued, I saw his legs go by and I'd heard the linesman's call, so I went after him once I heard Brian screaming.'

How anyone could have decided that there was no case to answer is unthinkable.

Tony Roche of the *Sun* probably summed it up best, and caught Woodward's sense of genuine outrage with a question-cum-statement: 'So you're saying the situation is that some bloke watches the video, on his tod, makes his decision and then buggers off somewhere you can't get a hold of him ... is that acceptable?'

Even though no action could now be taken Woodward was clearly outraged by what had happened; not just that his captain and star player had been removed from the fray but that nothing could be done about it. 'I'm not saying the two of them are guilty,' he said, 'but to ignore the incident and fly off is wrong. They should bring both of them in and discuss what happened. But we can't change what's happened and we'll just have to move on.'

Several times he repeated words to the effect that 'they

should at least be brought in to discuss the matter' and, on a casual viewing of the tapes, it is hard to disagree. While it's impossible to tell from the footage whether or not Umaga and Mealamu had intended to take O'Driscoll out, at very least, their side of the story should have been heard in a judicial setting. The fact that the citing commissioner disappeared without a trace and there is no remedy, no appeals' process through which the Lions can go, has clearly irked Woodward who, it later transpired, had gone to the lengths of visiting the Christchurch hotel of many of the travelling media and giving a midnight press briefing on the subject of the O'Driscoll incident. Of course, the citing of Grewcock probably didn't help his mood, although he did say – again on several occasions – that he was happy to accept whatever verdict the judicial panel reached on the matter. He reiterated time and again that the most important thing was that there be some sort of a process through which any unsavoury incidents can be investigated.

'If Grewcock has done something wrong,' he said, 'I'm delighted that it's being investigated and, if he's done something wrong, we will accept that.'

There was some suggestion that the New Zealanders had been provoked by the Lions' rather unusual response to the Haka. The Lions had removed their tracksuit tops, and stood stock still in a semi-circle, with O'Driscoll in the centre and Dwayne Peel behind him; as the Haka finished, O'Driscoll picked up a blade of grass and tossed it into the air. If nothing else, it was unique. Was it inflammatory?

'It was my idea,' was Woodward's explanation. 'I got an email from a Maori a few months ago and I actually ignored it until the opening ceremony we attended in Rotorua and I realised then that it made sense. The Haka is not performed until a piece of wood is placed on the floor and it's a sign of friendship to pick it up. So to show respect the chief goes out to the front with the youngest member of the tribe to show his respect. It's a sign of friendship, even up to taking our tracksuit tops off and not moving around. Even if the response to the Haka was taken the wrong way, I hope it wasn't related to what happened. I couldn't for one second think that that had been the case.'

Almost as soon as the press conference ended, misery was piled upon misery. Word came through that Grewcock had indeed been found guilty of biting Mealamu. A two-month suspension was handed down. 'I am obviously very disappointed at the outcome of the hearing,' the second-row said in a statement. 'I do not agree with the decision, because, as I argued to the hearing, I did not bite the player at all. But I have to accept the decision and that means for me the tour is over. I have decided therefore that I will return home as soon as I can. I think that is the best course of action for me and for the tour. I now hope that the rest of the Lions' squad go on to win the next two Tests. I'm just sad that they will have to do it without me, and wish them all the very best for the remaining matches on the tour.'

Then the whispering began. The general media consensus was that, even though the spear tackle on O'Driscoll was unfortunate, Woodward was deliberately stirring things up to deflect attention away from the performance on the pitch last night. Lions' legend, J.P.R. Williams, described it as 'pathetic' and there were few disagreeing. In the toilets, another former Lion-turned-journalist, Paul Ackford, agreed that the focus on the unfortunate injury to O'Driscoll was a 'smokescreen'.

'Oh, of course,' he chuckled as he dried his hands. 'We'll find out next Saturday, won't we?'

Entente Cools Down

Monday 27 June 2005, Wellington

This country is bigger than it looks. My odometer has gone over the 3,500 mile mark – not bad for four weeks' worth of driving – and my mood certainly hasn't been helped by yesterday's travails. Having had only a quick glance at the map before I booked my return ferry from the South Island I reckoned that Picton, from where the ship would depart, was only a short hop from Christchurch. In which case a 12.30pm sailing would be just right: have a few celebratory drinks on Saturday night – this was back when I too had succumbed to Sir Clive's 'warm feeling' – reasonably early – before dawn, that is – to bed, and a leisurely two-hour drive up the coast.

By the time I had made my way down to Christchurch a fortnight earlier, a journey which took in the region of five hours altogether, the error of my ways had become clear but, of course, by that stage, changing the booking was nigh-on impossible. Hence a 6.30am wake-up call and a 7am departure. Add to that five-metre high squalls on a crossing which allowed further rumination on the Lions' disastrous showing the previous night and my mood was none-too-good.

For all that, unlike the most of the print media, I remain sanguine about the Lions' chances. The New Zealand press predictably took as much delight in mocking the efforts of the head coach – for whom they have a very acute antipathy – and his Lions as they did in celebrating the performance of their own team. But the British and Irish media also delivered a damning verdict.

The venerable James Lawton, writing in the *Independent*, described Saturday night's 'rubbish' as a 'dire misadventure'. Stephen Jones of the *Sunday Times*, perhaps the journalist who is closest to Sir Clive, wrote that 'catastrophe upon catastrophe' amounted to the 'worst Lions' performance in 22 years'. The *Sunday Telegraph*'s Paul Ackford said the scenes which unfolded in Jade Stadium were 'carnage', that the result was a 'savage indictment' of Woodward's decisions, and labelled the Lions' head coach 'a chump'. In the *Guardian*, Austin Healey, a 2001 tourist who was a vociferous critic of Graham Henry's coaching on that tour, commented that Woodward had been 'completely out thought'.

Ouch. Everywhere, Sir Clive is being pilloried. Few would now disagree with Laurie Mains' pre-tour assessment of the Lions' party as the 'worst ever'. On Saturday night in Christchurch, as the night moved on, the Lions' fans continued to drink and make merry as the rain teemed down but the joviality of the afternoon had been chipped away at by melancholy. They weren't downbeat but they were bowed.

The verdict of the fans and media was the same: Clive got it wrong in his selection and in his tactics. Why was Henson left out? Why was Wilkinson picked at centre? Why was an out-of-form Robinson put in the firing line at full-back? Why did the Lions try from the start to play a kicking game? Why was the All Black front-five underestimated? Through all the criticism ran a particular theme: why couldn't the Lions play like Wales? Mike Ruddock, who took over as coach after, oddly, Henry and

The Last Great Tour?

Steve Hansen, oversaw an expansive running game which saw them sweep through the Six Nations, winning the country's first Grand Slam since the heady days of the 1970s. Why couldn't the Lions do that?

The criticism is as harsh as it is deafening. It is virtually impossible to say that Woodward got it wrong tactically or selectorially on Saturday. If the Lions had any ball with which to contest the game, one might be able to quibble but the reality was that, by the time they got any possession at all, the game was over. Will Greenwood's words bear repeating: 'In those conditions, you want it to be a three-or six-point game. Once it gets out to eleven, fourteen points, you really have to chase the game and it's very difficult'. At 21 points, to which the margin had been extended by the time the Lions got any serious amount of ball, the game was over. Simply, the Lions lost because neither their scrum nor their line-out functioned. How anyone could upbraid the head coach for tactical errors and selection mistakes is a mystery. Yes, the display was shambolic but when the line-out and scrum don't work, it's not hard to see why. When a pipe bursts in your building, you don't sue the electrician.

As for playing like Wales, one can understand why Woodward was reluctant to go down that road. Since Henry took over in 1998, through Hansen and now Ruddock, Wales have been moving towards playing the type of game they now play. That's about seven years; the Lions had seven weeks. In that space of time, building a solid, possession-based game is much more realistic; remember also that competing against a side as talented as New Zealand necessarily involves having an excellent defensive system, which is much easier to put together if a team plays in the Woodward style rather than the more chaotic Welsh style.

And, Woodward might legitimately ask, when was the last time Wales beat the All Blacks? Answer: 1953. And when was the last time Wales beat the All Blacks in New Zealand? There's no answer to that, the reason being that they've never done it. Sure, the current side ran them close in Wales in 2003 and in 2004, losing by only a point on the latter occasion, but neither time did they honestly look like winning. Woodward's England on the other hand not only won the 2003 World Cup but also beat the All Blacks on their own soil the preceding June; in fact, his England side had developed a seriously good record against New Zealand. Is it any wonder then that Woodward made the decision he did? And is it fair to hang a man for making a decision?

To the O'Driscoll incident then: the reaction of the New Zealand media and public was summed up by the front-page headline in the *New Zealand Herald* this morning: 'All Blacks win, Sir Clive spins'. The injury has dominated the post-match coverage, but it's hard to see how that could have been avoided: the Lions' captain being stretchered off in suspicious circumstances after a couple of minutes? Only one place that was going to end up: the front page. Even if Woodward had made no attempt at all to convince the world that Tana Umaga and Keven Mealamu had a case to answer, it would be the focus of intense discussion; the only problem for the Lions' head coach is that, with Alastair Campbell perceived to be pulling the strings, anything he says can be spun as spin.

Overall, the criticism is harsh. Woodward though is possessed of an immense self-belief which sometimes comes across as arrogance and makes him readily irritable, if not detestable, to outsiders and to those who prefer not to try and understand the complexities of his character. Thus, criticism rains down on his head. It is hard to communicate the depth of the loathing New Zealanders have for him. Perhaps even in his own country people view him with suspicion. Certainly, the British and Irish media have proved only too happy to give him a kicking. His response will be interesting.

Part Seven

Last Stop in the Provinces

BLACKOUT

Monday 27 June 2005, Palmerston North

Already the demeanour of the hosts has changed. That of the tourists has too. On the couple of hundred kilometres' drive from Wellington to Palmerston North today, no campervan coming in the opposite direction flashed us; no campervan driver waved; none made even the most cursory attempt at eye contact. This was in stark contrast to the behaviour that the legions of campervan pilots have exhibited over the last few weeks: if a van didn't flash or wave, it was most likely being driven by a swarthy man of Southern European origins or a similarly distinctive visitor from the Orient. But after the depression of Christchurch a pall has fallen over the travelling contingent.

The same cannot be said of the natives. They have changed almost beyond recognition. Before, being flashed by a New Zealand driver was rare; indeed, if a car's headlamps did light up there was usually a Lions' replica shirt behind the wheel. On today's journey, some went to almost death-defying lengths to acknowledge us. A lorry driver pointed in our direction; a motorist flashed; another driver waved; and, swerving violently, a motorcyclist gave us a one-handed salute. It was not the friendly, 'We're in this together' greeting that the touring drivers have been giving to each other though; rather, New Zealand was saying, 'Welcome to our country ... you're definitely welcome now because your rugby team isn't much bloody good'. In gardens along the route, people had erected signs: 'Hey Clive', one read, '21-3'; many more such signs, referring to the First Test result, were dotted along the roadside. The Lions were humiliated on Saturday night and no one is going to be allowed to forget it.

When we parked in Palmerston North, we immediately ran into a man handing out leaflets. 'You want some pies while you're here?' he cackled, wizened face bursting into a smile.

'Yeah, sure.' It would have been rude to refuse the flyers.

'Oh, you're Irish, are you?'

'Yeah.' Hard to get out of that one.

'What about your boy on Saturday, then?' I looked at Oisín. Here comes something about O'Driscoll. 'That bloke just didn't fancy it, eh? Pretended his shoulder was done for. Too cold for him.' We shrugged and, with another mad cackle, he was off.

***

The 'Barmy Army' concept is getting an unmerciful thrashing from the fans. Most Lions' supporters – virtually all the Celts and even the majority of the English – react with violent spasms and paroxysms of rage dotted by the f-word and various other expletives whenever the phrase is mentioned.

'We're Lions' supporters, not the bloody "Barmy Army",' runs the typical response. The New Zealand media, perhaps unaware of how easy it is to get people's backs up but in all probability looking for a good catch phrase, has been only too eager to employ the term, which has only worsened the mood of the travellers. Everywhere they go, they are confronted by natives who, having read the press, listened to the radio and watched the television, think they are dealing with the 'Barmy Army'.

Not so. As you'll recall the 'Barmy Army' was the description given by the Australian media to a group of English cricket fans; the fact that it was English fans alone who were given the moniker makes it highly unlikely that any Scot, Welshman or Irishman will ever embrace the term – even the English have misgivings; after all, the Lions is about a group of countries coming together as equals where nothing, not the team selection, management or even medical staff is dominated, much less monopolised, by one of the four. It's hard to think of anything as odious to the concept of the Lions as the 'Barmy Army'. As the Essex boys put it, all the way back in Stratford, 'It's a load of bollocks, innit?'

The suspicion of most is that the 'Barmy Army' is largely a commercial venture, despite the protestations of its self-styled leader, Freddie Parker. He claims he's doing it all purely for the love of the game; however, it's hard to believe he's selling T-shirts and other merchandise for the hell of it. They certainly aren't retailing for free. Parker's view of the tour probably isn't widely shared either. In his weekly diary in a Sunday tabloid, he describes the 'Barmy Army's' exploits, which, apparently, involve drinking all day, going to bed, moving town and drinking all day again. Which couldn't be more at odds with the actual experience: hundreds of red jerseys have trotted in and out of museums and other traditional tourist destinations over the past four weeks. Sightseeing and the enjoyment of local culture have not been neglected. Not everyone is drinking twenty pints a day; another reason the supporters' backs are up.

The decoration, in coloured sticky tape, on one campervan just about sums it up: 'Irish Army', it reads, 'Not Barmy'.

***

At the pre-match press conference in Palmerston North, the venue for tomorrow night's clash with Manawatu, the weakest of the sides being faced by the touring Lions, I mentioned the alteration in the natives' demeanour to second-row, Simon Shaw. Having toured here before with England, the second-row appreciated the change.

'It's become a united front,' he said, speaking of the cama-raderie in the camp. 'When you're combining different cultures and different countries, there needs to be a common aim, a goal and obviously, the goal is to win Test matches. But also, coming to New Zealand and touring helps to bring the thing together pretty quickly, given the kind of publicity we've had, the passion of the people anti-us, Lions-bashing. It brings things together pretty quickly. Actually, there's not much need-ed from the management point of view to create that. We're basically battling against a whole nation here, everyone's knowledge of rugby is that thorough.

'New Zealand's one of those places you just cannot

escape it. You tour Australia and South Africa and it's not the same. In Australia it's not that big a sport obviously, but in South Africa, which would be a comparable place where the passion's high about rugby, they're a different kettle of fish: they're a friendly nation, a very welcoming nation, and they tend to take it out on you on the rugby pitch, whereas New Zealand gets in your face the whole time. You're not just battling against the All Blacks, you're battling against every person on the street, every paper and every television programme.'

Can it hurt, the relentlessness of it all?

'It's pretty relentless but it's got to hurt, in a way, to bring out the best in the side. I think perhaps we haven't got offended enough by it!'

Whatever about the sudden shift in the climate on the streets, the Lions desperately need an impressive performance tomorrow night to help erase the disappointment of the First Test. They have yet to put in a comprehensive display, failing fairly miserably to do so last Tuesday evening in Invercargill but against Second Division opposition in Manawatu, they'll fancy their chances this time.

'Tomorrow's all about going out and putting in a really strong performance,' Shaw said. 'We haven't done that as yet on the tour, I don't think. The New Zealand press have been dogging us a fair bit – but you look back on the performances and sometimes understandably so: we haven't really come out of the blocks and put away a side.

'I think in most of the games so far, we think that we should have been fifteen to twenty points better than we have been. We've only been coming out in the end of the games, the last fifteen or twenty minutes and showing our strength, and that's the challenge: get out of the blocks and perform for 80 minutes. Judging by the training sessions over the past week, we couldn't be better prepared.'

If morale is low though the chances of putting together that top-notch display will fall.

'Obviously there's a fair bit of disappointment,' said Shaw of the mood in the camp. 'We watched the game and we've spoken about it as well but at the end of the day we didn't perform on the night. We were nowhere near where we needed to be. It's for us to put the tour back on track tomorrow night. A lot of guys playing tomorrow night would have felt, first time around, perhaps a bit aggrieved that they didn't get a chance, having put in some strong performances. It gives them another opportunity to stake a claim. Perhaps more a chance of being on the bench really but a strong game and we force the selectors to select us.'

It will also be critical for players to keep their individualism in check tomorrow night, making sure they focus on the task in hand rather than on improving their chances of making the Test team. In Invercargill, too much sevens-style rugby and individualism left the Lions unable to subdue moderate opposition. One of the Lions who would be renowned as a gifted individual is full-back, Geordan Murphy, and he's as good a person to ask as any; if anything this week, is it a bit more dangerous, given that the team has yet to be named and those who play well against Manawatu can harbour realistic ambitions of lining out on Saturday?

Murphy though proved to be more of a team player than one might think: 'Any time you go out in a Lions' shirt, or any shirt for that matter, the aim is to do well for that team, not to do well individually. You'll mess up pretty severely if you're going out to make yourself look good. That's the focus that everyone takes into the game. After that, selection wise, it looks after itself.

'The first thing you have to do when you get the ball is think ... I suppose, you can always do something that will make yourself look good but that won't do anything for the team. That's always the first thing you think of. I don't know of any player who thinks as an individual first. What's the best thing for the team: all anyone here would do is worry about the team.'

The team. Or, more importantly on a Lions' tour, the squad. And here's the big question: will they be able to bounce back?

'We had the best session of the tour so far yesterday,' Shaw said. 'That's not just my opinion: the coaches have been saying that as well, that it was the sharpest, most cohesive session of the whole tour. Most of the guys who played turned out as well, which shows the huge amount of unity within the squad, to prove to ourselves and show New Zealand that we're a better side than we showed on Saturday.'

Which bodes well for the Lions. Not so much for Manawatu, though.

Game 8: British & Irish Lions V Manawatu
Tuesday 28 June 2005, FMG Stadium, Palmerston North

Manawatu 6
Pens: J. Hargreaves (2)

Lions 109

The Last Great Tour?

Tries: S. Williams (5), M. Cueto (2), R. O'Gara (2), M. Corry, G. Murphy, J. Robinson, C. Hodgson, O. Smith, N. Back, G. D'Arcy, G. Cooper
Convs: C. Hodgson (7), R. O'Gara (5)

In the Town Square this afternoon, they erected a big stage. The mayor was there, other local dignitaries too. People in suits came and watched as a woman in a town crier's hat read out a poem dedicated to the occasion. In the background stood a pair of inflatable goalposts: a children's kicking competition had been held earlier. All around, Lions' fans watched, bemused and enthralled in equal measure. Those travelling in campervans were directed to a special site a five-minute walk away from the town centre: the authorities had sectioned off half of one of Palmerston North's main arteries to accommodate the legions of tourists. The local paper, the *Manawatu Standard*, has almost doubled in size each of the past few days, bloated by supplements celebrating tonight's game and recalling those which have gone before it in the region. At four in the afternoon, the captains of industry had left their offices, to cheer the arrival of the British and Irish Lions. They even held a parade.

'This is bigger than big, for our region, for our kids and for our community,' said Manawatu coach, Charlie MacAlister, even after his charges had been soundly thumped. 'We've been visiting a few intermediate schools in the last couple of days; we've been to three schools. It's been huge. And that's the fabric of our country, I think, particularly rugby, just going to schools and being humble, looking at these young kids singing songs to you. We were getting a lot from the game so we just wanted to give something back. It was awesome for us but for the region as a whole it was extremely gratifying. The support was fantastic, there was heaps of red jerseys out there; I guess we were used as a vehicle to get things back on track as far as morale was concerned but I'm very happy with the boys and they're just chuffed. Not chuffed at getting their butts kicked but chuffed in terms of the experience. They might tell a few fibs about tonight, about how awesome they were!'

'If they're trying to keep the game in the communities, the roots of the game, where the fabric of the game is,' he continued, 'I think it's kinda cool to keep one or two games in the Second Division, to keep giving young guys dreams in communities like ours. We haven't been in the First Division for the last fifteen or so years, and the last week, with the Lions coming over here, has just given it a massive profile, in the schools and to the kids. It brings some of the grumpy old has-beens back into town as well, gives them time to hook up, and maybe they haven't seen each other for a wee while. I think it's great for everybody. Sure, we were the doormat tonight but if it's an excuse for everyone to hook up together and raise the profile of the game, that's a pretty good reason, I guess.'

Even though Second Division opposition was obliterated by a midweek Lions' side, the day was suffused by a sense of history. The world's only rugby museum has Palmerston North as its home address. Throughout the day, hordes of replica jerseys poured in and out, eschewing the town's hostelries and the pleas of the 'Palmy Army' – don't ask – to drink their town dry.

In three rooms of walls and cabinets, the history of New Zealand rugby was told, from the first All Blacks who toured Britain and Ireland in 1905, the forwards keeping fit on a 42 day sea voyage by stoking the boilers in their vessel, through the 1924 Invincibles, who won all 32 of the 32 games they played on tour, a feat unequalled since, and onwards to the latter-day heroes, the 1987 World Cup winners. The Bledisloe Cup – played for by Australia and New Zealand – was on display too alongside the 'log o' wood' that Canterbury defended with ease last week: the Ranfurly Shield. Jerseys from all the New Zealand provinces lined one of the walls; jerseys from every-where else were dotted around too. Lions' memorabilia made its appearance too; the legendary crop of 1971, the only tour-ing party from Britain and Ireland to win a Test series against the All Blacks, was not ignored.

The treasure trove of history and knowledge survives on donations, a derisory $5 entry fee and the efforts of a few dozen volunteers. 'There must be about 30 of us, I suppose,' said one. 'Bob [Luxford, the curator] is here all the time, but there's someone with him all the time. We work one day a month so there must be 30 of us!' By early afternoon, the cash boxes were bulging. 'Oh, we've had hundreds of visitors,' answered another. 'But we won't know how many until we've counted all the money!'

'The fabric of the game,' MacAlister said. He wasn't wrong. In the professional era, teams don't travel to provincial out-posts like New Plymouth, Invercargill and Palmerston North, some of which could certainly be described as far flung; at the very least, they're off the beaten track. It's sad that the 're-scheduling' of the touring party's community activity meant that the parade was Lion-less; the hard-nosed, cynical, metropoli-tan observer might have scoffed and turned up his nose at the kitsch, might have cringed at the small-town pride but deep down, he couldn't help but appreciate that the visit of the Lions means something special in a place like Palmerston North. In more recent times, teams like Manawatu have drifted almost out of the public consciousness, never mind in Europe but even in New Zealand: a once-proud province has long been plying its trade away from even the heights of the Second Division (though, due to the restructuring programme, they will compete in the expanded First Division next season). Ireland, England, Scotland or Wales wouldn't play them on a tour of the land of the Long White Cloud, but, uniquely, the Lions will.

The tourists find themselves fighting against an awe-inspiring sense of history. New Zealand people know their rugby like no other race. The game here is possessed of an almighty aura, a mystique. In fact, the Lions' management recognises that almost supernatural quality: they have directed themselves and the players not to refer to New Zealand as the All Blacks: to do so would only add to the 'mystique'. The storied history of the British and Irish Lions gives off a ghostly shade of pale in comparison; New Zealanders know intimately of the history of the first All Blacks, the great feats of the Invincibles and the sundering of all but one of the British and Irish ships that have landed on their shores. Only in South Africa – and, perhaps Wales – does rugby have a similar command over the hearts and minds of an entire nation but even the South Africans and Welsh don't see themselves as standard bearers for the game the way New Zealanders do.

And it's in a place like Palmerston North that the whole mixture crystallises. The small town pride which drags businessmen early from the office and the love of the game which fills a stadium is brought together by a deep sense and appreciation of history and tradition.

Unsurprisingly, Ian McGeechan, a man who has been on more Lions' tours than anyone, appreciates this: 'Part of the idea of the tour is that you want to take the rugby around different parts of New Zealand, which I think is important. I think the Lions' tour is almost unique now for the number of games played in a country and it is important to bring it to as many different quarters as possible. All we could do was play as well as we could tonight and we didn't want to underestimate or undermine what might be opposing us. We didn't and that is a big statement about the attitude of the players. Hopefully the Manawatu players got something out of the game, a bit of experience, and we've got rugby at Palmerston North, which is also very important.'

It was good to see that the Lions' players had an appreciation of the occasion as well, even after such a crushing victory. 'We did swap jerseys with the lads, as has been the case throughout the whole tour,' said Donncha O'Callaghan, withdrawn at half-time after another good performance. 'It's such a big scalp for these teams and when you play against them they're lifting their game, as we would do at home, in a provincial side, if we were lucky enough to play against touring sides. We'd play that game as well. You know it's such an important day in their lives and that makes it so important for us then as well.'

'Unfortunately we weren't able to show what we had out there,' said Manawatu captain, Nathan Kemp. 'We were a bit over-awed in the first half; it was just a huge experience for us, just the trip, coming to the ground and seeing the crowd. It's all pretty new to someone who's used to a crowd of 1,000.'

Last Stop in the Provinces

It was indeed a pity that a weak Manawatu side ran into a Lions' midweek team looking to put a derailed tour back on track. 'Everyone was really disappointed after the weekend and we just wanted to go out and put a marker down really, that we're a lot better than that,' was Michael Owen's view. 'We know we've got things to improve on and we wanted to do that tonight. And there were a lot of boys out there tonight as well who maybe haven't had the chance that the others have had and they had a point to prove as well.'

'I think it was the biggest statement possible from this team that they wanted to put some rugby on the pitch that reflected the players,' said McGeechan. 'I thought they played as a team tonight; I think, last week, we got individual and our performance suffered because of it. Tonight I think the performance got stronger because that was a team playing for each other.

'It was very important to have a game like that. To be honest, I don't care who the opposition were tonight: I think that team were ready. It was important that we started to put good performances together and I thought there were some good individual and collective performances out there. It's miles away from a Test match, but nevertheless, to do what they did tonight, they had to play well. I thought the whole team performance was disciplined. You know, we could have had a scrappy 40 or 50 point win with a lot of mistakes and I think it was just the opposite: even with seven subs on, we kept our discipline about what we wanted to do. In that respect, it was important that we could show that we could do it.'

The Lions crossed for seventeen tries in the process of scoring more than 100 points. Simon Shaw noted yesterday that a dominant 80 minutes had not yet been put together on the pitch by the tourists: tonight was the first occasion in New Zealand on which an opposing side had been comprehensively put to the sword. As such, it must have been a massive relief for the squad as a whole.

'You just had to look at the smiles on the faces of the non-playing group when they came into the dressing room,' confirmed McGeechan. 'There was a good buzz and I think it said everything, that. It was important we showed we could play some rugby. Everyone was delighted with that. We know we have to raise our game for Saturday, but I think we'll be in the frame of mind to do that.'

The atmosphere in the ground was jovial too. Along the arcades of the FMG Stadium, Lions' fans strolled, wearing T-shirts dominated by the face of Tana Umaga and emblazoned with a slogan: 'Wanted for the assassination of Brian O'Driscoll.' Inside, towards the end of the second half, the injured captain was serenaded by supporters: 'We love you, Brian, we do. We love you, Brian, we do. We love you, Brian, we do, oh, Brian, we love you.' And, to give him his due, Brian smiled and waved. With his good hand, naturally.

'Everybody was delighted,' said Charlie Hodgson of the dressing room scenes afterwards. 'All the boys who weren't playing came down and were shaking everyone else's hand. It was important for us to get back on track after the disappointment of the weekend and put things right.'

In addition, unlike the game against Otago, some players genuinely shone this evening. Shane Williams dazzled his way to five tries; surely he's first in line for a wing berth in Saturday's Second Test. 'I just did the best I could and there's no more I can do', he answered when asked how he thought he had played. 'It's not up to me now. If I'm picked, I'm picked and if I'm not, I'm not. I tried my best.' His modesty can't overcome the fact that, after such an impressive display, it's important for the Lions' management to reward the top performers, and he was the stand-out player. Geordan Murphy showed some nice touches at full-back, Jason Robinson showed some signs of a return to his pomp on the other wing, Hodgson again looked accomplished at fly-half, O'Callaghan and Shaw did well in the second-row and Andy Sheridan was again in destructive form at prop.

The totality of the display was the most important thing though which is why the non-playing players won't have been too upset that they might find their place under threat.

But as the crowd, red and green intermingled, drifted back into town to try and meet the challenge of drinking 'Palmy' dry, a provincial outpost so small that even the real journalists were staying in motels, the overriding sense was that Woodward, whatever about the miserable result in Christchurch, and regardless of how the Test series turns out, might just have been right about this being 'the last of the great tours'.

The final words probably belong to Kemp who, even after the ferocious hiding, seemed a man content and at ease with himself. 'They were awesome,' he said of the Lions. 'The boys stuck their heads in and wanted to swap jerseys and gear. They actually initiated it and came in with a set of gear and some of them with socks and jerseys as well. They've given us a full kit ... we were all scrapping in there, trying to get as much free gear as we could. It was an awesome experience. They weren't any bigger than us; they just came in, sat down and had a talk to us, wanted to know about us. They're really good guys.'

Manawatu: F. Bryant; B. Gray, J. Campbell, M. Oldridge, J. Leota; G. Smith, J. Hargreaves; B. Matenga, J. Bradnock, H. Triggs; P. Rodgers, T. Faleafaga; K. Barrett, N. Kemp (c), S. Moore.

Subs: B. Trew for Smith 44, C. Moke for Matenga 50, N. Buckley for Oldridge 53, I. Cook for Barrett 64, D. Palu for Hargreaves 71, S. Easton for Bradnock 76.

Yellow Cards: N. Kemp 29, S. Easton 78.

Lions: G. Murphy; J Robinson, O. Smith, G. D'Arcy, S. Williams; C. Hodgson, C. Cusiter; M. Owen, M. Williams, M. Corry; D. O'Callaghan, S. Shaw; J. Hayes, G. Bulloch (c), A. Sheridan.

Subs: A. Titterrell for Bulloch 39, B. Cockbain for O'Callaghan h/t, N. Back for M Williams h/t, C. Cooper for Cusiter h/t, R. O'Gara for Hodgson 50, M. Cueto for Robinson 52, M. Stevens for Hayes 60.

Yellow Cards: M. Stevens 74

Referee: L. Bray (New Zealand)

Holding Court

Wednesday 29 June 2005, Wellington

It has become a truth universally acknowledged that the focus by the Lions' management on the Brian O'Driscoll/Tana Umaga/spear tackle incident has been a massive tactical error. Keven Mealamu for some reason has been erased from the picture, and the spotlight has fallen on the All Black captain. It may not, however, have been the brightest idea. New

Last Stop in the Provinces

Zealanders, in talk radio shows and on the streets, think two things about this: one, Sir Clive Woodward is trying to distract attention from last Saturday night's performance; two, he's doing so by attacking 'our Tana', who won the Pierre de Coubertin award for sportsmanship when he went to the assistance of Colin Charvis after the Welshman swallowed his tongue in a 2003 Test match, and an all-round nice guy. It's fair to say that they ain't too happy about this: the mere presence of Alastair Campbell, famous for his spin-doctoring on behalf of Tony Blair, has had an effect too, making it much easier to label Woodward's attempts to communicate his outrage as devilish, hideous spin.

It's fair to say that Umaga's team-mates ain't too happy about this either. Of course, they won't say that out loud but their body language does. What sort of effect, Richie McCaw was asked, will it have on the Second Test? McCaw, sitting back in his chair, suddenly froze and fixed the questioner with a stare as brief as it was ferocious. It lasted only a split second but it spoke a thousand words. 'We've totally forgotten about it,' he lied.

The only alternative response from the country's media was a leading editorial – what else, in this rugby-mad country – in yesterday's *New Zealand Herald*: 'Can any winner of the Pierre de Coubertin Trophy have had such a dramatic fall from grace? Little more than six months ago, All Black captain, Tana Umaga, was picking up the International Committee for Fair Play's premier award at a ceremony in Athens. Today, in Ireland and beyond, he is being branded a "thug" and a "coward" for the spear tackle perpetrated by him and Keven Mealamu that dislocated the shoulder of Lions' captain, Brian O'Driscoll, invaliding the Irishman out of the First Test and the tour.

'It was at the very least a reckless and dangerous act. As such it was unbecoming of a man who won plaudits for stopping play to tend to unconscious Welsh captain, Colin Charvis, during a Test in Hamilton. It may even have been malicious. Although that it unlikely we do not know and possibly never will. We do know that the tackle, the on-field aftermath and the subsequent reactions by the All Blacks bestow little credit on New Zealand rugby ...

'O'Driscoll's anger seemed directed as much at the All Blacks' reaction as the tackle itself. Quite reasonably he suggested it should have been a matter of "common courtesy" for Umaga to check on the condition of the opposing captain before he was taken by stretcher from the field. It is indeed unfathomable that a player of the All Black captain's reputation did not extend that courtesy. It can only be surmised that, with the game barely into its stride when the injury occurred, Umaga's judgement was clouded by adrenaline.'

Other than those strong words though the quiet, steely determination that McCaw displayed has been fed by a relentless show of support by the New Zealand public and press. A more accurate picture of the reaction is painted by this excerpt from a piece by Wynne Gray in the *Herald*: 'Move on, Sir Clive. Move on quickly, unless you want to alienate New Zealanders more than you have. It may be a play for the British and Irish media's affection but even that appears to have missed the mark. It was an unsavoury incident, granted, but the flawed judicial system everyone agreed to work to on the Lions' tour does not cater for any more action. No smokescreen or diversion about O'Driscoll can hide the greatest truth about

Last Stop in the Provinces

Saturday. The All Blacks played some superb rugby, the Lions were awful. Explain that to your fans and supporters. If you bang on about the alleged spear tackle much more, you risk a huge backlash.'

The man at the centre of the storm had, before today, not spoken about the injury to his opposite number. It was inevitable that he would have to do so at some stage and so, at the All Blacks' pre-match press conference, the team's media manager, Scott Compton, presented Umaga to the waiting press. 'I've been looking forward to meeting you guys,' he joked. Questions were not, as has been usual on tour, allowed to come at random from the floor.

'I'll call on people to ask questions,' said Compton. 'Just to keep things moving along.' Or, more realistically, to keep control.

'Obviously it's disappointing what happened to the Lions, losing Brian O'Driscoll and Richard Hill,' Umaga began, speaking in a slow, methodical style that allows him to measure his words and, when possible, imbue them with humour. 'It takes away some of the stars they had. I must say, the way I play I play hard, but in all my games I try to play as fair as I can. That's just the way I am. I don't have much else to say other than that. These things happen.'

Why, though, did he not make an immediate apology? Why did he not go over and see if O'Driscoll was OK?

'I feel I had a more important role to my team at that stage. I had to try and keep them together. It being such a lengthy period we had to sort some things out. First and foremost my allegiance is to the All Blacks. That's just the way it is.'

Has he approached Brian?

'I asked some of the Lions' players how he was, but I don't

try and do things through the media. We'll try and make contact and when we do, we will. Again, that's just how I am.'

Was the team offended by the Lions' response to the Haka?

'Not at all. It caught us on the hop. It was just different.'

Has he been disappointed that the media has covered this story at such great length?

'It has been a little bit annoying, especially with what our team achieved on Saturday. I feel more disappointed for our boys. The performance they put on, especially our tight-five, they deserved more. But what can you do? I can't tell you guys what to do.'

What of yesterday's *Herald* editorial? Does that hurt the game?

'I think it does. I believe we try and raise standards. I understand that we are role models to a lot of people in this country, through the standing which we have here. When that is attacked, that's the most disappointing thing for me.'

And that was pretty much that. The next questioner was told by Compton that he was 'going back over stuff we've already covered' and the players dutifully filed in to do their bit.

In another show of strength, the All Blacks' management today made three changes to the starting line-up. While the forward pack is the same – 'We've seen our forwards make big strides in the last couple of outings and the selectors believe they should have a chance to raise the level of their performance even higher,' was Graham Henry's explanation – the backline has been altered. Byron Kelleher replaces Justin Marshall at scrum-half, Rico Gear comes in on the right wing for Doug Howlett, who is axed from the squad in favour of Ma'a

Nonu and Leon MacDonald drops to the bench, replaced by Mils Muliaina.

'There is nothing separating our top players in some positions,' Henry said. 'The changes acknowledge the great form of some All Blacks who missed out on selection last week. Going forward the team needs to have more than one player ready for international rugby at every position. It is part of our strategy to develop and maintain that depth.'

'The boys were happy after last week,' said McCaw, 'but the job is only half started. We've got to play better on Saturday because they'll be hurting and when a team's hurting, they're going to throw everything at you. They've brought in a few new guys and they'll bring it to a new level. We have to do the same.'

Also the changes show that the All Blacks have remarkable strength in reserve: 'It shows the depth in the squad,' McCaw acknowledged. 'All the new guys are very excited about being involved and they've really got stuck in. It's brought the intensity up a notch. Healthy competition is good for any side, if it's handled right. It makes you try harder in games and in training and I think we're starting to see that on the pitch.'

In a corner of the room Dan Carter was also diplomatic about the Lions' chances: 'We know what they're capable of. We know they've got a good team, so we're not reading too much into last week. We're going to have to lift our own game to come out on top. The great thing about a Lions' series is to play against the best and see where you are.'

But whatever about the personnel on which the New Zealand selectors can call, the way the team plays the game is important too. Where the Lions look to slow things down and play a set-piece, possession-based game, their opponents aim to run the ball at almost every opportunity. Of course, in the Test arena, it won't always be possible to do so; nonetheless, there appears to be a significant divergence in the approach of the respective coaching teams. So the conversation turned to styles of play and the future direction of the international game. Stuart Barnes, a former England fly-half and Lions' tourist turned Sky Sports commentator and *Sunday Times* analyst, and I had Carter pinned down.

'We have a pretty strong attacking attitude,' he agreed. 'Keeping the ball alive is a big part of our game. But we're in it to win, not just to entertain. If we get a chance, sure, entertaining is part of our natural game but it's very much secondary. Definitely it's a style of play I like to see as a back but you need the players to do it. In New Zealand, the players' natural instinct is to have a crack, offload and play with an attacking attitude. That's probably the way rugby is heading, depending on the conditions. I mean, the Lions have definitely got the players to play that sort of game. Their back-three are all extremely dangerous runners.'

Diplomatic at the end but clearly the man has indicated his preference. And what's harder to defend against, in his experience? Is it the high tempo at which, say, Wales, play or the slower game the Lions seem to be embracing, the 2003 style of England? Carter was in no doubt.

'The high tempo, where they take it to us. It's quite hard because everything is happening so quick and makes it tough to defend against. If the 2003 style is done effectively though it's hard to combat. Both styles are dangerous if they're done well.

Last Stop in the Provinces

'You have to play to the conditions. Last Saturday we didn't get much of a chance to run and hopefully this week we'll be able to throw it around a bit more. A Test match is different to, say, Super 12. Territory is much more important, there's more kicking – and you have to do it – but you still look to move the ball.'

One more response is worth mentioning. Carter confided that he classes opposing openside flankers into two types: the smashers and the stalkers. The smasher gets in his opponent's face and tries to ruffle his plumage; the stalker, well, stalks. Lewis Moody, the chosen one this weekend, is very much a smasher.

'I don't mind playing against a smasher: it creates more opportunities. Thanks for the warning! I'll have to look at his previous games, what he's strong at and where opportunities may arise.'

Carter's body language as he answered was fascinating. He barely moved a muscle as he spoke calmly and surely about his opponent, giving off a breezy air of confidence. Clearly, he doesn't know much about Moody but the relaxed way in which he answered suggested that, come what may, Carter will be ready for the challenge. Imbued with total self-belief, he would back himself.

That is the other story of the First Test. The Lions let themselves down, of that there is no question, but in the conditions, New Zealand were awesome. They caught the ball as if there was glue on their hands and passed it as if by merely holding it in their grasp they had dried it. Where the Lions fumbled and groped, like a nervous teenager working his way towards second base for the first time, the All Blacks displayed the hands of an experienced Lothario. It was Don Juan versus Adrian Mole and the practised master, with grace and élan, won a decisive victory. Self-confidence and a steadfast belief in their own ability allowed New Zealand to overcome the elements and play sublimely. Almost everything they did when in possession worked; almost every decision they took was the right one. Had the night been dry, the margin would have been double what it was.

And then, there's the ability to change things. Just to make the squad a little more jumpy, just to keep them on their toes, there are three new faces in the line-up. A remarkable show of strength. It's worth betting that the confidence and belief won't have been even slightly damaged by those changes. As McCaw put it, it's time to take it to another level again.

***

'Last Saturday night, for someone who's been involved in coaching for a very long time, I'd put it top of the list of most disappointing nights I've been involved in. Prior to kick-off, going in to the game, I passionately believed I'd got lucky again, picked the right team, especially at ten and twelve when I saw the conditions and in terms of the line-out team we'd chosen. Then to see it all unfold was very, very disappointing for everybody involved. Now, we just have to look forward to Saturday night.'

No prizes for guessing the identity of the speaker. Sir Clive Woodward was a humble man as he addressed the media.

'Last Saturday night, things didn't go right from a Lions' point of view. It's not a development tour where you can spend a week training to put it right, so I don't think that was the appropriate step. We have made changes and it's important that we realise that these players have a chance to get everything back on the road. It was time to shake things up. It's disappointing for those I've had to leave out – there wasn't a single person in the team who didn't try their best – but Saturday night was a disappointment that I have to take responsibility for. So I have changed the team and I passionately believe we can win this game but we've got to really front up, which we obviously did not do, especially in certain aspects of the game, in the first Test match.'

The team that lined out in the First Test has been radically altered. Seven players have been axed from the starting XV. A new back-row has been picked *en bloc* and, in the backs, only Dwayne Peel plays in the same position as he did last time. Shane Williams' performance last night saw him push his way in; unsurprisingly, Jason Robinson moves from full-back to wing, with new captain Gareth Thomas reverting to the centre in place of Brian O'Driscoll; Gavin Henson has, to the delight of the media, been picked also; his fellow Welshman, Stephen Jones, has got the chop though, with Jonny Wilkinson moving to fly-half; of the entirely new back-row that has got the nod, two, Simon Easterby and Ryan Jones, were not in the original squad but will start nonetheless alongside Lewis Moody; Donncha O'Callaghan will partner Paul O'Connell, his Munster team-mate, in the second-row; and finally, Steve Thompson comes in to hook instead of Shane Byrne who, along with Ben Kay, is scapegoated for last week's line-out shambles though unlike Kay, he still earns a place on the bench.

It's a drastic transformation and Woodward has certainly

shaken things up. It's not asked but the selection of a totally new back-row – although Jones did come in early on – when those who played in Christchurch spent most of their time working the emergency pump as the tight-five listed alarmingly, seems a trifle harsh. The question that is asked is, has he overreacted?

'No. I don't believe I have. With the Lions we're in a different situation. I was coach of England for seven years and you're always developing a team and you can step back and don't have to overreact, but I just thought that last Saturday night was so disappointing for everybody and I take responsibility for that. You could put your head in the sand but obviously we needed to make changes.'

The midfield combination was also queried, especially the selection of Wilkinson at fly-half, even though the Englishman did little wrong in difficult circumstances in the First Test.

'To be honest,' Woodward replied, 'if O'Driscoll hadn't got injured. I was very excited about Jones and Wilkinson, but we never got a chance to see that develop because we got wiped out in the line-out. We can talk all night about individuals and selection but really I don't think whoever played in the back division on Saturday night would have made any difference. When your line-out goes to pieces and you don't win your own throws, it's difficult to actually look at. But once O'Driscoll was out it didn't look right, playing Jones and Wilkinson.'

'It is very competitive,' he continued, 'but I do believe Wilkinson is the number one fly-half in the party. I had to choose one and that's what I've done ... I think he had a tremendous Test match. I think, if you look at what he did in the Test match, he was probably the best back on the field – in terms of the Lions – and he's physically and mentally up for it. I thought what he did out there, in difficult conditions, was outstanding. That's not based on reputation, but on what he did in the Argentina game, what he did in the Wellington game and what he did in the Test match. He's a big match player.'

Certainly Wilkinson did reasonably well in the First Test; indeed he was arguably the best of the Lions' backs although, in the circumstances, that counts as rather a booby prize. While he didn't play particularly well against Wellington, he did turn in a good performance against Argentina and, if nothing else, he is reliable under pressure. The writing on one campervan probably summed up the rationale behind picking him: 'Play it safe. Always use a Jonny.' If nothing else, once the ball is placed on the kicking tee, the Lions can be 90 per cent certain that it will be travelling through the uprights. It's worth remembering too that, in South Africa in 1997, the Lions played Neil Jenkins out of position at full-back because they could rely on him to kick his goals; that decision probably won them the Test series.

The most surprising thing of all was the humility that the Lions' head coach displayed. Contrary to many people's perception of him as arrogant, he took responsibility, admitted mistakes and took what he felt was appropriate action: 'It went wrong Saturday night. I hold my hands up; we can't change that. We've got to move forward very, very positively now and I've got to put out a very attacking team. It's a game we have to win ... If I was building a team, it would be different, but not to make any changes would send the wrong message to the whole squad ... When you play that poorly, you have to change things. I still look at that initial Test team and, in my head, it still makes total sense, in terms of the game we were going to play.

No excuses but if we'd won all our line-out ball, I firmly believe it would have been a different story that night.'

Of course, he is right: the result would have been different if the Lions had been able to secure some possession. They may not have won but it's hard to disagree with that assessment. Whether or not this drastic shake-up will have the desired effect, only time will tell. Woodward put an awful lot of stock in being able to prepare a team on the training ground; whatever amount of time he had with his initial selection, he's had less than a week with this combination. It is, as one of modern rugby's clichés goes, 'a huge ask'.

The players too were holding their hands up. 'I was just gutted really, for the thousands of fans who've come over to support us,' said the ever-eloquent Josh Lewsey. 'They've been brilliant and we felt we left a lot of people down. As a sportsman, you live and breathe on what you do on the field and if you don't do what you say you're going to do and you don't do yourself justice, then you really let yourself down. That's the feeling we had, so it wasn't an enjoyable experience but experiences like that, they do make you stronger. Let's hope we can come out and perform this week; if we come out and perform to our potential, we'll beat this team. We've got to have that belief. If we don't then we'll get stuffed.'

Wilkinson too admitted that the opposition deserved to win last time but that things would be rather different on Saturday: 'The All Blacks were outstanding last week and they deserved to win. We were lucky it wasn't more. What we have to do is get the ball and show that we can put what we've worked at on the training ground into action on the pitch.'

That won't be easy without the ball though. 'Everything that

248

possibly could go wrong did go wrong,' said Paul O'Connell of the line-out debacle. 'The calling system was understood before the game but there were a few overthrows, a few misses and a few where they guessed right. Once a few happened people panicked. It didn't help that they had eight men in the line-out constantly.'

If they do have the ball things will, obviously, be different. 'We hope to get into the game this week, get a good start, get our feet planted on the ground and get moving,' said Wilkinson. 'Last week, we didn't have the ball and we couldn't fire any shots. When you spend all the time defending against world-class individuals the pressure will tell. To get the best out of a team you have to get the best out of individuals and you can't when you're clearing ball, defending and scrapping.'

O'Connell drew on the past to find hope for the future: 'We've had days with Munster when we've been absolutely hockeyed, away in France, or in Gloucester and people are writing about the end of Munster rugby all week in the papers, that it's the end of an era. And then we turn in our greatest ever performance the week after ... We've been there before and we know, and the supporters know, that we can turn it around.'

'To the fans who were there,' said Woodward, 'we've all had to apologise, we've all had to cop it, but since that night everyone's been fantastic, against Manawatu, everyone getting behind the team.'

The mention of last night's game, of course, is inevitable and important. Another stuttering performance would have done nothing for the Lions' morale but such a comprehensive thrashing, even of poor opposition, must have been a boost.

'Manawatu aren't the greatest side in the world but to see

people giggling and laughing in the dressing room afterwards, it gave us a huge boost,' O'Connell confirmed. 'It's a pity we haven't had more games and more results like that. But it was a massive boost: the boys were excellent last night.

'Ian McGeechan said at the time the First Test team was announced that the midweek team's attitude would define and make the tour. We needed something big like that last night to lift the tour and the boys did it. They've suffered their own disappointments themselves but they really lifted it.'

It's hard to know if that boost will be enough. Compared to the New Zealand squad who were, like Carter, cool and relaxed, the Lions seemed a little more edgy. Their self-belief must have been blunted by last Saturday night; while the hammering of Manawatu might have been a much-needed boost, the All Blacks, buoyed by last week's display, required no boost at all. More of the same please, Henry will be able to say. The exact opposite please, Woodward will have to say: this is showdown time.

New Zealand: M. Muliaina; R. Gear, T. Umaga (c), A. Mauger, S. Sivivatu; D. Carter, B. Kelleher; R. So'oialo, R. McCaw, J. Collins; A. Williams, C. Jack; C. Hayman, K. Mealamu, T. Woodcock.
Subs: D. Witcombe, G. Somerville, J. Gibbes, S. Lauaki, J. Marshall, M. Nonu, L. MacDonald.

Lions: J. Lewsey; J. Robinson, G. Thomas (c), G. Henson, S. Williams; J. Wilkinson, D. Peel; R. Jones, L. Moody, S. Easterby; P. O'Connell, D. O'Callaghan; J. White, S. Thompson, G. Jenkins.

Subs: S. Byrne, G. Rowntree, M. Corry, M. Williams, M. Dawson, S. Jones, S. Horgan.

A City Closes In

Thursday 30 June 2005, Wellington

Wellington's Opera House is located in Courtenay Place, the thriving, bustling focal point of the city's night life. Currently, Mozart's epic opera *Don Giovanni*, is playing for the benefit of Wellington's glitterati, its opera aficionados and its fur-clad upper-crust. And yet still there's no escape from the oval ball. A sign outside reads, 'Don Giovanni, he scores way, way more than Jonny'. Even at the home of a city's high culture rugby intrudes. Is it any wonder the walls appear to be closing in?

At a McDonald's in the shadow of 'the Colloseum', the atmosphere was no less aggressive. As ever I was in neutral colours and avoided the worst of the abuse; an Englishman, clad in his Mike Burton Tour jacket, got both barrels from the rotund native behind the counter, sweating almost as much as he was sneering.

'Who's gonna win on Saturday, then?' he bellowed, in a tone that went somewhere beyond goading, rude and offensive all at once.

'Oh, the All Blacks.' The reply was laced with humility, which rather sent the native back on his heels, his chance to scorn the visitor temporarily whisked away. Foolishly the Englishman continued, polite again. 'I can't think where he's going with selection. I mean, Robinson?' And, polite or not, the native spotted a chink of light.

'He's crap,' the reply erupted. 'He should have stuck to

league. Crap ...' The native continued, giving a magnificently uninformed discourse on the merits of rugby league converts across the world, particularly in Australia. The Englishman meanwhile stole a glance at me and in the meeting of two pairs of eyes, there was the equivalent of a resigned sigh.

'Sitiveni Sivivatu, now there's a good winger.' At least he got his pronunciation right. And yeah, Sivivatu isn't bad. But with one win under their belts, and momentum with their boys, the population's smiles have, at times, turned into sneers, their pleasant greetings into harangues. Never mind the city, the country is closing in.

***

The 'war of words' that was so amusing while the Lions trekked around the provinces has now taken on a strange twist. There was no carping before the First Test about referees, or any of that. Instead Sir Clive Woodward spoke incessantly of 'pressure'. Indeed he even went on national television this night last week and talked about the p-word. And, just to make sure that nobody ignored his comments, they were sent out by the Lions' media team.

Unsurprisingly, the p-word hasn't featured much this week. Instead the focus has been on the O'Driscoll incident, which has become the new 'war of words'.

On Sunday, Graham Henry blew off suggestions that the injury to O'Driscoll was a major incident: 'The O'Driscoll incident didn't strike me as anything different to any other part of the game, quite frankly ... There was an incident in the game when [Martin] Corry deliberately stomped on an ankle and I thought, "Why hasn't that been cited?"

'It hasn't been part of my policy to try and find fault with the opposition, but it seems to be becoming part of the game today ... I think our guys are a bit disappointed in the reaction [to the O'Driscoll incident]. Rather than saying, "Well done All Blacks, you've played pretty well", there's been a major concentration on the Brian O'Driscoll situation. We're all very sad about Brian O'Driscoll, just like we were with Lawrence Dallaglio. That's a genuine statement. But for the opposition to concentrate on one incident which I can't see anything wrong with, it struck me in the face.'

It probably won't have helped Henry's mood that, just when everyone thought the controversy had died away, Lions' assistant coach, Eddie O'Sullivan, fanned the flames of 'Speargate' this morning. Umaga phoned O'Driscoll yesterday to speak to him about the incident and his recovery but according to O'Sullivan, didn't apologise: 'To ring up and say he was sorry that he got hurt, without offering an apology, is disappointing. It's like kicking a ladder out from under somebody and commiserating that they had an accident. He was part of it, Brian is still a bit upset about that, and rightly so. You can't change what happened but in the cold light of day he could have handled it better as the skipper. Whatever happens from here on in, this incident will colour the whole Lions' tour and that's unfortunate ... Going back to amateur days, when an opposition player was injured, the captain always inquired about his well-being.'

The O'Driscoll incident has dominated print and airwaves to such a degree this week that the Lions' complaints about the All Blacks' habit of putting extra men in the line-out have been virtually ignored: Paul O'Connell's comments yesterday about the New Zealand habit of placing more players there than is legal are unlikely to have impact on Saturday's proceedings. Instead, there's renewed focus on Umaga, something which will only get the natives' backs up even more. A tactical error on O'Sullivan's part? Another thing the controversy has overshadowed are some rather cryptic comments made by the coaching team this week. After the line-out turned from farce to tragedy on Saturday night, Andy Robinson said it was impossible that the Lions' code had been broken by the opposition, as the calls had been changed the day before. But then, during the week, Sir Clive Woodward said, when quizzed about this, that 'Robbo was just spoofing'. The mind boggles.

Amidst all this fuss, it's worth mentioning that Carl Hayman, the All Black prop, has been ruled out of the Second Test: he has an infected toe, which may not heal in time for Saturday week either, and his place is taken by Greg Somerville, with Campbell Johnstone promoted to the reserves.

Alla Fine del Mondo
Friday 1 July 2005, Wellington

This week, we've been upgraded to club-class, specifically, a pair of mattresses in an outhouse in Oisín's cousin's house. The van is parked outside for $4 a day. Happy days. Well, apart from the neighbours: down the street is some sort of base for environmental activists, with 'no-nukes' symbols painted on its outer walls. So, it came as no surprise to me to wake yesterday morning and find my 'Bush-Cheney '04' sticker – no surprise either that, once they see it, far fewer people initiate conversation with me now – half-ripped off the back of the campervan. It was, I believe, either one of the eco-warriors or Simon Lewis of the *Irish Examiner*.

'Is that your campervan outside? The one with the "Bush-Cheney" sticker?' he upbraided me after that fateful All Blacks' press conference.

'It is. Proud of it, too.'

'Bloody hell. I don't believe it.'

So I've taken to calling him 'Leftie' Lewis – 'So someone is left wing just because they're anti-George Bush?' he asked in disbelief. All of which gives him a motive. I hope he has a cast-iron alibi.

The campervan came to mind when I was in the national museum, Te Papa, this afternoon. Nineteenth-century emigrants from Europe – at a time when the New Zealand authorities promised money, work and good times for all to lure people into what was then an even vaster, lonelier place than it is now – spent several months on a ship in a space that measured about six feet by four. Hours turned into days turned into weeks turned into months as they sailed slowly towards a destination the Italians called, *alla fine del mondo* – at the end of the earth. They'd have committed grievous bodily harm for a campervan and murder, at least, for a floor in an outhouse. So, I'm not complaining.

Across the road from Te Papa is the Wellington Brewing Company, scene tonight of a reception for the huddled masses of the British, Irish and New Zealand media. Before that though there was a special media quiz. Alistair Hignell of the BBC, an MS sufferer, was the quizmaster, with all the proceeds going to the Multiple Sclerosis Resource Centre. The quiz itself was good fun, but Hignell's introduction had his audience in stitches.

Some background: my relay of Sir Clive Woodward's press conferences has cut an awful lot out. Oft-repeated is his assertion that this is 'a great tour', that everyone's having a 'fantastic time', that the squad is a 'fantastic bunch of players', the 'best-prepared Lions' squad ever', that they're 'really happy' to be in New Zealand. Every match, it goes without saying, is a 'fantastic game' and a 'great occasion.' But, more than anything else, Woodward has continually had to defend the number of Lions he brought with him.

'I'd like to welcome you all to this evening's quiz,' Hignall began. 'Perhaps the last of the great quizzes. It is the best-prepared quiz ever to see action in New Zealand. All the questions have been given a chance. They're all delighted to be here. They've gone out into the community and met the people, which is all highly positive. Some people have wondered about the numbers of questions we've brought, but, as I say, every question has got a chance and, really, there's no way of doing this with less questions. I'm sure tonight will be a great occasion, all the questions are really looking forward to it, and it will just be fantastic…'

Graham Henry was certainly not laughing. The focus on the O'Driscoll/Umaga incident had pushed him close to boiling point, especially yesterday's intervention by Eddie O'Sullivan.

'I'm sure it's part of the policy,' Henry said. 'Mr Campbell and his policy: he gets another person to say the same thing the next day. I guess it's very irritating if everybody has to read that stuff all the time, but I guess that's what he's paid to do.'

Would the thousands of words written about Umaga be pinned to a dressing-room notice board to whip the All Blacks into a pre-match frenzy?

'I think we've grown up a bit,' Henry replied. 'Besides, there wouldn't be enough space on the wall to put all that crap on.'

'I don't think there will be any complacency,' he continued. 'We have to go out there and perform. We realise we have a wounded Lion and that a wounded Lion is a difficult beast.'

Just how wounded is the question and will Woodward's running repairs be enough to allow them to extend their claws?

A Warm Feeling, or just hot air?
Game 8: British & Irish Lions V New Zealand, Second Test
Saturday, July 2, 2005, Westpac Stadium, Wellington

New Zealand 48
Tries: D. Carter (2), T. Umaga, S. Sivivatu, R. McCaw
Convs: D. Carter (4)
Pens: D. Carter (5)

Lions 18
Tries: G. Thomas, S. Easterby
Convs: J. Wilkinson
Pens: J. Wilkinson (2)

It had all the ingredients, didn't it? I thought the Lions played much better than they did last week. They put a lot of pressure on us to start. We weren't quite there early on; we didn't defend particularly well. But it just showed the character of the team to bounce back and play some outstanding rugby. I thought they were quite phenomenal today

All Blacks' head coach, Graham Henry

7.37pm

Disaster.

Since Paul O'Connell conceded that penalty, New Zealand have been chipping their way back into the game.

'We talked about them having a start like that, with passion and intensity,' Tana Umaga will say later of the calm way in which his charges responded. 'Obviously, they had nothing to lose, they were backed into a corner and the only way they could come out was fighting and they caught us on the hop in the first couple of minutes.'

Dan Carter has kicked two penalties but the 6-7 deficit doesn't reflect just how dangerous the All Blacks have looked. Gavin Henson had to bundle Rico Gear into touch as the winger's fellow backs attacked with improbable width; just when it appeared as if they had run out of players, Gear materialised on the sideline. He had been lurking there all along; it simply seemed that the ball had travelled so far across the pitch that it couldn't possibly have been the work of just six backs.

That was from a set piece. From broken play, the All Blacks have looked even more dangerous.

The Lions collect good lineout ball on the opposition '22 and move it to Gareth Thomas in midfield. He knocks on though and New Zealand pounce. Suddenly, Carter is running. Henson gets to him but can't hold him. Carter goes on and on into the Lions' '22. When he can finally go no further he flips the ball to his captain, Tana Umaga. Try! And what a roar from the crowd. Tana is redeemed! His magnificent performance in the

258

Last Stop in the Provinces

First Test had been overshadowed by the O'Driscoll saga, but now, it's 'Ooh, Ooh, Ooh-Maga! Ooh, Ooh, Ooh-Maga!'

Perhaps there will be something else to write about tomorrow?

7.46pm

Or maybe not. The Lions are like over-inflated tyres, so pumped-up that they're ready to burst. Several times, the touch judge has had to warn the referee to tell Steve Thompson to 'calm down'. Even his own team-mates – 'It's our penalty, Thommo, it's our penalty' – have been having quiet words: Thompson has a manic look in his eye and he's not the only Lion on the point of exploding. Wilkinson nails a penalty from the five-metre line and the margin is down to three.

7.56pm: Half-time

The screw has been turned. All the muscle and passion in the world isn't enough against sheer class. The bludgeon, yet again, is trumped by the rapier. The gap on the scoreboard is only three, again thanks to Wilkinson's left boot. But the deficit in individual brilliance is a gulf, a canyon, a continent.

Whatever.

A try-saving tackle from Thomas denied Byron Kelleher but from the next play, New Zealand scored another epoch-making try. Moving left from a scrum on the right, Carter fed Umaga, who shaped as if to try and bash his way through but, as if the ball were being caressed by manicured hands, popped a silky pass back to Carter. He passed to Aaron Mauger but the Lions seemed to have it under control. They had plenty of numbers in defence and, even though Gear was steaming across from his wing, it looked as if the attack was going to break down. Jason Robinson's tackle on Mauger brought the All Black centre to the deck but, as the Lions shaped to defend the next wave, Mauger kept the move alive. He flipped the ball to the onrushing Gear who, in a split second, hurled a pass, basketball-style, to Sitiveni Sivivatu, lurking on the left wing. Like last week, Sivivatu needed not to be asked a second time. 21-13. Carter missed the conversion, spoiling an otherwise flawless first half. He was to make up for it in the second.

Carter's Half

A penalty after a minute was routine. Muscle memory guided that over the bar. But the rest? The rest was a man achieving greatness; everyone else was but a spectator as Carter dominated the stage.

After three minutes, he added a try to his name. A quick tap-penalty by Kelleher initiated the move and, from a ruck inside the Lions' half, the All Blacks moved the ball right. Keven Mealamu, amidst the chaos, found himself standing at fly-half. Without panicking, he kept his head up and spun the ball out to Rodney So'oialo. On the touchline was Carter and, with a spurt of acceleration, within a pair of strides, he had received the pass and burst past Lions' winger Shane Williams. As the crowd rose to its feet, Josh Lewsey came to meet him. Most players would have taken the tackle and looked for support. This time, Carter having broken free so unexpectedly, there was no support around. Some players would have taken Lewsey on, tried to sidestep him or run around him but really, in the narrow corridor of space that Carter found himself in, neither was an option. No support, no chance of beating the man, well, I'll just have to kick. Ninety-nine per cent of players would have chipped the ball skyward and hoped for the best. But that's not good enough when greatness is playing on the lyre. Carter picked out a spot behind the goal line, grubbered the ball through with satellite precision, swept past Lewsey and the ball stayed in play just long enough for the fly-half to touch it down. For good measure he stroked the conversion over as well. 31-13. Game over. Series over.

The Lions mounted a brief offensive after Carter landed another penalty – a product of his own skill and strength in shrugging off two would-be tacklers. Simon Easterby claimed a try in the corner yelling, 'Peely, Peely' to his scrum-half when a gap opened up. Even with that, the deficit was still sixteen, meaning the Lions would have to score three times to win. They didn't score again.

With just over ten minutes to go, Carter touched down once more. Off slow ruck ball on the right touchline, the All Blacks still fancied their chances. But a massive overlap looked like being lost when Mealamu received a twin present of the ball and Easterby. Somehow though the hooker – yes, the hooker – wriggled his arms free and released the ball to Carter, who ran straight and true for twenty metres to dive over for his second try.

From the restart, substitute Sione Lauaki ran 80 metres and nearly set up another try in the corner. On 76 minutes, New Zealand crossed again, Richie McCaw emerging with the ball. Carter, as cool and relaxed as he had been on Wednesday, knocked over the conversion to finish with a total of 33 points, the most any player has ever scored against the Lions and the joint third highest individual haul by a New Zealand international. The All Blacks' tally of 48 was the highest-ever registered against the Lions, by any side. Even those statistics don't do justice to the excellence of Carter's performance and that of the All Blacks. The former, again in tandem with Aaron Mauger and, when he was replaced at half-time, the captain, controlled the game. His passing, kicking and running were flawless and every decision he made was the correct one. Outside him, Umaga, after a tumultuous week, was colossal too.

'I thought the skipper had a very special game,' said Graham Henry. 'Tana Umaga, that is. He put up with a lot of rubbish during the week, from a person who doesn't know the game, hasn't got any passion for the game, which was disappointing. But he played an outstanding game.'

There was no doubting though that this, like the Matthews' Final, was the Carter Test. Even though the difference between the sides was about more than a single, individual performance, one man stood on the shoulders of giants this evening.

'To play alongside a special talent like Dan Carter is just unbelievable,' was Umaga's praise for his team-mate. 'To see what he's up to … his kicking, his nous, he runs the show. He's our leader. He leads us around all the moves we do; it's a lot for a young guy but he just loves it.'

'He played outstandingly,' smiled Henry, 'but I think credit must go to those around him. Aaron Mauger is a good voice outside him; he talks to him all the time. Captain's to his right as well and that helps. Richie McCaw: I thought his performance and his leadership was also superb. There were a number of people who helped Daniel in that regard.'

Mils Muliaina joined the chorus: 'Dan, mate, he's one of the best first-fives [fly-halves] I've seen. He's so cool, he's always relaxed. If he was any more relaxed, he'd be asleep, honestly. That's just the way he is. When he performs like that, good on him.

'He's got some leaders around as well, Aaron and Tana. They do all the talking and they're always in his ear. That just lets him relax and do his thing: get the backline firing.'

The headiest praise came from Lions' assistant coach, Eddie O'Sullivan: 'He had a superb game. He got really good service from his pack but his decision-making and his control of the game was excellent. He had a lot of options open to him as well and he used them well. It was a very complete performance. He's grown into his role and, on tonight, he's probably the top number ten in the world at the moment.'

But all over the pitch the All Blacks were remarkable. The Lions were almost 100 per cent better than they were last week but they could still have no complaints about the scoreline. They simply had no answers.

'Hats off to them', was all that Donncha O'Callaghan could say. 'Carter was just outstanding. And up front, they were just very good. I think tonight, you just have to put your hand up and say you were beaten by a better team.

'They dominated tonight, they were ruthless, they didn't take their foot off the pedal, and they finished us off. Sometimes, you get beaten and you just say, "Well done". We were beaten by a better team and we just have to put our hands up and admit that. You looked up with twenty minutes to go and it was well and truly over. You're just playing for pride then. You have this horrible, empty feeling that you've let so many people down. We're sorry for that.'

But what more could the Lions have done? They didn't play badly, did they?

O'Callaghan, head bowed and face numb, was at a loss. He almost had to choke the words out, like a mourning son stricken by disbelief: 'You look to areas: you look to say, was the lineout bad? It wasn't. Was the scrum bad? It wasn't. Was the breakdown bad? It wasn't. You just have to take your hat off to them. We played as well as we could and we just got beat.'

How though? What makes the All Blacks so good?

'This is what we do in the Super 12,' Henry said. 'This is how we play the game. It's an athletic game and the ideal breeding ground to play this type of rugby. I think people have to realise that. It gets a lot of criticism but it's great for developing athleticism and skill; we play at the right time of year; we were very lucky with the weather conditions tonight, that we could play that sort of game. But if you look at the Welsh and the way they play, they played superbly in the Six Nations. They use the ball a lot, the forwards can play and I guess there's a message there ... It's a great feeling to win in that manner, showing that sort of class.'

Class. What did the players think of that heady praise?

'This All Black team that I've been involved with, since the end-of-year tour last year, has probably been the best All Black team that I've been a part of,' said Chris Jack, after another fabulous display. 'We've been able to keep putting the performances together and that's something we're really proud of. It ranks very highly in my career of 39 Test matches ... There was a lot of things that went well for us but there were a few things we won't be happy with. You never have a perfect game. The day I have a perfect game is the day I hang up my boots, go home, sit down and say, "Never again".'

Is that part of what makes this team so good, this desire for continual self-improvement? Jack was diplomatic: 'We just try to be the best we can be, express ourselves, be proud of who we are and what we're doing.'

Standing nearby was Muliaina. From a distance, he moves with a swagger and cuts a powerful dash whether in his usual position of full-back, or centre, where he found himself for the second half tonight, after Mauger succumbed to injury. But what you see from afar doesn't do justice to how battle-hardened the man is. His face is criss-crossed by scars, from boots that went flying in this way, that way; his cheeks could pass for those of a middle-aged lumberjack. It's the face of a man who has fought on many a front-line. But Muliaina is only 25. In fact, the average age of the team is only a few fractions greater. We know of their ferocious appetite for work, we know of the intense environment in which All Blacks live and breathe, we know of their extraordinary skill level. But what of the leadership they display on the pitch? How is it that men so young play with old heads on their shoulders, as if they each have 100 caps?

'We've got some guys who've been around for a bit but we do have a leadership group,' was Muliaina's answer. 'That was probably what was lacking last year, that we didn't have enough leaders that could step up. But full credit as well to the coaches because they've listened to the players and we've got to this point.'

'The coaches have put faith in us,' added Jack. 'They've identified who they wanted to lead and how they wanted to do it. They've put the pressure on us to step up to the mark. And, if you don't step up to the mark, you're gone. That's how it's come about. The guys have taken it in their stride and decided to run with it.'

'The coaches have said that, with as many world-class players as we have, we can be an awesome team and it's about guys stepping up and wanting to be leaders, taking ownership, taking responsibility,' Muliaina continued. 'What can you say when it's coming off like that? The players believe in it, the coaches believe in it and it can only be a good thing.'

To the losing coach then. There was schadenfreude a-plenty in the press room. The members of the New Zealand media were delighted. Those of the British and Irish media who think the Lions should have played like Wales weren't too displeased either. Anyone who dislikes Sir Clive was happy. But there were glum faces too. Woodward's was foremost among them.

'There's nothing more we could have done,' he admitted. 'I'm very proud of them. No one gave up and I thought it was a tremendous Test match. I think the score went against us a bit: they scored at critical times and a few decisions went against us but we're playing against a very, very good team. From a Lions' point of view, we got a lot of things right tonight.'

But New Zealand were pretty bloody good too, weren't they?

'There's a lot of pace out there, all over the pitch, and the way they offload to each other is outstanding. I think Wales are probably the closest team to them in terms of the skill level. I believed we could come down here and win, if we got our game absolutely right. There's a lot of pace out there, and a lot of power as well. New Zealand backs have always been pretty special but now I think there's a good forward pack there as well. Let's not get carried away: they're a good team and they deserved to win tonight but I thought the Lions did very, very well.'

Where now for the Lions? Henry, to give him credit, was unwilling to criticise his opposite number's handling of the tour, coded references to his preference for the Welsh style of play apart: 'People come with ideas of how they can improve what happened in the past and you have to respect that. It didn't quite come together but most of the things the Lions have done on this tour, pre-tour, were suggestions from the 2001 management. It hasn't quite come together; people have ideas and sometimes they work, sometimes they don't.'

'I look forward to how my successor is going to handle it,' said Woodward. "It's not easy; you're trying to juggle so many things. The traditions: you're very conscious that a player on the trip be given every chance; you're also conscious that you haven't got many games to get your team prepared; a few more things cropped up on this tour, players not being available for various reasons, medical or playing in France. But you've just got to deal with these things and I have absolutely no regrets about the way I've gone about this tour.'

'There wasn't an area you could look at and fault,' said O'Callaghan, still shaking his head. 'Everyone did feel like they gave it their all and that's a funny feeling, when you feel like you couldn't have done any more and you just got beat. It was a weird mood really. Sometimes you lose and you might be moaning about refs, complaining about breakdowns and stuff but there was none of that tonight ... You don't know what to say now. You'd be kind of embarrassed to see these people who've saved for four years to come down here. You feel like you've left them down.'

But the final words have to be Woodward's. With the Test series gone, he still has to rally his troops for two more games. Though it brought quiet snorts of derision from some, he made a valiant effort to look on the bright side: 'We've got to move on quickly now. There's one week left in the tour and we're really looking forward to going to Auckland, and enjoying the last two games and moving things up a gear for next week's Test match.'

New Zealand: M. Muliaina; R. Gear, T. Umaga (c), A. Mauger, S. Sivivatu; D. Carter, B. Kelleher, R. So'oialo, R. McCaw, J. Collins; A. Williams, C. Jack; G. Somerville, K. Mealamu, T. Woodcock
Subs: L. MacDonald for Mauger 38, S. Lauaki for Collins 65, J. Marshall for Kelleher 65, D. Witcombe for Mealamu 68, M. Nonu for Sivivatu 72, J. Gibbes for Jack 74, C. Johnstone for Woodcock 76

Lions: J. Lewsey; J. Robinson, G. Thomas (c), G. Henson, S. Williams, J. Wilkinson, D. Peel, R. Jones, L. Moody, S. Easterby; D. O'Callaghan, P. O'Connell; J. White, S. Thompson, G. Jenkins
Subs: G. Rowntree for Jenkins 56, S. Jones for Wilkinson 60, S. Horgan for Henson 68, M. Corry for O'Connell 72, S. Byrne for Thompson 77.
Referee: A. Cole (Australia).

Part Eight

Blackwash

WINNING THE SINGING

Sunday 3 July 2005, Te Papa Museum, Wellington
Even after the lesson in rugby the Lions were treated to last night the fans are still not down-hearted. Disappointed, yes, but looking to make the most of the time that's left.

'Just have to get on and enjoy it as much as we can,' Tom Mulcahy, who enjoys the rare distinction of being a former Old Christians' coach as well as the current boss of the Munster Youths, sighed in a Wellington bar afterwards.

Inside, the beer flowed; outside, the crowds mixed amiably. And what a crowd there was. Thousands, equal numbers clad in red and black, thronged the streets around Courtenay Place, queuing, eating and drinking. Only the occasional boorish Kiwi, tongue and inhibitions loosened by too much to drink – 'Eh, Paddy, your boys were fucking shite. Time to fuck off home, mate' – came close to spoiling the party. The travelling support had finally arrived in droves; last week the, eh, delights of bland Christchurch had been forsaken for the pleasures of the flesh available in Queenstown but the narrow streets of Wellington, a city whose labyrinthine pathways boast more eateries per head of population than Manhattan, attracted an estimated 25,000 British and Irish Lions' fans, as indeed, to be fair to Christchurch, did the venue of the First Test on match-day. More remarkable than the number was their behaviour though: the police made 30 arrests last Saturday night – some for drunk and disorderly, others for drink-driving – but none of them were Irish, English, Scottish or Welsh. Accountants from the International Financial Services Centre. Dockers from Liverpool. Farmers from the Highlands. Unemployed miners from Aberavon. They came, they saw, they winced and then, they partied. All the time they behaved, even when those natives unable to hold their drink opened fire.

This afternoon, bellies bloated, throbbing heads gradually easing, a few hundred packed into Te Papa to hear the London Welsh male choir, who performed at half-time in the Westpac Stadium, and before the kick-off in Christchurch.

Though I had the distinction of being the youngest member of the audience who hadn't been dragged there by a parent, an auditorium packed with greying travelling supporters again disproved the notion that a 'Barmy Army', hell-bent on drinking New Zealand dry, is on the loose, pinting its way from town to town.

The choir's patron is John Dawes, the man who captained the Lions to their only series victory on New Zealand soil. That was, of course, in 1971, when he played with a who's who of all-time greats that dazzled its way around the country before triumphing over Colin Meads' All Blacks. After the choir's business was done, he addressed the crowd. 'Results may not be going our way on the pitch this time,' he admitted, 'but I think we're winning the singing.' And there is nothing like hearing a Welsh voice in song, whether in a bar, rickety old bandstand, or plush ballroom. It's natural; it's what they're good at; it's God-given. Down here though rugby is what's natural; it's what New Zealanders are good at; it's what's God-given.

Their firm sense of history and of their country's place in the world contributes to that too. The National War Memorial towers over a quiet corner of Wellington; the curator is a second-generation Irish immigrant, Martin Maher, whose parents were from Tipperary.

'Age shall not weary them,' a verse written near the entrance declares, 'Nor the years condemn. At the going down of the sun and, in the morning, we will remember them.' These are words which many of the natives might – with due respect paid to the vast difference between war heroes and rugby heroes – mischievously apply to those who have donned the crested fern.

As the choir sang its way through a half-hour of beautiful hymns the mind drifted, inevitably, towards the aftermath of last night's game and the comments of the Lions' head coach.

'I look forward to how my successor is going to handle it,' you'll recall Sir Clive Woodward saying. 'It's not easy; you're trying to juggle so many things. The traditions: you're very conscious that a player on the trip be given every chance; you're also conscious that you haven't got many games to get your team prepared; a few more things cropped up on this tour, players not being available for various reasons, medical or playing in France. But you've just got to deal with these things and I have absolutely no regrets about the way I've gone about this tour.'

He may not have been entirely honest about having absolutely no regrets; at the very least, there will surely be some quiet moments in which he will sit and wonder, 'if only' and 'what if?' What if: Dallaglio, O'Kelly and Taylor hadn't flown home injured; O'Driscoll hadn't been dumped unceremoniously out of the tour; Hill hadn't limped out shortly after; players like Mike Tindall and Phil Vickery had been available; Martin Johnson could have been persuaded to travel; other key players – Robinson, Wilkinson, Kay, Shanklin, D'Arcy – had been in their pomp and fighting fit; it had been a dry night against the province in Wellington and the Lions had been able to put a marker down in the form of a comprehensive performance; the All Blacks weren't so bloody good; the 50-50 breaks had gone their way in the First Test; New Zealand wasn't such a difficult place to tour? And then there's the biggest 'what if' of all: what if the line-out had functioned in Christchurch?

The question foremost in people's minds is the way Woodward marshalled his resources. Why did he bring so many players, they wonder. His explanation, all through, has been that the ravages of the modern game make it impossible to play two or three times a week. It might have worked in bygone times but today's attritional warfare doesn't allow it. 'I don't know how else it could have been done,' Michael Owen said after the Southland game. 'I think it's been done the best way possible. You mightn't get an awful lot of game time but you just have to take your chance when you get it. Everyone's aware of that and I don't think there was any other way to do it to be honest.'

Blackwash

Once Woodward was committed to bringing such numbers, for a limited number of games – 'We are one game short leading into the First Test,' McGeechan posited after the victory over Wellington – he was required to give all those players a fair shot. Rather than play the Test team he had decided on, or even units from it, it would be better for squad morale – which, remember, suffered in Australia four years ago – if every individual got a chance. That, as Woodward explained when asked if the Lions could ever win a Test series in the modern era, is what the concept of the Lions is all about: 'It's difficult but I think you would almost want to start, game one, and say, "This is my Test team". But I guess that's going to cause problems for the traditional Lions' tour. You've just got to look at the whole thing. It's been a balancing act. We all love the Lions and it's been a brilliant trip from my point of view although it's disappointing to lose these games. It depends on how you define what the Lions is about. If the only thing is to win Tests you may go about it differently.'

Woodward has spoken since the beginning of the tour of his idea of what the Lions is about: he wanted this to be 'the last of the great tours', with the game worming its way into every crevice in the country, with every player going home enriched as a rugby player and an individual, with four nations coming together in harmony both on and off the pitch. Bumpf, one might scoff, but it's unfair to hang a man for the crime of being idealistic.

It was that idealism, that cherished idea that 45 Lions wouldn't win just by turning up for three Test matches but by gelling together over seven weeks, that underpinned Sir Clive's decisions: 'I don't think that [focusing on the Tests] would have worked in terms of the Lions' philosophy of just wanting to give everyone a fair chance, which I've tried to do in a very small space of time. I do think the Lions is a quite a different team to that which I'm used to being in charge of and working towards a World Cup, as New Zealand are doing now, and preparing a group of players over a period of time. The Lions is different. You have to give everyone a chance but also make sure that it's enjoyable off the pitch and I think we've done all that. We gave everyone a chance and we possibly could have done better in the first Test match.

'I wouldn't have done anything differently. If it's just, just about winning that First Test, then I'd have probably picked the top 22 players, based them in Melbourne for four or five weeks for the first Test match, wrapped them in cotton wool. We'd have played a couple of practice games behind closed doors and then jetted over for the Test match. But I guess that wouldn't be too popular.'

The players too would have been denied the experience of travelling around this country – one of fascinating, bewildering diversity of landscape and people. As Woodward said on his arrival in New Zealand in late May, 'People say touring isn't touring any more and complain that there isn't time for a day off. I believe there should be. I've taken on board what people have said and that's why we're bringing 45 players. There will be days off to enjoy New Zealand, play some golf and visit the country. I want everyone to have learned from New Zealand and to come back having enjoyed the trip.'

Not to mention the experience of educating oneself from new coaches and new team-mates.

'Just hanging around with these type of people, how they

train and prepare for games, is just incredible,' said Donncha O'Callaghan, a renowned practical joker, last night. 'I know I'll probably get slagged when I get home that I've changed but yeah, I definitely feel that way. I've accepted higher standards now. I've matured. You have to, around these people: they've no time for a smart alec, doing the fool. You see the Neil Backs, the Richard Hills, and you just learn so much, on and off the field, the way they conduct themselves, the way they look after their bodies, the way they train. It's been a huge development for me – great exposure to great coaches as well – and I've come on an awful lot from it.'

Ideally Woodward would like every player to speak of the tour in similar terms to those chosen by O'Callaghan. At heart, the Lions' 2005 head coach is a romantic, and, barring the Barbarians – a scratch team composed of whoever accepts the invitation to play against international selections – there is nothing more romantic in the world of modern rugby than a traditional Lions' tour. Sir Clive is also possessed of tremendous self-belief which convinced him that his idealism and love of romance could be turned into reality; that, against the odds, New Zealand could be defeated. After all, the man represented his country and the Lions before becoming the first northern hemisphere coach to guide a team to World Cup victory; in between, he was a successful businessman. In short, he is entitled to his self-belief; and one ought not to begrudge him his love of romance either.

It is easy to say, in hindsight, that he made mistakes. Easy to say, and inaccurate. He didn't make mistakes: he made decisions. Some were right, some were wrong. He decided that he could replicate proper match conditions on the training pitch. He was wrong but his view was informed by years of coaching. He decided that he ought to bring 45 players to form two squads and six coaches to form two coaching teams. He was right. He decided that the best way to beat New Zealand was to employ the game plan that worked so well when England won the World Cup. He may have been wrong but this view was informed by, well, England winning the World Cup. He decided it would have been harmful, perhaps fatally so, to morale to play his Test team at an early stage on the tour. He was probably right. He did this, he did that. He was wrong, he was right. On and on we could go.

Deforestation will continue apace as thousands more acres – there have been many already – of newspaper pages are devoted to castigating Woodward's management of the tour, which – deeply personal – has been, is, and will be, desperately unfair.

Many of the journalists attacking Woodward with such rare abandon are now on their way home. A large number of them flew into New Zealand the week before the First Test – few of them were in New Plymouth, Hamilton, Dunedin or Invercargill – and quite a few have exercised their option to skip town after the Second Test. On a Lions' tour it's not only the Test series that matters: this is 'the last of the great tours' and what's great about it is that those who travel experience New Zealand and its people. It's not about three rugby matches against the All Blacks; it's about eleven rugby matches and six weeks of travel, sightseeing and culture. It's about six weeks of learning. As Woodward has made clear from the outset, winning isn't the only thing; although in the interests of balance a comment he made back in Auckland ought to be repeated: 'I just want to win, that's what sport's about. Once you come off the pitch with more points than the other guy, that's the key thing ... The history of sport only remembers the winners.'

Still, those who castigate, excoriate and just plain criticise would do well to recall the story of how, four times on a busy Friday afternoon, on the eve of a crucial Test match, the Lions' head coach took time to shake hands and talk with well-wishers. They would do well also to recall Tucker's words: ''E was a gentleman, Sir Clive.' And, of course, Murphy's First Law of sport: that when you lose, everyone's an expert. So, no chance that he'll be lurking near Umaga's house, axe in hand.

Dancing the Ayatollah
Monday 4 July 2005, Taupo

Thoughts of retribution have been in the air ever since the spear tackle incident in Christchurch. Prior to the Second Test, Paddy Power, the Irish bookmaker, placed tongue in cheek and offered odds of 1,000/1 that Tana Umaga would wield a spear during the Haka and, of course, throughout last week, Lions' fans were going around with Umaga's picture on their T-shirts, above the slogan 'Wanted for the assassination of Brian O'Driscoll'. Happily, it appears as if the injured Lions' captain has smoothed things over with Umaga.

'I've had an apology of sorts from Tana and, as far as I'm concerned, the matter is cleared up,' he said. 'I don't think, off the pitch, my relationship with Tana will change in any shape or form. I'll still go and have a drink with him after a game. I respect him hugely as a rugby player ... I've been the culprit of some bad tackles in my time too so you've just got to get on with it. The real disappointment for me was only getting the opportunity to play 45 seconds in the Test. Win, lose or draw, that's what you go on Lions' tours for.'

Tonight brought us to Taupo, a lakeside resort less than three hours from Auckland, temporary home to a few thousand Lions' supporters, the sound of their humming and hawing about whether or not they'll bother travelling north tomorrow, and of further proof that there is no such thing as the 'Barmy Army'. Before myself and Oisin demonstrated the intricacies – jumping up and down and patting your hands on your scalp – of 'Dancing the Ayatollah' to the locals, a performance improved, we felt, by eight pints of Steinlager and Mac's Gold respectively, I found myself talking to two elderly Welsh sheep farmers.

'It's the trip of a lifetime, son. I've been saving for about four years for it.'

'Who's looking after the farm?'

'Family.'

'Nice holiday.'

'We don't get many!'

'Are ye going to Auckland tomorrow?'

'Ah no. We wouldn't be fanatical about the rugby. Me, I've always wanted to come to New Zealand. This will be my only chance, so I want to see some things. Anyway, we've got a few things to do. We must go to a sheep farm up in Taupiro.'

'Well, if you guys are going travelling, there are some things which might be worth having a look at.'

'Oh yeah?'

So I told them about Martin Johnson Stadium in Tihoi and that the farm of All Black legend, Colin Meads, wasn't a million miles away from there either. 'He's only too happy to take in visitors. You might even get scones and sandwiches.' With two looks of gratitude, their eyes dancing and twinkling, they thanked me.

'We can drink to that. Pity about the rugby, though.'

'Never mind it. I wouldn't be anywhere else, son. This is the place to be.' 'Barmy Army'? Give me a break.

Running, passing, catching
Game 10: British & Irish Lions V Auckland
Tuesday 5 July 2005, Eden Park, Auckland

Auckland 13
Tries: I. Nacewa
Convs: B. Ward
Pens: B. Ward (2)

Lions 17
Tries: M. Williams
Pens: R. O'Gara (3), C Hodgson

Does anyone care any more? Ian McGeechan sported a broad grin afterwards, as he was well entitled to: his long association with the Lions most probably came to an end this evening – unless, he said, they bring coaches 'in wheelchairs' – in the happy circumstances of seeing his midweek side go through the tour unbeaten.

'I am very, very proud,' he said. 'It was a team full of character. They were intelligent in what they did, really dug in against a side that has some outstanding individual runners. It was a great team effort against a very good provincial side.

'Everybody gave everything tonight. At a time when it would have been easy to come off tour or show it didn't matter, we had a performance which showed how much the Lions means to a big group of people, and that includes me.'

For everyone else though it was a miserable winter's night in Auckland, rain teeming down as one team tried to play attacking, expansive rugby and the other tried to subdue them. At this stage no prizes can be awarded for guessing that it was Auckland, replete with Pacific Islanders – happily, the term 'corral hoppers' hasn't reared its ugly head since that night in New Plymouth – who were the ones running, passing and catching.

None of last Saturday's starting line-up featured tonight, which suggests that either the management was pleased that the Second Test performance was about as good as it could be or the players were just knackered. One or the other but it doesn't really matter: tonight's story was about the difference in approach between the two teams. Auckland tried to run their way to victory; the Lions tried to kick their way. A pair of incidents summed it up.

After seventeen minutes, Auckland fly-half Tasesa Lavea again elected to run the ball out of his own '22. He crabbed across the field slightly, looking for a team-mate to change the angle of attack by coming inside him. One duly came but by the time he was in a position to receive the pass, Lavea had changed his mind. Defending on the wing for the Lions was Simon Shaw. Facing him was Auckland centre, Ben Atiga. So Lavea, appreciating in an instant that Atiga would have too much pace for the second-row, ripped up the play book and fired a pass out wide. Sure enough, Auckland made huge ground. It got better. After the ball had been retained, Lavea then delayed, before delivering a sublime pass to Auckland second-row Brad Mika, who wasn't loitering out by the touchline. Once Mika was stopped, Lavea spun it wide and Joe Rokocoko – despite being one of the most prolific try-scorers in international rugby history, he still can't get a game with the All Blacks – was only bundled into touch five metres from the Lions' line.

By way of rather stark contrast, we move to the thirty-first minute of the opening half, with the Lions leading 6-3. Auckland once again attempted to run the ball out of defence but as had already happened on numerous occasions in the horrible, wintry conditions, they lost control and the Lions gained possession. There was no effort at expansive play from the tourists. Boos rang around the stadium as Ronan O'Gara, on as a sub for the injured Charlie Hodgson, sat well back and aimed a drop goal. No running the ball for the Lions.

Despite the boos, O'Gara's decision – if not its execution – was the correct one in the circumstances, particularly if a team is committed to playing a possession-based game in foul weather. Nonetheless, the boos were understandable: one team trying to perform the beautiful game; the other trying to bore them into submission? A crowd reared on running, passing and catching wasn't facing much of a play for its affections.

But Lavea's performance throughout tonight's game was another manifestation of one of the main reasons that no provincial side has been able to beat the Lions: their fly-halves are unable to kick the ball!

When Lavea did use his boot this evening the results were cringe-worthy, but even in the All Blacks' final trial, just over a month ago, the two contenders on display, Nick Evans and Luke Donald, kicked badly out of hand; Evans went on to run well but kick poorly in the Otago jersey, while Jimmy Gopperth, who was on the bench in Napier helped, by his failure to kick effectively, to contribute to Wellington's downfall in their game against the tourists. Dan Carter was right when he said last week that sometimes in the Test arena you have to ignore the voices and the aches of muscle memory imploring you to run the ball; to dust off a hoary old adage, you can kick the ball further than you can pass it. The All Blacks have struck a perfect balance, using big, booming clearances when they're under pressure and sneaky grubber kicks when they're attacking to turn the screw on the opposition but also getting the ball wide when the opportunity presents itself. The Lions may not have the balance that New Zealand have but against the provincial teams the fact that, when they clear the ball, they clear it effectively and, when they get the chance, they kick the ball well offensively, is a huge advantage.

In the first half tonight, this part of the Lions' game wasn't working though. Will Greenwood, Gordon D'Arcy and Denis Hickie all found themselves kicking poorly. Hickie had the misfortune of producing the runt of the litter: he had one effort charged down, an error that almost led to an Auckland try. But another huge advantage that the Lions have is that, well, they are, from one to fifteen, seasoned internationals. They ain't no dummies and, so, in every game on tour there have been flashes of brilliance. Martyn Williams knocked on over the try line after Greenwood had made a half-break and offloaded excellently in the tackle; Hickie too almost redeemed himself when he just failed to control a perfectly-guided O'Gara crossfield kick. And then, there was the game's critical score. On the stroke of half-time, Auckland scrum-half, Steve Devine, missed touch with a clearance, finding Mark Cueto instead. Winger, Isa Nacewa, made a kamikaze effort to tackle, Cueto stepped away from him and danced his way to within five metres of the line. Seconds later Matt Dawson was popping the ball to Williams, the Welshman was touching down and the Lions found themselves in what was, considering the conditions, a commanding 14-3 lead.

The second half produced only more of the same for those who had made the long trek north from Wellington: province running; Lions boring. Sigh. And the twelfth minute contained a moment that revealed another of the Lions' difficulties on this tour. The tourists won good, clean line-out ball and moved it wide but when the tackle came, the first three Lions to the ruck sported eleven, twelve and fifteen on their backs. Unsurprisingly, a penalty was conceded.

The All Blacks wouldn't have made the same mistake. If they had gone wide like that, Rodney So'oialo and Richie McCaw would have been in the same frame; but generally New Zealand play a different sort of game: close to the ruck and, broadly speaking, in the centre of the pitch, the forwards, from one to five, dominate the proceedings; their job is to make inroads up the middle, clear the ball quickly and then get it to their backs; again, McCaw and So'oialo will be in support, so the backs' job is mainly limited to running, passing and catching. But, because their skill levels are so high, it's almost inevitable that, when they do pass the ball wide, they will make ground, which makes it easier to retain the ball no matter what number is on the back of the first player to the ruck; often there won't even be a ruck, as the All Blacks' ability to offload in the tackle and their excellent support running allows them to keep the play moving. Sometimes, as on this occasion, the Lions have been guilty of going wide too early, without building up momentum. That makes it close to suicidal to have three of your smallest players trying to secure ruck ball. And, of course, it means that, if you do manage to retain the ball, three of your quickest players are immediately unavailable to receive it. There is a contrast in styles – England 2003 V New Zealand 2005 – and, at the moment the All Black star is in the ascendancy. The funny thing is it doesn't take a degree in theoretical physics to decide that using big forwards to do the donkey work and the small, quick guys to do the flashy stuff is a sensible approach to the game of rugby. Of course, each member of the All Blacks' XV is possessed of good positional sense, awareness and appreciation of the game, which gives them an added advantage but keeping things simple, rather than complicated, has been a virtue preached by thousands of coaches in dozens of different sports. Maybe now it will find itself back in *vogue* on the rugby pitches.

The only thing to cheer me up was the well-deserved try that Auckland scored after 22 minutes of the second period. My friend, Lavea, made a break and found Atiga in support. He went to ground but, despite an attempt by Martin Corry to kill the ball, two Auckland forwards rumbled on, offloading the ball out of the tackle for Nacewa to touch down. The offload at pace, a skill evident in the New Zealand game since that final trial and used to devastating effect in the Test Series, again proved effective. Only rarely could the Lions manage to pass like that; indeed the only man in a red jersey tonight who seemed capable of doing so was Greenwood.

That Nacewa score, duly converted, reduced the margin to just a single point, but try as they might, Auckland couldn't breach a well-drilled Lions' defence again. After missing with a drop goal, O'Gara scored a penalty to extend the lead and, when the hosts knocked on after a final, brave attempt to run, pass and catch their way to victory, the curtain came down on the midweekers' tour.

'I'm sick of the place, to be honest,' O'Gara said afterwards. 'I'm supposed to be flying out to Fiji on Sunday but I just need to go home. My girlfriend's come out this week and she thinks she's going on a two-week holiday, but ...' Behind him though the coaching team of McGeechan, Mike Ford and Gareth Jenkins looked, understandably, like happy men. Their work here is done and, with an unblemished scorecard, their reputations have been enhanced.

Auckland: B. Ward; I. Nacewa, B. Atiga, S. Tuitupou, J. Rokocoko; T. Lavea, S. Devine; A. MacDonald, D. Braid, J. Collins (c); B. Williams, B. Mika; J. Afoa, S. Telefoni, S. Taumoepeau.
Subs: J. Kaino for Mika 45, N. White for Taumoepeau 56, K. Haiu for MacDonald 65, G. Williams for Nacewa 70, J. Fonokalafi for Telefoni 76, I. Toe'ava for Atiga 76.

Lions: G. Murphy; M Cueto, W. Greenwood, G. D'Arcy, D. Hickie; C. Hodgson, M. Dawson; M. Owen, M. Williams, J. White; B. Kay, S. Shaw; J. Hayes, G. Bulloch (c), A. Sheridan.
Subs: R. O'Gara for Hodgson 21, S. Horgan for

The Last Great Tour?

Greenwood 49, M. Corry for White 54, M. Stevens for Hayes 59.

Referee: S. Walsh (New Zealand)

McGeechan's influence on the tour cannot go unmentioned. The respect he drew, even when speaking to the press, was remarkable. One can only imagine what it must have been like for the players who fell under his tutelage. They all spoke glowingly of him.

'I think he's probably one of the greatest rugby coaches that there is,' said Graham Rowntree. 'He's one of the top two guys I've worked with. His whole demeanour, his whole manner, is just incredible. I think a good coach says what he has to, when he has to. If he's just barking at you all the time, like a little dog, you start ignoring him. But when "Geech" speaks, you listen to him. He doesn't speak just for the hell of it. He's very good with players, at bringing confidence out in them.

'Have you heard him speak? You should hear him speak before a game. To the team. Christ.' Rowntree came close to being lost for words. 'It's emotional,' he eventually concluded.

Add this from Geordan Murphy: 'It's a real pleasure to be coached by a legend like Ian McGeechan. He's been there and done it, seen it all, so you know he's got a huge amount of knowledge and it's nice to be coached by a guy like that. On top of that he has a great reputation as a player from his day, and he speaks about that and he makes some fantastic speeches.'

It is indeed a nice way for a great to bow out. Well, bow out on one stage: not yet 60, he will take over the reins at London Wasps next season and bring his unique brand of man-management, in-depth rugby knowledge and oratorical brilliance to them. And who knows, when the Lions go to South Africa in 2007, perhaps the 'Geech' will, once more, answer the call of the wild. Wheelchair and all.

***

On the subject of the media's treatment of Sir Clive Woodward, there's a good example from today's newspapers. James Lawton wrote in the *Independent* that: 'All that is left is a degree of recognition that almost everything about this Lions' expedition was wrong: its excessive, unwieldy size, its lack of proper match preparation, even its moral base as represented by that unprecedented campaign of spin. It may be that in the next few days Woodward will step out of a mood of denial that in the wake of the Second Test was painful to see. He may finally grasp that just as he got almost everything right in his World Cup campaign with England, here his misjudgements have fed on each other.'

While one can argue the toss on many of Lawton's points – and, I suspect, more will agree with him than me – attacking the morality of this Lions' tour is surely too much. And if the attempt to hold someone to account for the tackle on O'Driscoll formed part of an 'unprecedented campaign of spin' can someone please explain why, at the press conference last Wednesday, Woodward refused, even when asked, to comment any further on the O'Driscoll injury? Though Eddie O'Sullivan raised the matter again the following morning, it's impossible to know whether he was under a direct order to do so. Some of the media management has been distasteful – a photograph of Gavin Henson speaking to Sir Clive after his omission from the First Test team turns out to have been staged, for example – but there's quite a difference between something being distasteful and immoral.

The Walking Wounded ... bruised egos among them
Wednesday 6 July, Maritime Museum, Auckland

Titters all round.

'Maybe I should have let James take a few more press conferences.' His tongue may have been in cheek but Sir Clive Woodward's sentiments were warmly received. Dr James Robson, the head doctor for the Lions, had been running through the list of injuries suffered by various crocked members of the touring party. The damage to each player was announced in Robson's soft Scottish tone and a hearty dollop of humour lurked very close to every sentence. It made a difference from hearing that everything is fantastic, it's a great occasion and we've all had a super time. But, a joke's a very serious thing, as Charles Churchill once wrote, and the situation facing the Lions is grim. After the rigours of last night's battle against Auckland, combined with the scars remaining from the Second Test and the general wear and tear of a six-week tour, the tourists resemble a band of walking wounded.

'We didn't actually train this morning,' Woodward said. 'We literally had too few players to do so.'

There were no complaints though. Sir Clive's upper lip looked as if it had been starched into place: 'Despite all the injuries, we're still going flat-out to win this Test match ... We'll have a full session tomorrow and together again on Friday ...

Blackwash

The dressing room was a great place to be last night: we've really bounced back. Some players from last night's game will back up for Saturday's Test but you can't do it constantly. We've replaced thirteen players through injury, but that doesn't take account of the players who are unable to play through injury or aren't able to play more than one game a week because of the state of their bodies. So we're protecting the players to a certain degree. There has to be some perspective about it. It's been a case of proceeding very carefully.'

Repetition was one of the Woodward quirks that Alistair Hignell made fun of last Friday night but in this case the head coach's quirk has won the battle. Eyebrows that found themselves raised when he announced that he was bringing 45 players to New Zealand have now sunk back to their starting positions. The rigours of the modern game, plus the intensity with which the game is played in the provinces of this country, as Woodward has repeatedly insisted, required flying in such a large squad for this itinerary. It's worth mentioning as well that Woodward had no control over when and where the games were played: the schedule was set in stone before he took office. Anyway, by repeatedly focusing on those two factors, bringing them up again and again, Sir Clive has convinced the press and the public that he was right. So perhaps there is something to be said for his media strategy.

However, not everyone would agree. Alastair Campbell, it turns out, in telling the players how to handle the press, said that they should, 'go out there and tell those fuckers nothing'. Indeed the reason that Robson hasn't been wheeled out more often is because, early on in the tour, he gave a press briefing at which, he was told, he had given too much away. This is the sort of thing that has got journalists' backs up; perhaps the coverage would not have become so scathing, personalised and unfair had the media not become so miffed at their treatment. The mere presence of Campbell irritated experienced journalists who are used to covering the home nations and enjoying virtually unfettered access to top players, rubbing shoulders in hotel elevators and shooting the breeze over breakfast: as if, the press corps' sentiments have been, we need to be micromanaged by a devious spin doctor. Who, to make matters worse, is a soccer fan. Sadly the question was never explored at any length, though Woodward has said that when he asked for the identity of the best media consultant available, Campbell's name came up; this was to be the best-prepared Lions' tour ever and thus only the best would do. Another decision which was logical but in hindsight, probably not correct, especially when one considers the galvanising effect that 'Speargate' had on the All Blacks last week. Woodward would have concentrated on the incident whether or not Campbell was in his entourage, solely because of his outrage. However, the fact that Campbell was present allowed the New Zealand team, media and public to spin it as a devious attempt to attack the All Black skipper and distract attention from a lamentable Lions' performance in Christchurch. But back to the on-pitch failures.

'If I had my time again,' Woodward said, 'I'd wrap the best 22 players in Britain and Ireland in cotton wool and go out to win that first Test match. But if I went with that suggestion to the Lions' committee, they'd rightly turn it down: that's not what a Lions' tour is about. If everyone had stayed fit for the whole tour maybe we could have an argument about the numbers but with the intensity of the games we've had, the midweek games, injuries were inevitable. We've lost players who would have been in the Test team: Dallaglio, O'Kelly, O'Driscoll.

'But that's what New Zealand is like. It's the hardest Lions' tour of them all and the injury toll shows that ... There's no way you could play the number of games we've played with any fewer players. It would be absolutely impossible. You wouldn't have a Test team! My number one priority has been the players. When I was England coach in 2001 the players came back from the Lions' tour absolutely exhausted. We've now lost eleven out of twelve tours down here; obviously, we wanted to win for the second time but I was also determined that the players would come back in the best possible shape.'

Again there's a reference to the spirit of the Lions. Woodward's use of the word 'rightly' is another manifestation of his sense of romance: the Lions should trek up and down a country; dozens of players should be exposed to a different culture, to different styles of play, to different opponents and different team-mates; they should get out and meet people, as they would have on the tours of old. That's why there was a hint of regret in his voice over a month ago, in the Hilton Hotel, when he described this as 'the last great Lions' tour'.

It wasn't all Woodward being defensive: there was the occasional humorous intervention from Dr Robson and the head coach also launched an offensive against the press: 'I've never seen players of so many different nationalities get on so well together. I've been taken aback by some of the British and Irish media. I think, to be honest, they've lost a bit of perspective about what's going on here.'

I couldn't agree more. A group of Lions, a team patched together from four countries, short through injury of four of its best players, took on an All Black side – possibly the best on the planet at the moment – the nucleus of which has been in place since the last World Cup two years ago. Woodward took decisions to try and overcome the gulf in preparation but the gap proved to be unbridgeable. Even if he had answered some questions in the alternative, the gap would, in all probability, still have been unbridgeable.

'You have to go with the decisions that you've made,' he said. 'There's not a lot I would have changed. I wanted the players to be fresh and fit going into the first Test match and I think we achieved that. I'll be sorry to go home on Sunday. I've really enjoyed it. It's a fantastic country to go to and it's the greatest test in world rugby.'

Glastonbury
Thursday 7 July 2005, Alexandra Park, Auckland

I want to go home. Yesterday morning, the NZRU hosted a special function in central Auckland to brief the media on their bid to host the 2011 Rugby World Cup. I was very excited about going – they had made a promise of 'refreshments' – but when I awoke, it was to the sound of torrential rain pummelling the roof of the campervan. To hell with that.

The rain hasn't let up either, which is a problem. Along with hundreds of other vans, our vehicle is pitched up in Alexandra Park, normally a racetrack but for this week, a temporary motor camp. With the rain belting down, however, it's not as much fun as it sounds. In fact, it's more like Glastonbury, except with fewer facilities where one can attend to personal hygiene. There must be over 1,000 Lions' fans here; there are four portable showers – which are cold.

Even though there is a long line of Portaloos stretching down the grassy area in the middle, the complete absence of drainage means that whenever you need to go, unless you packed a pair of wellingtons, or keep a plastic bag wrapped around your shoes, the water ends up seeping into your socks. There is no permanent power, which means that the heater doesn't work. All of which adds up to one written-off pair of runners. And, when you factor in the muck element, an awful lot of unpleasant-looking brown stuff on the floor of the van.

'I can't wait to get home at this stage,' said the Irish guy living next door. 'The rugby's been bloody awful, and now the weather's the same.'

I too have Ronan-it is: I want to go home.

I suspect, however, that Mr O'Gara may now have recovered from his bout of Ronan-itis. With Charlie Hodgson and Jonny Wilkinson ruled out of the Third Test through injury, he's got a place on the bench. The pack is the same but behind the scrum it's all change. In on the right wing is Mark Cueto, who caps a remarkable rise: when the Lions toured Australia four years ago, Cueto had never played a game of professional rugby but his starting berth is just reward for his performances on this tour. Geordan Murphy was right when he said, in Palmerston North, that the Test teams were never 'set in stone': he starts at full-back, with Josh Lewsey shunted to the wing. Will Greenwood partners Gareth Thomas in the centre, though the new captain, according to Dr James Robson, has been suffering from the flu. The most remarkable part of the team announcement was the list of injuries accompanying it: Charlie Hodgson (simple concussion incurred V Auckland);

The Last Great Tour?

Simon Shaw (neck and forearm); Ben Kay (severe bruising to right eye plus virus); Ollie Smith (rib bruising); Gavin Henson (left arm); Jonny Wilkinson (left shoulder/neck); Andy Sheridan (left lower-leg); Gordon D'Arcy (general fatigue).

The D'Arcy one is a little odd. Sir Clive Woodward said last night that D'Arcy had ruled himself out of contention, which seems unusual; then again, the centre missed much of the season through injury and, on this tour, hasn't really found the spark that made him the player of the 2004 Six Nations. Maybe it's D'Arcy-itis I have. Like me, Gordon just wants to go home.

The mood of Lions' fans might have been buoyed by the naming of the All Blacks' team yesterday. Dan Carter, Aaron Mauger, Richie McCaw, Carl Hayman and Anton Oliver are all injured. Leon MacDonald starts at fly-half, Rodney So'oialo is named at openside flanker, Conrad Smith comes in to partner Tana Umaga in the centre and Sione Lauaki gets a run at number eight. The team is still a strong one but the absence of the injured quintet is cause for cheer. Then again, the gap between the sides has hardly been down simply to the influence of one group of players. They could have played Carter's girlfriend, ice-hockey international, Honor Dillon, at fly-half last week and the margin wouldn't have been affected. The Lions still won't be favourites to win.

New Zealand: M. Muliaina; R. Gear, C. Smith, T. Umaga (c), S. Sivivatu; L. MacDonald, B. Kelleher; S. Lauaki, R. So'oialo, J. Collins; A. Williams, C. Jack; G. Somerville, K. Mealamu, T. Woodcock.
Subs: D. Witcombe, C. Johnstone, J. Ryan, M. Holah, J. Marshall, L. McAlister, D. Howlett.

Lions: G. Murphy; M. Cueto, W. Greenwood, G. Thomas
(c), J. Lewsey; S. Jones, D. Peel; R. Jones, L. Moody, S.
Easterby; D. O'Callaghan, P. O'Connell; J. White, S.
Thompson, G. Jenkins.
Subs: S. Byrne, G. Rowntree, M. Corry, M. Williams, M.
Dawson, R. O'Gara, S. Horgan.

'What are they going after ordinary people for? They are the
innocent people. Why?'

I had no answer for the Afghan cab driver. I had been
standing in an Irish bar with the two McDermotts – celebrating
my success in finally managing to buy a round of drinks for
them – when word came through that there had been 'incidents' in London. As the awful events unfolded – dozens dead,
hundreds wounded – my own moans and whinges fell away. It
was a depressing end to what has been a depressing week.

The cabbie who took me back to Alexandra Park was a qualified lawyer, but he'd left Afghanistan in 1997. 'The Taliban was
coming into power. I could see things were getting bad. So I took
my family out. And this is it all over again. These crazy people.'

London's Burning
Friday 8 July, Auckland

A pall hung over Alexandra Park this morning. There were
rumours that a few fellow travellers knew people on the missing list in London or, worse, amongst the fatalities of the terror
attacks there during yesterday's rush hour. Notepads, microphones and television cameras moved around from one early
riser to the next. Suddenly, the rugby doesn't matter that much

any more, and everyone feels a little bit ashamed that, yesterday morning, they were complaining that the showers are only ever lukewarm at best.

Apparently there has been some suggestion that the game tomorrow ought to be cancelled as a mark of respect to those who were killed and maimed. No such drastic action will be taken though. 'Life will still go on,' assistant coach, Andy Robinson insisted. 'You have to live for the next day and that's the attitude of all the squad'.

Robinson and Eddie O'Sullivan were on pre-match media duty in the Hilton Hotel, which was a welcome relief from the depression of the temporary motor camp. Both coaches were bullish about the Lions' chances in the Third Test. Incidentally there has been a change on the New Zealand team. Leon MacDonald is out so Luke McAlister, who played at centre for the New Zealand Maori, will make his Test debut at fly-half for the All Blacks, with Nick Evans of Otago coming onto the bench. But the change, in the greater scheme of things, should not make a huge difference. The most important questions are: (a) Do the Lions have the energy and pride left to turn in a big performance? (b) Do New Zealand have the motivation to produce another top-quality display?

'The mood this week has been quite exceptional, surprisingly so,' said O'Sullivan. 'I would have expected, after a long, hard season, that the players would be a bit down but that hasn't been the case. We want to go out tomorrow and end the tour on a high note ... Fellas could be looking to get on a plane but that hasn't been the case. We had a really good session this morning.

'The team would like to prove that we can win a Test match

in New Zealand. That's the motivating factor and if something's worth doing, you want to do it.'

Across town, Graham Henry was insisting that the numerous changes to the All Black line-up were 'exactly' what they need: 'It gives us another challenge, four or five changes from last week, one in the role of number ten, who really navigates the team. It's now how the team pulls together to make it the best it can be. It's a challenge for us and I'd like to see how we handle it. I've got every confidence they'll handle it well.'

Back in the Hilton it was also an opportunity to hear the views of O'Sullivan and Robinson on the quality of the opposition. 'The All Blacks are playing great rugby at the moment,' the former conceded. 'They can go wide and they can go up the middle if they need to. We're not at that level on this tour. We've made changes but they've made changes too and we'll see how that affects them. It's a big challenge, players getting to know each other. It's challenging even at international level because you're not with guys week in, week out, and it's even more of a challenge on a Lions' tour. It's something we haven't really done on tour; hopefully, we will do it tomorrow night.'

Robinson too praised New Zealand but like O'Sullivan noted that the Lions still have a chance to prove a point tomorrow night: 'The New Zealand forwards can run and carry the ball and get continuity into the game. That's been the difference, I think. We have it in the Lions' players to do that, and it's about bringing it out in them. We have the ability to play with that sort of pace and width and it's something we aspire to but we haven't got there yet. Maybe tomorrow night we will.'

The question of numbers came up again, albeit in a different guise this time. Had the use of two coaching teams spoiled the

Lions' rhythm somewhat? 'One of the things that has been successful on this tour has been the two coaching teams,' came a sharp rebuttal from O'Sullivan, 'which means that players have a steady coaching team. You have to give the players the best preparation possible and, because time levels have gone up so much, it has become very time consuming. It would have been impossible for three people to deal with two teams and I think the success of the midweek team has shown that.'

It was hard not to feel some sympathy for the two coaches, both of whom looked like men who've been toiling solidly for the last six weeks. O'Sullivan, who is rumoured to have had a major bust-up with Phil Larder, the defence coach, became particularly tetchy when he was challenged by Dave Ferguson of the *Scotsman*. O'Sullivan made the mistake of saying that there's never a '50-50 call' when deciding which player to pick in a certain position: something will always tip the balance in one direction. Ferguson's hand shot up.

'But you said last week, Eddie, that the selection of Matt Dawson over Chris Cusiter was the toss of a coin.'

Somehow, O'Sullivan managed to wriggle his way free, performing a Houdini-esque manoeuvre with a dyspeptic grimace on his face. It's fair to say that Ferguson won't spend the next few festive seasons waiting anxiously for an IRFU Christmas card.

The rumour of the Larder-O'Sullivan face-off – apparently, it involved their nose hairs making intimate acquaintance – is worth mentioning. It appeared in the *Sunday News* last weekend, as did a story alleging that Gavin Henson had threatened to quit the tour. Both, of course, were dismissed by the Lions' management.

'It's nonsense that I've had to work hard with Gavin,' Sir Clive

Woodward said last weekend. 'He has been fantastic. I have not had to speak to him at all on this trip about anything like that. If I had I wouldn't have picked him for the Test. Behind the scenes, the players have been very professional and I would put him at the top of that list. It is a shame these stories would be made up. When I see things like that I can just say it is complete nonsense.'

And he knew nothing of a brawl either: 'Seriously, I know nothing about that at all. All the coaching staff get on well, Eddie and Phil sit together on the bus every day, so I know nothing about any incident.'

But the problem is that all the players and coaching staff are bound by terms in their contracts that prevent them from disclosing anything about the tour until mid-November, otherwise they won't receive the considerable fee they've earned in the Land of the Long White Cloud.

'I've never seen players of so many different nationalities get on so well together,' Woodward said on Wednesday. Well, we'll see. Something like the disagreement between Larder and O'Sullivan wouldn't be particularly unusual in such a highly-charged environment, where shoulders and other bodily items are being rubbed on a daily basis; and Henson is a notoriously complex character: when he played there, the management at Swansea allegedly used to have to order him to make conversation with staff at the club. One is tempted to say that there will doubtless be unhappy utterances from some players: for example, Ronan O'Gara didn't exude happiness and delight after the game on Tuesday night and mentioned that 'some' of the management questioned his ability to defend after his performance against the Bay of Plenty; then again, it's just as likely that O'Gara expected the tour to be as difficult and draining as it has been and, like the good pro he is, won't moan at all. And critics a-plenty will come crawling out of the woodwork: Clive got this wrong, Clive got that wrong. Easy to do that now. We'll just have to wait and see.

***

One man who may be entitled to gloat a little is Barry Glendenning of the *Guardian*. He wrote the Lions off on the eve of the First Test, in no uncertain terms either. He began by focusing on the dominance of the line-up by English players: 'In an adjacent stand, Ireland's Geordan Murphy, arguably the most creative tourist to have pulled on the number fifteen jersey since the Lions' arrival in New Zealand, will be seen scratching his head with the standard-issue giant red foam finger handed to him by the official Lions' tour Morale Co-ordinator, wondering what he has to do to get a break from Clive Woodward short of swearing off potatoes for life while burning a copy of the 1916 Irish proclamation in the back of the team bus ...

'In polite society it [Woodward's preferred style of play] is known as "control rugby", although those of us who aren't blinkered by allegiance to any of the England teams it has served can think of far less flattering adjectives to describe it. An affront to everything that is good about the game, the brand of metronomic, smash-and-bash, wham-bam-kick three points if you can anti-rugby advocated by Woodward is even more painful to watch than it is to play. Hoof the ball to the opposition, draw an infringement from the ensuing melée and smile your trademark thin-lipped rictus as your place-kicker keeps the scoreboard ticking over three points at a time ...

Blackwash

'Well, I'm sorry, Sir Clive, but it may come as a huge shock to you to learn that there are those of us in Great Britain and Ireland who are of the strong opinion that as far as this Lions' tour is concerned, winning most certainly is not everything. There are those of us in Great Britain and Ireland who greeted your appointment as Lions' head coach with groans of despair. There are those of us in Great Britain and Ireland who find it incredibly difficult to wish any team under your tutelage well, and what's more, there are those of us in Great Britain and Ireland who are seriously questioning the wisdom of dragging our weary, hungover carcasses out of bed at some ungodly hour of the morning to watch your British and Irish Lions try to "England" New Zealand into submission in a Test match.'

My favourite paragraph though was this one: 'Was it for this that thousands of boorish, deck shoe-wearing city boys took six weeks out of the city to aroo-cha-cha halfway around the world at great expense in order to stand on pub tables with their trousers around their ankles while drinking pints of lager through a sock? It probably was but they're all floppy-fringed imbeciles and quite frankly the rest of us deserve better.' I still can't read that paragraph without doubling over.

There were some suggestions as to what should be done to Mr Glendenning. Paul Hayward of the *Daily Telegraph* said that the aforementioned 'city boys' should form a giant ruck, using Mr Glendenning as the ball. If Mr Glendenning had been in the Claddagh Bar in Newmarket, near Alexandra Park, this evening he might just have retracted his words. While there are certainly many upper-crust fans here – spending six weeks on the other side of the world doesn't come cheap – the vast majority are ordinary people. The Claddagh is run by a midget from Limerick, a man named Noel, who used to play for Young Munster. Unsurprisingly, the place was chock-full of 'Cookies' – Young Munster supporters – this evening. There were no floppy-fringed imbeciles to be seen; hell, there wasn't even a fringe in sight.

And what did they think of it all? A man from Newcastle West probably spoke for most of them when he said, 'Teeeessssfoookunmiiiightycarrraacckaltaaaaguddder'.

Flotsam on the fringe of hell
Game 11: British & Irish Lions V New Zealand, Third Test
Saturday 9 July 2005, Eden Park, Auckland

New Zealand 38
Tries: T. Umaga (2), C. Smith, A. Williams, R. Gear
Convs: L. McAlister (5)
Pens: L. McAlister

Lions 19
Tries: L. Moody
Convs: S. Jones
Pens: S. Jones (4)

> Pity for the tired men
> Up the line and down again
> Tramping where their comrades fell
> Flotsam on the fringe of hell.

It would, of course, be overkill to compare the mind-numbing effects of the Great War on soldiers thousands of miles from home with the travails of a mere rugby team, a trifling irrelevance by comparison. But the quote on the wall of an exhibition in Auckland Museum celebrating the sacrifice of New Zealanders in World War One might just have brought a wry smile to the lips of Lions' fans, players and management.

But, smiles or no smiles, the tramping continues. The Lions turned in another decent performance tonight. Slightly slower of thought and deed, they always looked a class below the All Blacks, even though the hosts were ravaged by injury, but played with plenty of pride and passion. Josh Lewsey said in Wellington before the Second Test that his one fear in rugby was 'not fronting up, not giving the best account of yourself'; the Lions certainly 'fronted up' for the last two Tests.

And the fans? Well, the media box atop the main stand in Eden Park is a state-of-the-art facility, which seats over 100 journalists in sound-proofed casing. During the game, the roars of the crowd barely filtered through, even at the most exciting moments. Before the match though the shouts of 'Lions! Lions! Lions!' could clearly be heard, the travelling support bursting into song after a minute's silence for the victims of the terrorist attacks in London.

'The fans have been absolutely amazing,' said winger, Mark Cueto. 'From the first day we landed, there were 40 or 50 of them at Auckland airport, shouting and roaring, and that was four weeks before the First Test. And they're still there now, roaring and encouraging. As we got closer to the Tests, to see the number of red shirts, it was something special.'

'The supporters have been absolutely outstanding,' added Paul O'Connell. 'You'd half-expect them to turn at some stage but they've been great. It's been a long tour, everyone's tired and the series is over but they've still been there. There were hundreds at the hotel today and there were thousands at the game. We weren't good but they were very good.'

While the Lions did 'front up', to use Lewsey's phrase, again tonight, once more, they came off second best. Only very early on in the contest did it appear as if they had any chance of victory. The first line-out they won, with Shane Byrne a late replacement for the ill Steve Thompson at hooker, turned into a maul that travelled twenty metres upfield and forced a penalty that Stephen Jones converted. From the restart, they poured forward again, Lewsey and Gethin Jenkins combining to get within sight of the line. Then though, with a four-man overlap, Donncha O'Callaghan elected to go for the line himself. It was not a mistake that a New Zealand forward would have made. As O'Connell put it afterwards, speaking generally about the All Blacks' advantage upfront: 'Their pack is more skilful than ours at the moment: you see their forwards throwing passes and beating people all the time.' They also have an awareness of time and space that would have, in that instance, seen them cross underneath the posts for a seven-pointer. As it was, the Lions forced a penalty and, as an extra reward, Tana Umaga was yellow-carded. 6-0 to the Lions, with the opposition skipper in the sin-bin for ten minutes? Not a bad start, even allowing for the try that ought to have been. The fans thought so: on the radio link to the referee's microphone, 'Bread of Heaven' could be heard ringing around the ground.

Then, it all went wrong. From a scrum on the Lions' ten-metre line, New Zealand were awarded a free kick. Sione Lauaki took it quickly and made ground. Byron Kelleher passed the ball left to Jerry Collins. Showing the awareness and passing skills that O'Callaghan didn't, the flanker saw that Will Greenwood, clearly thinking that Collins would attempt to bash his way forward, had stepped in, leaving space out wide. Collins gave a soft pass to his team-mate, Conrad Smith, and the centre cut through a poor attempted tackle by Geordan Murphy to score near the posts. 'It was a bit weird, because it all just opened up for me,' was how Smith saw it. 'Everyone ran to cover Jerry and that opened the gap for me.' 7-6 to New Zealand, with ten minutes gone. Not such a good start.

From there, it didn't get any better for the Lions. Playing in his first ever Test match, the fourth-choice All Black fly-half – after Dan Carter, Aaron Mauger and Leon MacDonald – Luke McAlister, was mixing the occasional bad with lots of good. Most of the time, he was chipping or grubbering the ball in behind the Lions. It was not, coach Wayne Smith, said later, a deliberate tactic: 'We try to make decisions on the pitch, logical decisions, based on the opportunities we see, and communicate them. Hopefully, the communication is good and the kick is good. It's responding to what you see and communicating it.' Both execution and communication were excellent tonight and, two minutes after Smith's try, they combined to produce another score for the home team. Once more, a beautifully judged chip caused panic in the Lions' ranks and the All Blacks retained the ball. When McAlister swung the ball wide, Gareth Thomas nearly intercepted, but the ball went loose and Sitiveni Sivivatu was stopped just short of the line. This time, McAlister elected to kick and, though it went straight to Dwayne Peel, the scrum-half fumbled the ball over the goal line and Ali Williams, the second-row who fulfilled Steve Hansen's prophecy that he would be one of the stars of the series, pounced for his second try in three games. That gave New Zealand a 14-6 lead and, by the time their captain returned, they still led by five, 14-9. 'Maybe the boys don't need me that much,' Umaga joked.

What was remarkable was Umaga's boys' approach while their skipper was confined to the sidelines: never did they let their intensity drop and they didn't change their style of play either. Many sides would have exploited every opportunity to slow the game down. Not New Zealand: Lauaki's quick tap – most teams would have delayed taking it for as long as possible – led to their first try; McAlister continued to chip the ball, a risky strategy at the best of times, even more so when the opposition has a numerical advantage; and at one stage they even took a quick line-out.

With rain continuing to fall, McAlister continued to kick short, though it wasn't always the correct option, notwithstanding the greasy conditions. He and Stephen Jones traded penalties until, two minutes before the break, New Zealand's greater class and penetration told once more. Another McAlister chip forced a knock-on from Lewsey and, from the resultant scrum, the fly-half powered through the tackle of his opposite number, popped the ball to Umaga and the captain burst over for New Zealand's third try. It was double scores, 24-12, at the break and, in truth, the scoreline didn't flatter the All Blacks. Nonetheless, it was far from vintage stuff: 'We played our best rugby in that first ten minutes,' said Conrad Smith, 'but it petered out the longer the game dragged on ... Graham had some stern words for us at half-time.'

'Maybe the challenge was gone, after three Tests,' the centre continued. 'I was still pretty hot but the game changed a bit.

Blackwash

They never got within a try and maybe some of us were looking ahead to the end. It's been a hard-won series. I don't think
the second half will have impressed him [Henry] too much
either. We'll have to improve a lot for the Tri Nations.'

While the All Blacks' display after the interval wasn't anything like as good as their performances in the first two Tests, it
was still mightily impressive; the fact that Conrad Smith was
aware that it was a level below that which the players demand of
themselves demonstrates just how much he and his team-mates
thirst for perfection. But, as Smith said, after a long series, it
can become difficult to maintain the intensity.

Yet another try for his centre partner and captain after 49
minutes effectively sealed the game and allowed New Zealand
to rest back on a significant pile of laurels. The All Blacks were
awarded a penalty after a five-metre scrum and elected to run
through a set move that resulted in Umaga crashing through
Jones and O'Connell to dive in underneath the uprights.
'Forward, forward', the touch judge had bellowed to the referee
of the scoring pass, but his advice was ignored, the try stood
and New Zealand had a massive 31-12 lead. To win, the Lions
would need to score at least three tries. The manner in which
the hosts had worked themselves into position for their last
score didn't augur well for them though. At one stage, Smith
had thrown out an inch-perfect, twenty-yard pass to Sivivatu,
who was bundled into touch at only the last possible moment;
the Lions simply weren't possessed of that sort of cutting edge
and, without such a cutting edge, a nineteen-point deficit, in wet
conditions, became an insurmountable obstacle. For the
tourists to have had any chance, in any of the Tests, the margin
would probably have had to remain two scores or less.

But for a second intervention from that same touch judge, the points' record that the All Blacks racked up in Wellington would have been under threat. Jones knocked on in the centre of the field and, once more, New Zealand counter-attacked. Chris Jack of all players, placed an elegant chip behind the Lions' defence and Sivivatu won the race to touch down. But those of us hooked up to the referee knew that the score would probably not be awarded: after Jones had knocked on, the touch judge saw him being tackled 'high and late' by Collins. Though the decision seemed, at best, marginal the flanker went to the sin-bin and the Lions had the reprieve of a penalty on the ten-metre line rather than making the acquaintance of a 24 point deficit.

They kicked for touch and pounded away at fourteen All Black opponents for four minutes before Lewis Moody touched down for a try. In the first half, playing an open, expansive, high-tempo game, New Zealand – minus a man – scored two tries in the same period of time. The Lions' efforts to maul the opposition over the line were close to embarrassing; it was only on their third attempt, against an understrength pack, that they managed to cross. By way of contrast, consider the performance of Sir Clive Woodward's England team in Wellington in 2003. At one point, they had been reduced to thirteen men, with the hosts camped on their line. In a remarkable show of courage, grit and steel, they held New Zealand at bay, scoring a crucial psychological victory in the run up to the World Cup. That England team wouldn't have taken three attempts to dispose of the All Blacks' maul defence.

More importantly, it showcased the difference in approach between the sides. New Zealand would never commit that much effort to trying to maul their way to victory: under Henry, Hansen and Smith, they play a much more attacking game. It's worth noting that, if the Sivivatu try had been allowed, the aggregate margin of victory would have been even greater.

It was no surprise that afterwards, Josh Lewsey, one of the most thoughtful, insightful members of the touring party, recognised that New Zealand have, through their style of play, set a new template for those who want to succeed at the highest levels in international rugby.

'When we go back to England, we have to start playing like them,' he said. 'That's how England became World Champions: we changed our game because we needed to change it. You can't blame the players for effort. Everyone gave it everything. And, when you're not good enough, you have to take the lessons and learn from it. The lads gave it everything; you couldn't ask for more. As long as you can go off that field with your head held high, that's all you can do, and we certainly did that in the Second and Third Tests. But when you lose three Tests convincingly you have to learn the lessons of that. It's difficult to turn on an attacking game overnight. It's something you have to work at, develop a structure and that takes a long time. New Zealand are doing it day in, day out, but it takes years to develop.'

To be fair to the Lions' management, it's not as if the players haven't attempted, at times, to put width on the game. 'Well, the word had come through that they would try some stuff, try to open it up and create some opportunities,' Conrad Smith admitted afterwards. 'And it went that way: we were stretched a few times but we scrambled quite well. They do have a good forward pack and they do drag players in, so there is space out wide.' It's just that the Lions have had a much more cautious way of going about it, with too many forwards loitering in wide positions, unlike the All Blacks, who prefer to keep such areas free for the players with identifiable hair partings.

Sure enough, in the closing twenty minutes, the Lions never looked like scoring again, not even possessing the ability to take advantage of overlaps. Ronan O'Gara came on, with Stephen Jones shifting to inside centre, Lewsey to full-back and Shane Horgan, another substitute, from centre, where he had been introduced to right-wing but if ever the words deckchairs and *Titanic* were to come to mind, that was the time. The difference was negligible, although O'Gara, who has enjoyed a good tour in terms of his own game, again looked sharp. 'Tonight, at the end,' said Woodward, 'we had O'Gara, Stephen Jones and Greenwood, who have never played together before, against the best in the world.' There is some truth in that, to give the head coach his due, but it also ought to be noted that, of the All Black team that started the First Test, only one back, Sivivatu, lined out in the same position tonight; it isn't necessarily continuity of selection that makes the All Blacks so good: it's the style of play they employ. Afterwards, Umaga understated how good his side was: 'We studied the Lions and we knew that's how they'd play. We created a game plan that we thought could combat that and we're very happy we did.'

The captain didn't protest enough methinks. With a game plan that employed such élan and flair, it was fitting that New Zealand scored the last try of the series and the circumstances in which they scored it were fitting as well. The Lions were, as the clock ran down, trying belatedly to introduce some width into the game but a pass from Will Greenwood found only the lurking Rico Gear, who intercepted and cantered away to score. Even when the Lions had to play expansive rugby they couldn't and the fact that it was Greenwood, a vital cog in the English team in 2003 but a pale shadow of his former self on this tour, was symptomatic of the Lions' difficulties this time. As they trudged back under the posts one last time they must truly have felt like flotsam on the fringe of hell. Even the post-final whistle walk around to clap their loyal supporters must have been penitential.

The good-natured ribbing from Henry mightn't have improved their mood: '[The] 2001 [Tour to Australia] was a great series, with seven tries each. I don't want to make much of that, but there were seven tries each in 2001 – I'll just repeat that – and we should have won the Second Test. The try count in this series? I've lost count.'

For the record, it was twelve to three in favour of the All Blacks. 'New Zealand's execution rate is very high,' sighed Eddie O'Sullivan. 'You don't need to ask them twice. There's a small difference in the skill level of individual players and we haven't been as efficient as New Zealand.'

Typically, the home team's post-match focus was on challenges yet to come: 'I'm very happy,' Umaga said. 'It's the result of the combination of a lot of work from these three guys [Henry, Steven Hansen and Smith] and Sir Brian Lochore [the selector] and the players. There was a lot of pressure on but we worked through it and stuck together. I think that's the best thing about the series: that we've come closer together as a unit. It's a happy bunch of players and we look forward to our next challenge.'

It's a sad way for Woodward to bow out of international

rugby: soon, he will take up a position with the football club, Southampton, but he protested that he has no regrets and is unconcerned about his legacy being tarnished. 'I can't say I'm too interested in my legacy and whether it's been tarnished by our failure to win here,' he said. 'I accepted this job and did it to the best of my ability. We can analyse what happened until we're blue in the face but in the end, it's sport. You have good days, you have bad days.'

Still, there can be little doubt but that he would have liked the curtain to come down in more auspicious circumstances.

New Zealand: M. Muliaina; R. Gear, C. Smith, T. Umaga (c), S. Sivivatu; L. McAlister, B. Kelleher; S. Lauaki, R. So'oialo, J. Collins; A. Williams, C. Jack; G. Somerville, K. Mealamu, T. Woodcock.
Subs: M. Holah for Lauaki h/t, C. Johnstone for Woodcock 44, J. Marshall for Kelleher 46, J. Ryan for Jack 76.
Yellow Cards: Umaga 7, Collins 55.

Lions: G. Murphy; M. Cueto, W. Greenwood, G. Thomas (c), J. Lewsey; S. Jones, D. Peel; R. Jones, L. Moody, S. Easterby; D. O'Callaghan, P. O'Connell; J. White, S. Byrne, G. Jenkins.
Subs: M. Dawson for Peel 49, G. Rowntree for Jenkins 49, S. Horgan for Thomas 50, R. O'Gara for Murphy 66, M. Corry for R. Jones 68, G. Bulloch for Byrne 70, M. Williams for Moody 75.

Referee: J. Kaplan (South Africa)

EPILOGUE

THE GATES OF EDEN

Sunday 10 July , Mount Eden, Auckland

From the top of Mount Eden, a dormant volcano, a bus ride and a climb away from the city centre, you can see all of Auckland's suburbs, goalposts – soccer and rugby alike – glittering under a pale, wintry sun. Eden Park can be seen in the distance, the hundreds of twinkling campervans in Alexandra Park too, but in truth there is little to mark Auckland out as different from any other capital city. Then the eye is caught by some vast swathes of green, with goalposts scattered about them as if an afterthought. The most remarkable thing is the location: just on the fringes of the Central Business District, acres of rugby fields roll away from Auckland Museum. Not a soccer ball in sight. Who says they aren't serious about their rugby?

With the wind sweeping across the rim of the crater, buffeting the locals who had come for a familiar stroll and the foreigners who had come to marvel, memories of last night's press conference came flooding back. With the tour at an end, thoughts inevitably turned to answering the broader questions, a contemplative task hardly out of place on a windswept mountaintop. The biggest of the broader questions is, 'Why?' Why did the Lions fail, not only to win but also to make an impression on the New Zealand public, never mind an impression in the Test arena? Yesterday afternoon I saw Ollie Smith in the city centre, running up the street. Nobody paid a blind bit of notice. Even the Lions' fans didn't seem to know who he was.

'The Lions did their best,' was Graham Henry's magnanimous response. 'The All Blacks played some quality rugby and in a different style which the Lions found difficult to handle. But the Lions' players always give it their best shot and I'm sure they did that.'

They certainly played with plenty of pride and passion in the last two Tests and demonstrated good spirit in the midweek games, when they were being pummelled by psychopathic locals playing in the games of their lives. As the saying goes, Christmas comes but once a year; the Lions only arrive in New Zealand once every twelve. Of those who donned provincial jerseys on this tour, only Gordon Slater, the veteran Taranaki prop, played against the Lions in 1993. In short, there is something special about a tour like this. 'It doesn't happen very often, the Lions,' said Tana Umaga. 'It's a great concept and, for us, it's the second biggest thing, after the World Cup.' It's a big thing for their fans as well: from coffee shops in Amberley to a barbershop in Auckland – 'You follow rugby?' I asked the woman who was tending to me. 'Well, you bloody well have to, mate, in this job. It's pretty much all I talk about.' The uniqueness of the Lions, added to the passion that already exists, is a potent mix.

'Before this tour, the Lions had lost nine out of ten Test series in New Zealand [the 1888 crop didn't play a Test series, though they did tour],' said Sir Clive Woodward. 'Now it's ten out of eleven. We were under no illusions about how difficult it would be. Everything should be kept in perspective, but I have to accept that this is how I will be judged.'

'You have to look at our record down here: the record is better everywhere else,' added Bill Beaumont. 'If we had the same bunch of players, without injuries, I'm pretty confident that we would have done well in South Africa or Australia.'

'You can see from the midweek games that we've played why it's so difficult to come here,' Woodward also said. 'They have such a talented bunch of players to pick from that they will challenge you.'

What makes New Zealand rugby special is that, at every level, there is something to play for. Club players want to wear the provincial jersey, provincial players want Super 12 contracts, Super 12 players lust after an All Black cap. At every level, the players are looking over their shoulders. 'They've put the pressure on us to step up to the mark,' Chris Jack said after the Second Test, speaking about the demands placed on him and his team-mates by their coaches. 'And, if you don't step up to the mark, you're gone.'

Even apart from the desire of those in the lower tiers to displace those above them, the combined weight of history and expectation might lead to pressure to perform, but something that Jerry Collins said in Wellington still resonates: 'Yeah, there's a lot of pressure there. You get it from the supporters, from the bus driver, from the guy at the butcher's. Yeah, there's more pressure if you lose but you've got to take the good with the bad and you've got to try and take the good out if it. Work the bad to your good.'

The Last Great Tour?

New Zealand rugby players respond to challenges – otherwise they end up driving buses or slicing corned beef. The challenge, this time, wasn't to beat the opposition up in the provinces: it was to win the Test series. The internationals were kept far from the risk of injury, wrapped in cotton wool, training 80 minutes a day and participating in only a glorified training session against Fiji before the showdown in Christchurch. And that defeat, that crushing defeat, in which the Lions were reduced to kicking a penalty goal to remove the big, round zero from the scoreboard, must have had a devastating psychological effect.

'The Lions came with high hopes and I think it really hurt them, the New Zealand performance in the first game,' Conrad Smith said last night, echoing what Dorothy, the retired airport volunteer, told me back in Auckland airport. 'The Lions rely on their forward strength but we really broke them up front. Then the backs could take over. That gave us a big advantage.'

Big, huge, massive: the dominance of the New Zealand pack allowed them to dictate the pace of the game; the Lions were never able to slow proceedings down to a level more suited to their gameplan. Perhaps one could say that the seeds of that forward display were sown in 2003, when the All Blacks, possessed of dazzling talent in the backs, came undone in the World Cup because their forwards struggled to dominate; unusually, a nation once feared for its forward strength and kicking game had come to rely on the men behind the scrum to win matches for them.

'We're definitely better,' admitted hooker, Keven Mealamu, 'but I couldn't put a figure on it. I guess we have more games under our belt now, and more experience. And we took the experience from 2003 and learned from it and maybe don't make the same mistakes that we did then. There's nothing better for a forward than seeing the opposition scrum going backwards. It gives us more opportunities to score as well.'

As Graham Rowntree told me back in Christchurch, 'My dad always used to say, "forwards win games, backs decide the score".'

Then, quite apart from the performance in the First Test, when the Lions couldn't even erect a platform on which to perform, there were the injuries. Mike Tindall and Phil Vickery, if fit, would almost certainly have started. Then there were Lawrence Dallaglio – a born leader, a three-time Lions' tourist and former England captain – and Brian O'Driscoll – talisman and captain – being removed from the fray on medical carts. Richard Hill and Tom Shanklin, two more top performers, also limped out of the tour. Simon Taylor and Malcolm O'Kelly, seasoned, skilful internationals, preceded them. And that list of eight ignores another battalion of players who were simply out of form – D'Arcy, Greenwood, Robinson, Kay and Grewcock. Even Jonny Wilkinson, who has been plagued by injury since dropping the goal that won England the World Cup, was not at his best, even though he played well in the Test series and is far from being, as some suggest, 'finished'. By contrast, New Zealand, but for Anton Oliver, who may not have started anyway, reported a clean bill of health; their starting XV was backboned by the Canterbury Crusaders, the 2005 Super 12 champions. To boot, by the time they arrived here, the Lions' players already had a full season under their belts; this is a perennial problem: when the southern hemisphere sides tour the north in the autumn, they are at the end of their season and, when the

European teams venture south of the equator at this time of year, they are on their last legs. So it was for the Lions.

And then, while events conspired to paint Dallaglio and O'Driscoll out of the picture, New Zealand had someone special wearing the captain's armband.

'Tana is a great leader,' said Smith, who also plays alongside him for the Wellington Hurricanes. 'He can play anywhere; he's just one of those wonderful players who come around now and again. I'm lucky enough to have the opportunity to play alongside him.'

And Henry was fulsome in his praise yesterday evening: 'I'd like to compliment the skipper, Tana Umaga, who I thought was the player of the series and was quite outstanding again tonight.'

Outstanding and all as New Zealand were, a Lions' tour presents difficulties of its own. The core of the opposition had been in place since 2003; the Lions didn't have the luxury of a long period in which they could get to know one another. And, as Ian McGeechan reiterated on Tuesday night, they could have done with more time: 'You need a minimum number of games leading into the First Test and we were probably two games short of that here ... It certainly helped in 1997 [when the Lions beat South Africa] to have that extra time to put combinations together, and it is the balance leading up to the First Test that's the critical one because you're pulling four groups of players together.'

As Eddie O'Sullivan mentioned last week, 'It's a big challenge, players getting to know each other. It's challenging even at international level, because you're not with guys week in, week out, and it's even more of a challenge on a Lions' tour.'

Epilogue

'The Lions is different,' said Woodward. 'It's not like a national team where you can build up a team; it's a different challenge. New Zealand have the same core of players that lost in the last World Cup and they've learned from that and moved on. With the Lions, you have three or four weeks to bring together four countries against that team. It's one of the more difficult things that I've tried to achieve in my coaching career. So, you have to keep some perspective: it's not easy.'

As for the style of play Woodward employed, something he said last night, when speaking about what makes the All Blacks so good, bears repeating: 'I think Wales are probably the closest team to them in terms of the skill level.' It's not as if Sir Clive is ignorant of the fact that, of the Home Nations, Wales played the best rugby this season; indeed, he commented on television prior to the First Test that the 40 minutes they played after half-time in Paris this spring was the best he's ever seen. Woodward merely felt that his style, with the players to implement it, would be more effective in the Land of the Long White Cloud. It's worth remembering that Wales haven't beaten the All Blacks since 1953 and have never beaten them outside the UK.

Though it lacked grace to say it last night, after such a comprehensive series defeat, the Lions' head coach also noted that the lack of preparation time he had enjoyed with his charges made things easier for New Zealand. That wouldn't be the case in the future, he said: 'I'd like to caution New Zealand with a warning: in sport, you have your good days and you have your bad days, and when you get to something like a World Cup, reputations can be destroyed in one game ... I'm looking forward to the Grand Slam tour [when the All Blacks tour the British Isles this autumn], where they play each of the four countries one after another, week after week, when they're fresh and fit and the New Zealand team has been battered. I'd just like to see how they get on then.'

There were other fighting words from the Lions' head coach. Surely, the questioners asked, the Test series, the aggregate score, the try-count, proved that there was a gulf between the way Super 12 countries play the game and the methods preferred in Europe?

'I don't think there's any gulf between the northern and southern hemisphere. You can only judge teams like New Zealand in the World Cup, where all the teams are coming in with the same amount of preparation and you're up against the best-prepared teams in the world. There's no difference between the north and south as long as they're on a level play-ing field. Who holds the World Cup at the moment?'

Quite apart from being the only coach in the history of sport to gloat in defeat, Woodward may be slightly wrong about this. Paul O'Connell lamented the fact that the New Zealand for-wards were more skilful than their Lions counterparts and Eddie O'Sullivan admitted there was a slight difference in skill levels. It may not amount to a gulf, but the way the All Black forwards are big and strong, yet light on their feet, gives them a marked advantage over British and Irish opponents, who hail from lands where, in the muck and rain, hard men are preferred to soft hands. Still, as the World Cup is the only occasion on which north and south meet in peak physical condition, rather than at the end of a long domestic campaign, Woodward is right to say that it is the true test of a team; it is too early to judge how good this New Zealand side actually is. Then again, last night was neither the time nor the place to make that point: credit ought to have been given to Graham Henry and company.

Sir Clive had one last dig at those who had questioned his decision to bring such a large squad:

It's staggering how much people write about the numbers. It's black and white for me: players can only play once a week ... To be brutally honest, I'd prefer to have brought more players and play more games. I'd like to make it bigger. But, if I were being brutally selfish, as I've said, I'd take the top 22 players, not play them in the provincial games, base them in Melbourne and fly them in for the Tests but that would be the end of the Lions.

The comment about more games brought laughter from the press corps when he made it, in a television interview. Henry was amused too: 'I assume he said that in jest.'

'No!' chuckled the audience.

'He didn't?' A pause. 'Oh dear, I'm flabbergasted.'

Woodward did say though before the tour began, that he would have liked to bring 60 or 70 players: touring a country like New Zealand should be an experience in itself; and learning from new coaches and new players can enhance the game in the home nations. Certainly, a few more games in the lead up to the First Test wouldn't have hurt the Lions' cause and, considering the injury list, a few more players might have helped matters too. But the Lions' head coach ought to have been more circumspect about that particular idea: it was a suggestion that, without being fleshed out, was bound to draw only derision from the media and public.

O'Connell, a half-empty bottle of Steinlager clutched in his hand, giving off the air of a man who was only too happy that the flight home was fast approaching, sighed that the Lions might have had a chance of victory but things didn't fall in their favour: 'Possibly if we'd a bit of luck with injuries but if you look at the tour for outstanding players or player, there's none really. No one really inspired us and that's the one thing that hits me. But you still need things to go your way as well.'

So we're back to the 'what ifs' and 'if onlys' again. But O'Connell's point about the lack of inspiration is an important one too. There were few outstanding performances on tour: Josh Lewsey against the Bay of Plenty; Ryan Jones against Otago; Shane Williams against Manawatu; and maybe Simon Easterby in the Second Test did stand out but there was no sustained excellence, no one standing there in front of the New Zealand public, beating his chest and saying, 'Be afraid, folks, be very afraid'. Again, one might be tempted to argue that, if anyone had got a run of games, if there had been a Test squad picked from the outset, that some totem might have emerged, but then, we're back to 'what ifs' and questioning decisions that Woodward took for logical reasons.

Ultimately though, it's hard to know, no matter what team had been picked, no matter what style of play had been employed, no matter how many of the 'what ifs' fell in their favour, whether the Lions could have won. It might just be that the All Blacks are the world's outstanding team at the moment, boasting world-class performers at prop – Carl Hayman and Tony Woodcock – second-row – Chris Jack and Ali Williams – openside flanker – Richie McCaw – scrum-half – Byron Kelleher – fly-half – Dan Carter – centre – Aaron Mauger and Tana Umaga – wing – Sitiveni Sivivatu – and full-back – Mils Muliaina.

Epilogue

Anton Oliver, Keven Mealamu, Jerry Collins, Rico Gear, Joe Rokocoko and Leon MacDonald could all feel aggrieved at not being on that list. And then there's Rodney So'oialo, Greg Somerville, James Ryan, Jono Gibbes, Sione Lauaki, Ma'a Nonu, Conrad Smith and Doug Howlett, who would get into any of the current English, Irish, Welsh or Scottish teams. That's an embarrassment of riches in any language.

To the second big question then: can the Lions survive in the modern era?

'The Lions is the greatest brand in world rugby and we wanted it to continue to be,' said Beaumont. 'In the dressing room there's disappointment but everyone says they wouldn't change a thing; it's been a great rugby experience. I look at it myself and ask, "What would I change?" Apart from the result of the Test series, nothing. I'd like to congratulate the All Blacks on their victory.'

The tour manager made a pledge too: 'We will be very competitive in South Africa in 2009. Of this tour, there's nothing we would change. We brought the right amount of players – just look at the amount of injuries we've suffered. I have to say though that we were two or three games short of what a real Lions' tour has been in the past: maybe the coaching staff would have wanted a few more.'

However, rumours are already circulating that, in future, the tours will be much more condensed, with perhaps a handful of warm-up games against strong provincial opposition before a Test series. How that ultimately develops, only time will tell but if those suggestions are implemented, no tour will ever again reach places like New Plymouth, Palmerston North and Invercargill and dozens of players won't get the same exposure to the joys of the highways and byways of the southern hemisphere. This could be the end.

'It's very, very important to keep the Lions' ethos,' added Woodward. 'I'm proud of everyone who's gone on this tour, players, management, everyone. There hasn't been a single problem with anyone in the party. The players have been fantastic ambassadors. It's a tough country to come to, especially to play Tests and midweek games; no one else does it. It's very difficult. But it's a challenging thing to do and that's why you do it. Fundamentally, I have no regrets about this tour.'

'The Lions must survive,' his opposite number, Henry, said. 'The Lions' brand is something special; every time they tour, it's a major occasion and they've had some great teams down the years. I think it's essential. There's still a bit of Lion in me. They're a special team: the players in each of the four countries, England, Ireland, Scotland and Wales, see it as the peak of their career to be selected for the Lions and it would be very disappointing if that went away.

'The Lions must continue.'

PS: The Last Bus Home
Wednesday 13 July, Auckland International Airport
'Oh, we're not going straight home,' he answered, in a broad Scottish accent.

'No, off to Bangkok for a bit of R 'n' R,' another elaborated.

'Well for some ...' sighed an Irishman.

'Ah, now, we'll be taking it fairly seriously. There's a nice thing there we want to see. A fruitmarket, is it?' He wasn't being serious.

Epilogue

'Meat market, more like,' said another Irishman. Chuckles all round. The Lions' fans are still all friends. Everyone's had a good time.

I was forced to give thanks again to the easygoing nature of the New Zealand people. Due to a cornering error early on in my travels my campervan – now minus the 'Bush-Cheney '04' sticker, which was finally whipped off in a car park in Whangarei – had sustained an injury to its left side. Pythagoras I ain't.

'Ah, don't worry about it, mate. Only a scratch,' said the rental car assessor. 'Hey, you boys have suffered enough already, eh?'

The Press newspaper was good enough to pen a gushing editorial on the behaviour of the travelling fans after, naturally, poking some fun at the knight at the head of the party: 'But if [Sir Clive] Woodward himself will not be sorely missed, the same cannot be said of the thousands of British (*sic*) supporters who turned parts of New Zealand stadiums into seas of red. These fans were not part of the "Barmy Army", a group which was over-hyped by its self-styled leader, Freddie Parker. Several businesses, beguiled by Parker's claims of the numerous fans he would bring to their establishments to drink and party, found to their cost that many British and Irish fans firmly rejected any association with the "Barmy Army".

'Rather, the touring supporters who will be remembered fondly are the legions of friendly and good-natured fans that packed the streets and bars of New Zealand cities. Unlike their rugby team, these supporters could teach New Zealanders a thing or two. They showed that it is possible to have a civilised approach to drinking, without the violence that is too often part of the New Zealand culture of alcohol.

'Above all, despite having paid large sums to be part of what was a losing campaign, their reaction was not one of bitterness. Instead, they demonstrated a spirit of sportsmanship too often lacking among New Zealand sporting crowds.'

Consider then this extract from Doug Golighty's column in the *Truth* (a fine publication, the front-page headline of which reads, 'Babe Goes Barmy For Rugby Stud'): 'Leaving Wellington's Ron Jarden Stadium on Saturday night, I was bloody embarrassed to be a New Zealander. And it was all to do with the attitude of drunk, boorish, pig-headed, arrogant All Blacks' supporters. At the best of times, they can be vitriolic, foul-mouthed and abusive, but they surpassed themselves on Saturday. I'm not talking about gumboot wearing, overall-clad working-class types here ... Rather it was the actions of the chardonnay-swilling, beer-guzzling corporate types who soured one of the better nights in New Zealand's rugby history. In gutless fashion and fuelled by the fire water, in they went. "How much for your fucking jersey now, you wankers?" a middle-aged, smartly-attired idiot shouted at a group of four Scotsmen in kilts.' The abuse chronicled by Golighty actually got worse and there is no doubt that, after drink, some New Zealanders metamorphose into lager louts.

Poor Freddie Parker, subject of a few unflattering stories involving percentages and promises in last weekend's papers, has disappeared. As Paul Smith of the *New Zealand Herald* wrote in his online blog: 'Since the call for a coup against the "Barmy Army" commander-in-chief, Freddie Parker [made by Smith a few weeks ago], nothing has been seen or heard of the man. He has disappeared from TV screens and cannot apparently be contacted by media organisations. Concerns are rising that the request for an overthrow of the Great Leader has been taken too seriously.' Poor Freddie.

From matters trivial to serious. Sir Clive might have thought that, on Saturday night, he was firing the last shots in the war of words by giving New Zealand a warning about the fickleness of sport and the need to prove oneself in the World Cup on the only stage that counts. Graham Henry though immediately launched a strong riposte.

'I guess that's an attempt at camouflage,' the All Blacks' head coach said. 'You can spin these things any way you like, but what are we supposed to do? Deliberately not win the series we play in the run-up to a World Cup?

'It's ridiculous. Not worth commenting on really. What did we bring to the series? I think we played some quality rugby. What did they bring? They came over here thinking they would win the first Test with a particular style and a particular selection: thoughts that proved to be mistaken. In my opinion, the game has moved on since England won the World Cup in 2003 and the shift is irrevocable. I don't believe it is possible to simply pick a huge pack of forwards and a goal-kicking fly-half and win a game that isn't being played in a blizzard. Rugby is multidimensional now, and that has to be more stimulating for everyone involved. What more can I say? We had more gamebreakers in our side than they did in theirs. It's the way of the world. One team was better than the other.'

A clear win for Henry: a victory on points against a dogged opponent who refused to stay down. The above statement is an eloquent summary of the Test series but the final words were really uttered yesterday in Waitangi. Situated towards the north of the North Island, a little town known before then as the 'hell hole of the Pacific' was where the Treaty of Waitangi was signed in 1840. The document, signed between a representative of the Queen and hundreds of Maori chiefs, remains the basis of New Zealand's constitution, even today. A group of Welsh Lions' supporters on a package tour was wandering around the central attraction, Treaty House, at the same time as me.

'End of the line, now,' one said to me.

'Homeward bound. Cracking holiday. Pity about the rugby.'

He thought for a minute, pursed his lips and raised his eyebrows pensively. Then, he nodded.

'Yup. You've said it, mate.'

The Tour In Detail

Game 1 V Bay of Plenty,
Saturday 4 June 2004, Rotorua International Stadium, Rotorua

Bay of Plenty 20
Tries: C. Bourke, M. Williams
Convs: M. Williams (2)
Pens: M. Williams (2)

British & Irish Lions 34
Tries: J. Lewsey (2), M. Cueto, T. Shanklin, D. Peel, G. D'Arcy
Convs: R. O'Gara (2)

Bay of Plenty: A. Cashmore; F. Bolavucu, A. Bunting, G. McQuoid, A. Tahana; M. Williams, K. Senio; C. Bourke, N. Latu, W. Ormond; B. Upton, M. Sorensen; B. Castle, A. Lutui, S. Davison.
Subs: W. Smith for Bourke 48, A. Stewart for Bolavucu 53, T. Filise for Davison 62, P. Tupai for Sorensen 62.

Lions: J. Lewsey; M. Cueto, B. O'Driscoll, G. Henson, T. Shanklin; R. O'Gara, D. Peel; L. Dallaglio, M. Williams, R. Hill; B. Kay, P. O'Connell; M. Stevens, G. Bulloch, G. Jenkins.
Subs: M. Corry for Dallaglio 16, S. Thompson for Bulloch 65, A.

Sheridan for Stevens 65, G. D'Arcy for Henson 68, M. Dawson for Shanklin 76.

Referee: P. Honiss (New Zealand)

Game 2 V Taranaki
Wednesday 8 June, Yarrow Stadium, New Plymouth

Taranaki 14
Tries: C. Masoe, B. Watt
Convs: B. Watt (2)

British & Irish Lions 36
Tries: G. Murphy (2), M. Corry, S. Horgan
Convs: C. Hodgson (2)
Pens: C. Hodgson (4)

Taranaki: S. Ireland; S. Tagicakibau, M. Stewart, L. Mafi, C. Woods; S. Young, C. Fevre; T. Soqeta, C. Masoe, J. Willis; S. Breman, P. Tito (c); G. Slater, A. Hore, T. Penn.
Subs: B. Watt for Ireland 16, M. Harvey for Tagicakibau h/t, J. Eaton for Breman 64, R. Bryant for Willis 66, J. King for Fevre 67, H. Mitchell for Penn 68.
Yellow cards: A. Hore 53.

Lions: G. Murphy; S. Horgan, W. Greenwood, O. Smith, D. Hickie; C. Hodgson, C. Cusiter; M. Owen, L. Moody, M. Corry (c); D. Grewcock, D. O'Callaghan; J. Hayes, A. Titterrell, G. Rowntree.
Subs: G. Jenkins for Hayes 48, S. Byrne for Titterrell 68, G. Cooper for Cusiter 74.

Referee: K. Deaker (New Zealand)

330

Game 3 V New Zealand Maori

Saturday 11 June 2005, Waikato Stadium, Hamilton

New Zealand Maori 19
Tries: L. MacDonald
Convs: L. McAlister
Pens: D. Hill (2), L. McAlister (2)

British & Irish Lions 13
Tries: B. O'Driscoll
Convs: S. Jones
Pens: S. Jones (2)

Maoris: L. MacDonald; R. Gear, R Tipoki, L. McAlister, C. Ralph; D. Hill, P. Weepu; A. MacDonald, M. Holah, J. Gibbes (c); S. Hohneck, R. Filipo; C. Hayman, C. Flynn, D. Manu.
Subs: C. Spencer for Hill 42, G. Feek for Manu 52, D. Braid for Filipo 72

Lions: J. Lewsey; T. Shanklin, B. O'Driscoll (c), G. D'Arcy, S. Williams; S. Jones, M. Dawson; M. Owen, M. Williams, R. Hill; P. O'Connell, S. Shaw; J. White, S. Thompson, A. Sheridan.
Subs: G. Jenkins for Sheridan 48, S. Byrne for Thompson 72.
Yellow cards: Sheridan 38.

Referee: S Walsh (New Zealand)

Game 4 V Wellington

Wednesday 15 June 2005, Westpac Stadium, Wellington

Vodafone Wellington Lions 6
Pens: J. Gopperth (2)

The Last Great Tour?

British and Irish Lions 23
Tries: G. Thomas
Pens: J. Wilkinson (6)

Wellington: S. Paku; L. Fa'atau, M. Nonu, T. Tu'ipulotu, R. Kinikinilau; J. Gopperth, P. Weepu; T. Waldrom, B. Herring, K. Ormsby; L. Andrews, R. Filipo; T. Fairbrother, M. Schwalger, J. McDonnell (c).
Subs: K. Thompson for Herring h/t, L. Mahony for Schwalger 59, C. James for Kinikinilau 67, J. Purdie for Filipo71, R. Flutey for Weepu 73, J. Schwalger for Fairbrother 76, T. Ellison for Tu'ipulotu 76.

Lions: J. Lewsey; G. Thomas, B. O'Driscoll (c), G. Henson, J. Robinson; J. Wilkinson, D. Peel; M. Corry, N. Back, S. Easterby; B. Kay, D. Grewcock; J. White, S. Byrne, G. Jenkins.
Subs: S. Jones for Henson 62, S. Horgan for Lewsey 68, M. Stevens for White 72, C. Cusiter for Peel 72.

Referee: P. Honiss (New Zealand)

Game 5 V Otago
Saturday 18 June, 2005, Carisbrook, Dunedin

Otago 19
Tries: B. Lee
Convs: N. Evans
Pens: N. Evans (4)

British & Irish Lions 30
Tries: W. Greenwood, R. Jones, S. Williams
Convs: C. Hodgson (3)
Pens: C. Hodgson (3)

Otago: G. Horton; H. Pedersen, N. Brew, S. Mapusua, M. Saunders; N. Evans, D. Lee; G. Webb, J. Blackie, C. Newby (c); T. Donnelly, F. Levi; C. Dunlea, J. MacDonald, C. Hoeft.
Subs: J. Shoemark for Brew 47, J. Aldworth for Dunlea 52, J. Vercoe for MacDonald 62, C. Smylie for Lee 75.

Lions: G. Murphy; D. Hickie, W. Greenwood, G. D'Arcy, S. Williams; C. Hodgson, C. Cusiter; R. Jones, M. Williams, S. Easterby; D. O'Callaghan, S. Shaw; M. Stevens, G. Bulloch (c), G. Rowntree.
Subs: O. Smith for D'Arcy 52, M. Dawson for Cusiter 61, A. Sheridan for Rowntree 62, S. Thompson for Bulloch 62, D. Grewcock for Shaw 62, R. O'Gara for Hodgson 70, M. Owen for Jones 77.

Referee: L. Bray (New Zealand).

Game 6 V Southland
Tuesday 21 June 2005, Invercargill

Southland 16
Tries: H. T-Pole
Convs: R. Apanui
Pens: R. Apanui (3)

Lions 26
Tries: G. Henson (2)
Convs: R. O'Gara (2)
Pens: R. O'Gara (4)

Southland: J. Wilson; M. Harrison, B. Milne, F. Muliaina, W. Lotawa; R. Apanui, J. Cowan; P. Miller, H. T-Pole, H. Tamariki; D.

Quate, H. MacDonald; A. Dempsey, J. Rutledge, C. Dermody (c).
Subs: J. Wright for Miller 40, D. Hall for Rutledge 59, P. Te Whare
for Milne 63.

Lions: G. Murphy; M. Cueto, O. Smith, G. Henson, D. Hickie; R.
O'Gara, G. Cooper; M. Owen (c), M. Williams, L. Moody; D.
O'Callaghan, S. Shaw; J. Hayes, A. Titterrell, M. Stevens.
Subs: A. Sheridan for Stevens h/t, G. Bulloch for Titterrell 50, T.
Shanklin for Smith 50, C. Cusiter for Cooper 50, S. Easterby for
Owen 68, G. D'Arcy for Murphy 75.

Referee: K. Deaker (New Zealand)

Game 7 V New Zealand, First Test
Saturday 25 June 2005, Jade Stadium, Christchurch

New Zealand 21
Tries: A. Williams, S. Sivivatu
Convs: D. Carter
Pens: D. Carter (3)

British & Irish Lions 3
Pens: J. Wilkinson

New Zealand: L. MacDonald; D. Howlett, T. Umaga (c), A.
Mauger, S. Sivivatu; D. Carter, J. Marshall; R. So'oialo, R.
McCaw, J. Collins; A. Williams, C. Jack; C. Hayman, K. Mealamu,
T. Woodcock.
Subs: G. Somerville for Woodcock 67, B. Kelleher for Marshall
67, M. Muliaina for MacDonald 68, R. Gear for Umaga 74, D.
Witcombe for Mealamu 74, S. Lauaki for Collins 76.

Lions: J. Robinson; J. Lewsey, B. O'Driscoll (c), J. Wilkinson, G.

Thomas; S. Jones, D. Peel; M. Corry, N. Back, R. Hill; B. Kay, P. O'Connell; J. White, S. Byrne, G. Jenkins.
Subs: W. Greenwood for O'Driscoll2, R. Jones for Hill17, S. Thompson for Byrne 56, S. Horgan for Robinson 56, D. Grewcock for Kay 56, M. Dawson for Peel 72.
Yellow Cards: P. O'Connell 12.

Referee: J. Jutge (France)

Game 8 V Manawatu
Tuesday 28 June 2005, Palmerston North

Manawatu 6
Pens: J Hargreaves (2)

Lions 109
Tries: S. Williams (5), M. Cueto (2), R. O'Gara (2), M. Corry, G. Murphy, J. Robinson, C. Hodgson, O. Smith, N. Back, G. D'Arcy, G. Cooper
Convs: C. Hodgson (7), R. O'Gara (5)

Manawatu: F. Bryant; B. Gray, J. Campbell, M. Oldridge, J. Leota; G. Smith, J. Hargreaves; B. Matenga, J. Bradnock, H Triggs; P Rodgers, T Faleafaga; K. Barrett, N. Kemp (c), S. Moore.
Subs: B. Trew for Smith 47, C. Moke for Matenga 50, N. Buckley for Oldridge 53, I. Cook for Barrett 64, D. Palu for Hargreaves 71, S. Easton for Bradnock 76.
Yellow Cards: N. Kemp 29, S. Easton 78.

Lions: G. Murphy; J. Robinson, O. Smith, G. D'Arcy, S. Williams; C. Hodgson, C. Cusiter; M. Owen, M. Williams, M. Corry; D. O'Callaghan, S. Shaw; J. Hayes, G. Bulloch (c), A. Sheridan.

Subs: A. Titterrell for Bulloch 39, B. Cockbain for O'Callaghan h/t, N. Back for M Williams h/t, G. Cooper for Cusiter h/t, R. O'Gara for Hodgson 50, M. Cueto for Robinson 52, M. Stevens for Hayes 60.
Yellow Cards: M. Stevens 74.

Referee: L. Bray (New Zealand)

Game 9 V New Zealand, Second Test

Saturday 2 July 2005, Westpac Stadium, Wellington

New Zealand 48
Tries: D. Carter (2), T. Umaga, S. Sivivatu, R. McCaw
Convs: D. Carter (4)
Pens: D. Carter (5)

Lions 18
Tries: G. Thomas, S. Easterby
Convs: J. Wilkinson
Pens: J. Wilkinson (2)

New Zealand: M. Muliaina; R. Gear, T. Umaga (c), A. Mauger, S. Sivivatu; D. Carter, B. Kelleher; R. So'oialo, R. McCaw, J. Collins; A. Williams, C. Jack; G. Somerville, K. Mealamu, T. Woodcock.
Subs: L. MacDonald for Mauger 38, S. Lauaki for Collins 65, J. Marshall for Kelleher 65, D. Witcombe for Mealamu 68, M. Nonu for Sivivatu 72, J. Gibbes for Jack 74, C. Johnstone for Woodcock 76.

Lions: J. Lewsey; J Robinson, G. Thomas (c), G. Henson, S. Williams; J. Wilkinson, D. Peel; R. Jones, L. Moody, S. Easterby; D. O'Callaghan, P. O'Connell; J. White, S. Thompson, G. Jenkins.

Subs: G. Rowntree for Jenkins 56, S. Jones for Wilkinson 60, S. Horgan for Henson 68, M. Corry for O'Connell 72, S. Byrne for Thompson 77.

Referee: A. Cole (Australia)

Game 10 V Auckland

Tuesday 5 July 2005, Eden Park, Auckland

Auckland 13
Tries: I. Nacewa
Convs: B. Ward
Pens: B. Ward (2)

Lions 17
Tries: M. Williams
Pens: R. O'Gara (3), C. Hodgson

Auckland: B. Ward; I. Nacewa, B. Atiga, S. Tuitupou, J. Rokocoko; T. Lavea, S. Devine; A. MacDonald, D. Braid, J. Collins (c); B. Williams, B. Mika; J. Afoa, S. Telefoni, S. Taumoepeau.
Subs: J. Kaino for Mika 45, N. White for Taumoepeau 56, K. Haiu for MacDonald 65, G. Williams for Nacewa 70, J. Fonokalafi for Telefoni 76, I. Toe'ava for Atiga 76.

Lions: G. Murphy; M. Cueto, W. Greenwood, G. D'Arcy, D. Hickie; C. Hodgson, M. Dawson; M. Owen, M. Williams, J. White; B. Kay, S. Shaw; J. Hayes, G. Bulloch (c), A. Sheridan.
Subs: R. O'Gara for Hodgson 21, S. Horgan for Greenwood 49, M. Corry for White 54, M. Stevens for Hayes 59.

Referee: S. Walsh (New Zealand).

Game 11 V New Zealand, Third Test

Saturday 9 July 2005, Eden Park, Auckland

New Zealand 38
Tries: T. Umaga (2), C. Smith, A. Williams, R. Gear
Convs: L. McAlister (5)
Pens: L. McAlister

Lions 19
Tries: L. Moody
Convs: S. Jones
Pens: S. Jones (4)
New Zealand: M. Muliaina; R. Gear, C. Smith, T. Umaga (c), S. Sivivatu; L. McAlister, B. Kelleher; S. Lauaki, R. So'oialo, J. Collins; A. Williams, C. Jack; G. Somerville, K. Mealamu, T. Woodcock.
Subs: M. Holah for Lauaki h/t, C. Johnstone for Woodcock 44, J. Marshall for Kelleher 46, J. Ryan for Jack 76.
Yellow Cards: Umaga 7, Collins 55.

Lions: G. Murphy; M. Cueto, W.. Greenwood, G. Thomas (c), J. Lewsey; S. Jones, D. Peel; R. Jones, L. Moody, S. Easterby; D. O'Callaghan, P. O'Connell; J. White, S. Byrne, G. Jenkins.
Subs: M. Dawson for Peel 49, G. Rowntree for Jenkins 49, S. Horgan for Thomas 50, R. O'Gara for Murphy 66, M. Corry for R. Jones 68, G. Bulloch for Byrne 70, M. Williams for Moody 75.

Referee: J. Kaplan (South Africa)

APPENDIX II

Lions Tour Statistics
Game Time

	Games	Minutes
Josh Lewsey	6	468
Geordan Murphy	6	461
Martyn Williams	7	445
Donncha O'Callaghan	6	440
Gethin Jenkins	7	409
Simon Shaw	5	400
Paul O'Connell	5	392
Julian White	5	392
Michael Owen	6	391
Martin Corry	7	376
Will Greenwood	5	367
Dwayne Peel	5	353
Mark Cueto	5	348
Simon Easterby	5	332
Denis Hickie	4	320
Shane Williams	4	320
Lewis Moody	4	315
Gordon D'Arcy	6	309
Ben Kay	4	296
Gareth Thomas	4	290
Ryan Jones	4	288
Gordon Bulloch	6	286

The Last Great Tour?

	Games	Minutes
Ronan O'Gara	6	283
Andy Sheridan	6	281
Gavin Henson	4	278
Stephen Jones	5	278
Jason Robinson	4	268
John Hayes	4	247
Brian O'Driscoll	4	242
Ollie Smith	4	238
Matt Stevens	6	234
Shane Byrne	6	227
Matt Dawson	6	222
Charlie Hodgson	4	221
Jonny Wilkinson	3	220
Chris Cusiter	5	213
Steve Thompson	5	206
Neil Back	3	200
Shane Horgan	6	189
Tom Shanklin	3	186
Danny Grewcock	3	184
Andy Titterrell	3	179
Richard Hill	3	177
Graham Rowntree	3	137
Gareth Cooper	3	96
Jason White	1	54
Brent Cockbain	1	40
Lawrence Dallaglio	1	16
Malcolm O'Kelly	0	0
Simon Taylor	0	0
Iain Balshaw	0	0

* Does not include warm-up game V Argentina

Points for the Lions*

	Pens	Convs	drop goals	try	points
Charlie Hodgson	8	12	0	1	53
Ronan O'Gara	7	9	0	2	49
Shane Williams	0	0	0	6	30
Jonny Wilkinson	9	1	0	0	29
Stephen Jones	6	2	0	0	22
Mark Cueto	0	0	0	3	15
Geordan Murphy	0	0	0	3	15
Josh Lewsey	0	0	0	2	10
Gordon D'Arcy	0	0	0	2	10
Martin Corry	0	0	0	2	10
Gareth Thomas	0	0	0	2	10
Gavin Henson	0	0	0	2	10
Tom Shanklin	0	0	0	1	5
Dwayne Peel	0	0	0	1	5
Shane Horgan	0	0	0	1	5
Brian O'Driscoll	0	0	0	1	5
Will Greenwood	0	0	0	1	5
Ryan Jones	0	0	0	1	5
Jason Robinson	0	0	0	1	5
Ollie Smith	0	0	0	1	5
Neil Back	0	0	0	1	5
Gareth Cooper	0	0	0	1	5
Simon Easterby	0	0	0	1	5
Martyn Williams	0	0	0	1	5
Lewis Moody	0	0	0	1	5
Total	30	24	0	38	328

* Does not include warm-up V Argentina

Most points V Lions 2005

Dan Carter (New Zealand), Second Test
33 points (2 tries, 4 convs, 5 pens)

Murray Williams (Bay of Plenty), Game 1
15 points (try, 2 convs, 2 pens)

Nick Evans (Otago), Game 5
14 points (2 convs, 4 pens)

Richard Apanui (Southland), Game 6,
11 points (1 conv, 3 pens)

Dan Carter (New Zealand) First Test
11 points (1 conv, 3 pens)

Lions' Records

Single Game
Points: Alan Old, 37, V SW Districts (South Africa), 1974
Tries: David Duckham, 6, V West Coast/Buller (New Zealand), 1971;
J.J. Williams, 6, V SW Districts (South Africa), 1974

Single tour:
Total Points: Barry John (New Zealand), 188, 1971

Total Tries: Randolph Aston (South Africa), 30, 1891

Total Appearances: Harry Eagles (Australia/New Zealand), 35, 1888

Career
Points: Andy Irvine, 281, 1974-1980

Appendix II

Tries: Tony O'Reilly 38, 1955-1959

Appearances: Willie John McBride, 71 (one as sub), 1962-1974

Most tours: Willie John McBride, 5; Mike Gibson, 5

Overall Records:
Biggest win: (106) 116-10 V Western Australia (Australia), 2001
Highest score conceded: (39) 67-39 V Northern Free State (South Africa), 1997

Worst defeat: (28) 10-38 V Waikato (New Zealand), 1993

Lions' History in New Zealand

1888 tour

Date	V	Score	Venue
28 April	Otago	8-3	Dunedin
2 May	Otago	4-3	Dunedin
5 May	Canterbury	14-6	Christchurch
9 May	Canterbury	4-0	Christchurch
12 May	Wellington	3-3	Wellington
14 May	H Roberts' XV	4-1	Wellington
16 May	Taranaki Clubs	0-1	New Plymouth
19 May	Auckland	6-3	Auckland
24 May	Auckland	0-4	Auckland
8 September	Auckland	3-0	Auckland
12 September	Auckland	1-1	Auckland
15 September	Hawke's Bay	3-2	Napier
17 September	Wairarapa	5-1	Masterton
20 September	Canterbury	8-0	Christchurch
22 September	Otago	0-0	Dunedin
26 September	South Island	5-3	Dunedin
29 September	South Island	6-0	Christchurch
2 October	Taranaki Clubs	7-1	Hawera
3 October	Wanganui	1-1	Wanganu

Appendix III

1904 tour*

Date	V	Score	Venue
6 August	Canterbury/ South Canterbury/ West Coast	5-3	Christchurch
10 August	Otago/Southland	14-8	Dunedin
13 August	New Zealand	3-9	Wellington
17 August	Taranaki/ Wanganui/ Manawatu	0-0	New Plymouth
20 August	Auckland	0-13	Auckland

*This was primarily a tour of Australia

1908 tour

Date	V	Score	Venue
23 May	Wairarapa Bush	17-3	Masterton
27 May	Wellington	13-19	Wellington
30 May	Otago	6-9	Dunedin
3 June	Southland	14-8	Invercargill
6 June	New Zealand	5-32	Dunedin
10 June	South Canterbury	12-6	Timaru
13 June	Canterbury	8-13	Christchurch
17 June	West Coast/Buller	22-3	Greymouth
20 June	Nelson Bays/ Marlborough	12-0	Nelson
27 June	New Zealand	3-3	Wellington
1 July	Hawke's Bay	25-3	Napier
4 July	Poverty Bay	26-0	Gisborne
8 July	Manawatu/ Horowhenua	12-3	Palmerston North
11 July	Wanganui	9-6	Wanganui
15 July	Taranaki	0-5	New Plymouth
18 July	Auckland	0-11	Auckland
25 July	New Zealand	0-29	Auckland

1930 tour

Date	V	Score	Venue
21 May	Wanganui	19-3	Wanganui
24 May	Taranaki	23-7	New Plymouth
28 May	Manawhenua	34-8	Palmerston North
31 May	Wairarapa Bush	19-6	Masterton
3 June	Wellington	8-12	Wellington
7 June	Canterbury	8-14	Christchurch
11 June	West Coast/		
	Buller	34-11	Greymouth
14 June	Otago	33-9	Dunedin
21 June	New Zealand	6-3	Dunedin
25 June	Southland	9-3	Invercargill
28 June	Ashburton/		
	South Canterbury/		
	North Otago	16-9	Timaru
5 July	New Zealand	10-13	Christchurch
9 July	New Zealand		
	Maori	19-13	Wellington
12 July	Hawke's Bay	14-3	Napier
16 July	Poverty Bay/		
	East Coast/		
	Bay of Plenty	25-1	Gisborne
19 July	Auckland	6-19	Auckland
26 July	New Zealand	10-15	Auckland
30 July	North Auckland	38-5	Whangarei
2 August	Waikato/		
	King Country/		
	Thames Valley	40-16	Hamilton
9 August	New Zealand	8-22	Wellington

The Last Great Tour?

Date	V	Score	Venue
12 August	Marlborough/ Nelson/ Golden Bay/ Motueka	41-3	Blenheim

1950 tour

Date	V	Score	Venue
10 May	Marlborough/ Nelson/ Golden Bay/ Motueka	24-3	Nelson
13 May	Buller	24-9	Westport
16 May	West Coast	32-3	Greymouth
20 May	Otago	9-23	Dunedin
23 May	Southland	0-11	Invercargill
27 May	New Zealand	9-9	Dunedin
31 May	South Canterbury	27-8	Timaru
3 June	Canterbury	16-5	Christchurch
6 June	Ashburton/ North Otago	29-6	Ashburton
10 June	New Zealand	0-8	Christchurch
14 June	Wairarapa Bush	27-13	Masterton
17 June	Hawke's Bay	20-0	Napier
21 June	East Coast/ Poverty Bay/ Bay of Plenty	27-3	Gisborne
24 June	Wellington	12-6	Wellington
1 July	New Zealand	3-6	Wellington
5 July	Wanganui	31-3	Wanganui
8 July	Taranaki	25-3	New Plymouth
12 July	Manawatu/ Horowhenua	13-8	PalmerstonNorth
15 July	Waikato/ King Country/ Thames Valley	30-0	Hamilton

The Last Great Tour?

Date	V	Score	Venue
19 July	North Auckland	8-6	Whangarei
22 July	Auckland	32-9	Auckland
29 July	New Zealand	8-11	Auckland
2 August	New Zealand Maori	14-9	Wellington

1959 tour

Date	V	Score	Venue
20 June	Hawke's Bay	52-12	Napier
24 June	Poverty Bay/		
	East Coast	23-14	Gisborne
27 June	Auckland	15-10	Auckland
1 July	New Zealand		
	Universities	25-13	Christchurch
4 July	Otago	8-26	Dunedin
8 July	South Canterbury/		
	Mid-Canterbury/		
	North Otago	21-11	Timaru
11 July	Southland	11-6	Invercargill
18 July	New Zealand	17-18	Dunedin
22 July	West Coast/Buller	58-3	Greymouth
25 July	Canterbury	14-20	Christchurch
29 July	Marlborough/		
	Nelson/		
	Golden Bay/		
	Motueka	64-5	Blenheim
1 August	Wellington	21-6	Wellington
5 August	Wanganui	9-6	Wanganui
8 August	Taranaki	15-3	New Plymouth
11 August	Manawatu/		
	Horowhenua	26-6	Palmerston North
15 August	New Zealand	8-11	Wellington
19 August	King Country/		
	Counties	25-5	Taumarunui
22 August	Waikato	14-0	Hamilton
25 August	Wairarapa Bush	37-11	Masterton

The Last Great Tour?

Date	V	Score	Venue
29 August	New Zealand	8-22	Christchurch
2 September	New Zealand Juniors	29-9	Wellington
5 September	New Zealand Maori	12-6	Auckland
9 September	Bay of Plenty/ Thames Valley	26-24	Rotorua
12 September	North Auckland	35-13	Whangarei
19 September	New Zealand	9-6	Auckland

1966 tour

Date	V	Score	Venue
11 June	Southland	8-14	Invercargill
15 June	South Canterbury/		
	Mid-Canterbury/		
	North Otago	20-12	Timaru
18 June	Otago	9-17	Dunedin
22 June	New Zealand		
	Universities	24-11	Christchurch
25 June	Wellington	6-20	Wellington
29 June	Marlborough/		
	Nelson/		
	Golden Bay/		
	Motueka	22-14	Nelson
2 July	Taranaki	12-9	New Plymouth
6 July	Bay of Plenty	6-6	Rotorua
9 July	North Auckland	6-3	Whangarei
16 July	New Zealand	3-20	Dunedin
20 July	West Coast/Buller	25-6	Westport
23 July	Canterbury	8-6	Christchurch
27 July	Manawatu/		
	Horowhenua	17-8	Palmerston North
30 July	Auckland	12-6	Auckland
2 August	Wairarapa Bush	9-6	Masterton
6 August	New Zealand	12-16	Wellington
10 August	Wanganui/		
	King Country	6-12	Wanganui
13 August	New Zealand		
	Maori	16-14	Auckland

The Last Great Tour?

Date	V	Score	Venue
17 August	Poverty Bay/ East Coast	9-6	Gisborne
20 August	Hawke's Bay	11-11	Napier
27 August	New Zealand	6-19	Christchurch
31 August	New Zealand Juniors	9-3	Wellington
3 September	Waikato	20-9	Hamilton
6 September	Counties/ Thames Valley	13-9	Papakura
10 September	New Zealand	11-24	Auckland

1971 tour:

Date	V	Score	Venue
22 May	Counties/		
	Thames Valley	25-3	Pukekohe
26 May	Wanganui/		
	King Country	22-9	Wanganui
29 May	Waikato	35-14	Hamilton
2 June	New Zealand		
	Maori	23-12	Auckland
5 June	Wellington	47-9	Wellington
9 June	South Canterbury/		
	Mid-Canterbury/		
	North Otago	25-6	Timaru
12 June	Otago	21-9	Dunedin
16 June	West Coast/		
	Buller	39-6	Greymouth
19 June	Canterbury	14-3	Christchurch
22 June	Marlborough/		
	Nelson Bays	31-12	Blenheim
26 June	New Zealand	9-3	Dunedin
30 June	Southland	25-3	Invercargill
3 July	Taranaki	14-9	New Plymouth
6 July	New Zealand		
	Universities	27-6	Wellington
10 July	New Zealand	12-22	Christchurch
14 July	Wairarapa Bush	27-6	Masterto
17 July	Hawke's Bay	25-6	Napier
21 July	Poverty Bay/		
	East Coast	18-12	Gisborne
24 July	Auckland	19-12	Auckland

The Last Great Tour?

Date	V	Score	Venue
31 July	New Zealand	13-3	Wellington
4 August	Manawatu/		
	Horowhenua	39-6	Palmerston North
7 August	North Auckland	11-5	Whangarei
10 August	Bay of Plenty	20-14	Tauranga
14 August	New Zealand	14-14	Auckland

Appendix III

1977 tour

Date	V	Score	Venue
18 May	Wairarapa Bush	41-13	Masterton
21 May	Hawke's Bay	13-11	Napier
25 May	Poverty Bay/		
	East Coast	25-6	Gisborne
28 May	Taranaki	21-13	New Plymouth
1 June	King Country/		
	Wanganui	60-9	Taumarunui
4 June	Manawatu/		
	Horowhenua	18-12	Palmerston North
8 June	Otago	12-7	Dunedin
11 June	Southland	20-12	Invercargill
14 June	New Zealand		
	Universities	9-21	Christchurch
18 June	New Zealand	12-16	Wellington
22 June	South Canterbury		
	/Mid-Canterbury/		
	North Otago	45-6	Timaru
25 June	Canterbury	14-13	Christchurch
29 June	West Coast/		
	Buller	45-0	Westport
2 July	Wellington	13-6	Wellington
5 July	Marlborough/		
	Nelson Bays	40-23	Blenheim
9 July	New Zealand	13-9	Christchurch
13 July	New Zealand		
	Maori	22-19	Auckland
16 July	Waikato	18-13	Hamilton

The Last Great Tour?

Date	V	Score	Venue
20 July	New Zealand Juniors	19-9	Wellington
23 July	Auckland	34-15	Auckland
30 July	New Zealand	7-19	Dunedin
3 August	Counties/ Thames Valley	35-10	Pukekohe
6 August	North Auckland	18-7	Whangarei
9 August	Bay of Plenty	23-16	Rotorua
13 August	New Zealand	9-10	Auckland

1983 tour

Date	V	Score	Venue
14 May	Wanganui	47-15	Wanganui
18 May	Auckland	12-13	Auckland
21 May	Bay of Plenty	34-16	Rotorua
25 May	Wellington	27-19	Wellington
28 May	Manawatu	25-18	Palmerston North
31 May	Mid-Canterbury	26-6	Ashburton
4 June	New Zealand	12-16	Christchurch
8 June	West Coast	52-16	Greymouth
11 June	Southland	41-3	Invercargill
14 June	Wairarapa Bush	57-10	Masterton
18 June	New Zealand	0-9	Wellington
25 June	North Auckland	21-12	Whangarei
28 June	Canterbury	20-22	Christchurch
2 July	New Zealand	8-15	Dunedin
6 July	Hawke's Bay	25-19	Napier
9 July	Counties	25-16	Pukekohe
12 July	Waikato	40-13	Hamilton
16 July	New Zealand	38-6	Auckland

1993 tour

Date	V	Score	Venue
22 May	North Auckland	30-17	Whangarei
26 May	North Harbour	29-13	Auckland
29 May	New Zealand Maori	24-20	Wellington
2 June	Canterbury	28-10	Christchurch
5 June	Otago	24-37	Dunedin
8 June	Southland	34-16	Invercargill
12 June	New Zealand	18-20	Christchurch
16 June	Taranaki	49-25	New Plymouth
19 June	Auckland	18-23	Auckland
22 June	Hawke's Bay	17-29	Napier
26 June	New Zealand	20-7	Wellington
29 June	Waikato	10-38	Hamilton
3 July	New Zealand	13-30	Auckland

Other Titles from The Collins Press

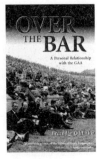

Over the Bar
A Personal History of the GAA
Breandán O hEithir

Growing up on the Aran Islands Breandán O hEithir became a passionate follower of hurling and football. After dropping out of university, a variety of jobs brought him into close contact with the GAA all over Ireland. He developed a deep interest in its social life and folklore plus the warmth and fun behind the official goings-on. Here he records his memories of journeys to matches, great players and personalities, and pays his own tribute to the dynamic and enduring influence of this organisation on Irish society.

ISBN: 1-903464-74-9   PB   Price: €12.95   2005

Croke Park: A History
Tim Carey

Headquarters of our largest sporting and cultural organisation, the GAA, its arena has witnessed many dramas. Thousands have played on its stage while millions have watched. Today it is one of the world's most impressive stadiums – the third largest in Europe – and a symbol of the GAA's strength. This history tells the story of 'Croker'.

ISBN: 1-903464-54-4   HB   Price: €30.00   2004

Dowtcha Boy!
An Anthology of Cork Slang
Morty McCarthy

Becoming familiar with Cork 'lingo' isn't easy but *Dowtcha Boy!* can make you 'crabbit' (cute, wise to) with little effort. It's 'simple out', like! Morty McCarthy went out on a mission to record Cork's quirky words and unique expressions. On his travels around his native city Morty collected over 400 words and phrases voiced by Corkonians. Memories will be jogged and the humorous illustrations by Fergal Keane will surely make it worth a sconce!

ISBN: 1-903464-68-4   PB   Price: €7.99
Reprinted 2005

That's Cork
Tom Galvin

Cork is synonymous with Shandon Bells, the River Lee, Echo Boys, tripe, rebels and hurleys; so what else is there to learn about 'de real capital'? Find out everything you ever wanted to know about Cork – and everything you thought you didn't want to know! Written by an outsider with the help of a few insiders, it is packed with quirky and witty observations about the city.

ISBN: 1-903464-76-5   PB   Price: €7.99   2005

The Height of Nonsense

Paul Clements

Visit the 32 counties of Ireland with Paul Clements, armed with his own rules of the road, e.g., 'Forsake all twenty-first century Celtic superhighways in favour of boreens'. Paul travelled the GMRs (Great Mountain Roads) in search of the county tops. He explores remote corners of little-known counties, some very flat, and spent time with the eccentric and quaint. Listen to tales of druids, banshees, highwaymen and loose women.

PS. Why did he only find 28 county tops?

ISBN: 1-903464-69-2   PB   Price: €13.95   2005

Irish Folk, Trad and Blues
A Secret History

Colin Harper and Trevor Hodgett

Great pioneers of Irish folk, trad and blues, such as Sweeney's Men and Rory Gallagher, lived when the media and record industry showed scant interest. This fascinating history reveals their frustrations and triumphs. Infighting, personality clashes and musical differences led to bust-ups and new collaborations. Forgotten heroes intertwine with 'honorary' visitors, like Bob Dylan and Arlo Guthrie.

ISBN: 1-903464-45-5   HB   Price: €25.00   2004
ISBN: 1-903464-90-0   PB   Price: €16.95   2005

Towpath Tours
A Guide to Cycling Ireland's Waterways
John Dunne

The towpaths of Ireland are a perfect amenity, a treasure trove of tranquil settings, which offer a safe, fume-free environment without the access problems of our hills and mountains. Availing of the paths once used by horses to pull barges along canals, the author documents and maps 29 recommended off-road tours along some of Ireland's most scenic and historic waterways.

ISBN: 1-903464-75-7   PB   Price: €12.95   2005

Munster's Mountains
30 Walking, Scrambling and Climbing Routes
Denis Lynch

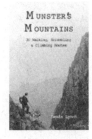

While including some well-known routes the book explores alternative routes, thus offering a sense of exploration and adventure in a 'new' environment.

ISBN: 1-903464-17-9   PB   Price: €12.95
Reprinted 2005

Stone Mad

Seamus Murphy

ILLUSTRATIONS BY WILLIAM HARRINGTON

This account of time spent as an apprentice stonecarver is an acclaimed Irish classic. The young Seamus Murphy took the unusual step of apprenticing himself to a master stonecarver to learn the ancient craft of the mason. *Stone Mad* tells the story of his seven years of growing knowledge, of the challenges and joys of stone – and of the men who worked it. The result is a book of unsurpassing beauty, full of warmth, humour and profound perception.

ISBN: 1-903464-81-1   PB   Price: €12.95   2005

A Doctor's War

Aidan MacCarthy

INTRODUCTION BY PETE MCCARTHY

Researching *McCarthy's Bar*, Pete McCarthy entered MacCarthy's Bar in Castletownbere, west Cork. While there Adrienne MacCarthy gave him a copy of her father's wartime memoir. Pete found it 'unputdownable'. An RAF medical officer, Aidan served in France, survived Dunkirk, and was plunged into adventures in the Far East. In Nagasaki his life was literally saved by the dropping of the atomic bomb and he was an eyewitness to the horror and devastation it caused.

ISBN: 1-903464-70-6   PB   Price: €12.95   2005